Mass Communication

Mass Communication
A Sociological Perspective

Charles R. Wright
University of Pennsylvania

THIRD EDITION

RANDOM HOUSE   NEW YORK

Library of Congress Cataloging in Publication Data

Wright, Charles Robert, 1927–
  Mass communication.

  Bibliography: p.
  Includes index.
  1. Communication—Social aspects.   2. Mass media—
Social aspects.   I. Title.
HM258.W74 1985   302.2'34   85-8260
ISBN 0-394-33244-X

Manufactured in the United States of America

To
Anne Marie Wright
and
Herbert and Helen Hyman

PREFACE

This new edition of *Mass Communication: A Sociological Perspective* elaborates upon the sociological orientation to the study of mass communication that was introduced in the previous editions. It builds upon, modifies, and extends the earlier treatments to take into account more recent research developments.

Mass communication research, an active and productive scholarly field in the 1970s, when the second edition was written, continued full speed into the 1980s. Some of this new research bears directly on our subject—the sociology of mass communication—providing us with new information for understanding mass communication as a social process and its structure as a social institution.

When the first edition was written the sociology of mass communication was a relatively young academic specialty. Even then, however, the field was so broad in scope that it was necessary to be selective about what to present in a short book such as this. Today it is even more necessary that our presentation be selective, given the field's rapid growth and the considerable body of literature being published about the mass media and mass communication.

This book presents a sociological approach to mass communication. Thus it complements works that stress a psychological, economic, literary, humanistic, philosophical, journalistic, historical, technological, or other orientation. I have selected for consideration some recent and some "classic" studies of mass communication that are sociological in nature and that address an important array of research problems in the field.

A great deal of mass communication research has been published in the United States during the past several decades, and this work receives most of our attention here. Even so, our discussion is not limited to American mass media or to American research. Chapter 2, for example, describes and compares features of mass communication systems in several societies. Selected research from outside the United States is cited in other chapters. And our discussion of American studies focuses mainly on their theoretical and empirical contributions—findings that shed light on sociological points of general interest and significance to the field.

Each chapter in this new edition has been revised, and some have been almost completely rewritten, incorporating new ideas, topics, research findings, and citations. A number of new studies have been included, but I have not hesitated to present an old study if it best serves to illustrate a sociological point. I believe that it is important for students to see contemporary research problems in the context of prior work in the field. I have occasionally cited findings from recent research by graduate students, especially those with whom I have worked, that helps illuminate a point. Thus, for example, the discussion of interpersonal communication and opinion leadership (in Chapter 4) has been enriched by examples from several graduate theses not easily available in the general literature. I believe that it is important for students, who are tomorrow's research scholars, to see that this is a field to which they can contribute.

The basic framework that guided the earlier editions serves us here. The book begins with a theoretical challenge: to explore the characteristics of mass communication and their social significance. In Chapter 1 we suggest one theoretical orientation—a functional perspective—that can guide a discussion of the social consequences of mass communication as a social method for handling news, mass persuasion, entertainment, and socialization. We present a functional inventory as a heuristic device for organizing claims and findings about mass communication effects. (We return to an examination of social consequences later in the book.)

But our sociological perspective draws upon other theoretical orientations too—on concepts taken, for example, from social psychology and from the sociological study of organizations, occupations, and professions—some of which are used more explicitly in subsequent chapters, especially in the treatment of mass communicators and audiences.

Chapter 2 describes selected features of the organization of mass communication in several societies, including the Soviet and Chinese Communist systems of newspapers and broadcasting and the British, Canadian, and American broadcasting systems. These cases are not comprehensive descriptions of the mass media in these countries or current journalistic accounts of media events there. Rather, each case illustrates some special feature of the media's structure and operation within that social system, and together the examples demonstrate a variety of alternative arrangements of mass communication as a social institution. These comparative cases help us to appreciate that each mass communication system needs to be seen as a part of its particular society and as having features potentially functional or dysfunctional for it. They also give us some contrasts with our own media system that put our research interests and social concerns about mass communication into a wider framework.

Chapter 3 presents research on the sociology of the mass communicator, focusing on studies of key occupational roles in the production of mass-communicated news and popular entertainment.

Chapter 4 examines the sociology of the audience, with special attention to research linking mass communication and interpersonal communication and examining opinion leadership as a communication role.

Chapter 5 considers some social and social psychological characteristics of the audiences for mass communication and their behavior.

Chapter 6 looks at some studies of mass communication content. It directs attention to the cultural content of mass-communicated news and entertainment—to the kinds of people, social roles, values, and social norms presented.

Chapter 7 presents research on the apparent social consequences of mass-communicated news and efforts at mass persuasion.

Chapter 8 considers public concerns about the social consequences of mass entertainment.

Chapter 9 examines studies of mass communication and the socialization process.

Chapter 10 presents a brief discussion of the possible sociological significance of some current developments in mass media technology.

While I accept full responsibility for the treatment given to the study of mass communication in this book, my sociological perspective owes a great deal to the many people whose work I have drawn upon and to teachers, colleagues, and students who have influenced my ideas over the years.

My interest in the study of society's symbol makers and communicators was stimulated at Columbia College by a master undergraduate teacher of sociology, William C. Casey. Subsequently, the graduate training in sociology and the research experience I enjoyed at Columbia University made a significant contribution to my orientation toward sociology and mass communication.

I was—and continue to be—indebted to three pioneers in the field: Herbert H. Hyman, Paul F. Lazarsfeld, and Robert K. Merton. With their encouragement, I introduced Columbia College's first undergraduate course in the sociology of mass communication, in 1954. I introduced a similar course for both advanced undergraduate and graduate students in the Department of Sociology and Anthropology at UCLA in 1956. During those experiences with the course, I felt the need for a book that organized the field in a sociological way for my students. That is what motivated the first edition of this book, published in 1959.

Since writing that first edition, my ideas about the sociology of mass communication have been enriched and sharpened through discussions with excellent colleagues and students at Columbia University, UCLA, and elsewhere. During the past sixteen years I have learned much from my colleagues and students at the Annenberg School of Communications and the Department of Sociology, both at the University of Pennsylvania. It would be a pleasant but impossible act to name each of these generous people here. I hope that they will accept this collective acknowledgment.

Several former students helped as research assistants during the preparation of this edition or earlier ones and deserve special mention and thanks: Judith Beinstein, Juli Benini, Colleen Cool, Julie Dobrow, Josephine Holz, Hoonsoon Jang, March Kessler, Hannah Kliger, Chien Joanna Lei, and Linda Park.

I have benefited from advice about this edition or earlier ones from Mary E. W. Goss, Josephine Holz, Herbert Hyman, Raymond J. Murphy, Charles H. Page, ElDean Bennett, Del Brinkman, Carl J. Crouch, Thomas P. Dunn, Walter Gantz, Gene N. Levine, Jerry M. Lewis, and Dennis Wenger. Charles Page was especially helpful as consulting editor to the original series of sociology books in which the first two editions appeared. All editions have benefited from a fine job of editing at Random House. Murray Curtin, Walter Kossmann, and Jane Cullen were especially helpful editors on the second edition; and Roth Wilkofsky and Fred Burns on the third.

I am indebted to several friends and colleagues who have shared their work with me.

Ray L. Birdwhistell has shown his friendship and generosity by sharing his observations and insights into the nature of human communication and by his constant reminder that it is social.

Muriel Cantor has helped to reinforce my sociological orientation to mass communications by her valued comments and research.

Ralph Turner generously provided several volumes of reports from his study of mass-communicated earthquake predictions in southern California.

Sandra Ball-Rokeach and Milton Rokeach kindly sent me a prepublication manuscript copy of their book reporting on *The Great American Values Test.*

George Gerbner, Larry Gross, and Nancy Signorielli helpfully supplied reports from the Cultural Indicators project.

Paul Messaris kindly provided copies of research papers on his study of how families use television during their socialization of children.

And Paul Tichenor thoughtfully sent me copies of the *Sociology of Rural Life,* containing accounts of studies on mass communication and rural conflicts, by himself and colleagues at the University of Minnesota.

I thank all these generous people. If I have overlooked someone, I hope to be forgiven.

Parts of this book were written during a scholarly leave from the University of Pennsylvania. I wish to express my thanks to the university and to the Annenberg School of Communications for their support. I also thank Maxine Beiderman and Hillary Guenther, who helped enormously by typing several chapters of an earlier draft of the manuscript.

It is important that the special help of two persons be recognized here, and I do so with pleasure and appreciation. I have learned a great deal from Herbert H. Hyman—teacher, colleague, co-author, friend—with whom I have worked and shared family adventures for more than thirty years. And I have received invaluable help from my wife Anne Marie, without whose encouragement and good judgment this book could not have been completed—in any of its three editions.

C. R. W.
Havertown, Pennsylvania
March 1985

CONTENTS

Mass Communication

CHAPTER 1

The Nature and Functions of Mass Communication

Shortly after the accident at the nuclear power plant at Three Mile Island, Pennsylvania, in March 1979, more than fifty thousand people held an antinuclear demonstration in Hanover, Germany. Mass-communicated news is said to have given the events at Three Mile Island transoceanic immediacy. At least eight out of every ten German adults, for example, followed the news closely, according to public opinion polls. And demonstrators throughout Western Europe are reported to have chanted, "Pennsylvania is everywhere."[1]

Yet within a few miles of Three Mile Island, some Pennsylvanians did not learn of the nuclear accident until a week after it happened, despite the fact that it was a major news topic in local and national mass media. How could this happen? Who could escape the daily barrage of radio and television coverage, speculation and commentary—the threats of a massive release of radioactivity, a potentially explosive hydrogen bubble, and the remote possibility of a meltdown at the nearby atomic plant? It is no mystery: These Pennsylvanians are members of the Old Order Amish community in Lancaster County. They do not use electricity.

"In case of an emergency," one of their leaders informed a governmental committee looking into the Three Mile Island accident, "you will realize that the Old Order Amish do not have telephones, radios or TV." Less than half of the community learned about the Three Mile Island experience by reading newspapers. In an emergency, he said, some Amish families could be warned through loudspeakers operated by volunteer fire companies from the surrounding communities, and farm workers might be alerted by ringing family dinner bells. But even these modes of communication may not be available in some outlying Amish areas, where news and instructions would have to reach members through word of mouth from the leader in each church district.[2] So much for the awesome power of the mass media under some social circumstances!

Most of us take for granted our "right" to be regularly informed and entertained by the mass media. It is difficult for us to imagine life without them, especially in a technologically modern country. We may become more conscious

---

[1] See Dorothy Nelkin and Michael Pollak, "A Pregnant Pause: The European Response to The Three Mile Accident," in *The Three Mile Island Nuclear Accident: Lessons and Implications*, eds. Thomas H. Moss and David L. Sills (New York: The New York Academy of Sciences, 1981), pp. 186–195. The chant is quoted on p. 186.

[2] Jill Lawrence, "Amish Got TMI News Week Later," *The Philadelphia Inquirer*, August 8, 1979, pp. 1B, 2BW. The person quoted is Andrew Kinsinger, chairman of the national branch of the Old Order Amish Steering Committee.

of our dependence on the mass media for news and for entertainment when they are missing for some reason, when things go wrong, or when we hear about other citizens who seem to do without them. Sometimes our awareness is heightened in times of social crisis and threat. These moments also may make us more aware of our dependence on interpersonal as well as on mass communication for our daily survival and well-being. For communication is a social process that is not defined by the technical apparatus of the mass media.

As a social process, communication is essential to society and to human survival. Every human society—so-called primitive or modern—depends on communication to enable its members to live together, to maintain and modify working arrangements about the social order and social regulation, and to cope with the environment. Participation in the communication process establishes a person as a social being and as a functioning member of society.

It is not surprising that a matter so basic to human life has been a topic for study and speculation throughout history. From antiquity to modern times, the subject of human communication has attracted the attention of a long line of authors representing a rich variety of intellectual orientations, and including artistic, humanistic, and political approaches. Only relatively recently, however, has it become a popular topic for investigation by social scientists. Communication has been studied by social scientists trained in anthropology, political science, psychology, social psychology, sociology, and other disciplines, in addition to those specializing in the study of communication itself. Our book proceeds from a *sociological* orientation, an approach which gives special emphasis to mass communication as a social process and to its structural, organizational and cultural context.[3]

We shall present a sociological analysis of the nature, process, and social consequences of mass communication. In doing this, we will consider some points about interpersonal communication as well, where they add to our understanding of mass communication as a social phenomenon. To start, we need to specify those activities with which we will be most concerned, regardless of the means of communication being used—that is, mass or interpersonal.

FOUR MAJOR COMMUNICATION ACTIVITIES

Harold Lasswell, a political scientist who was a pioneer in mass communication research, once distinguished three major communication operations: (1) surveillance of the environment, (2) correlation of the parts of society in responding to

---

[3] We focus on treatments of communication consistent with this sociological approach, and even then have had to be selective. We omit, for example, nonsymbolic animal "communication," since our concern is with human and especially mass communication. And since we consider mass communication as more than the transmission of bits of information from sender to receiver, engineering and information science also fall outside the scope of our study. It is worth noting here, since it tends to get overlooked when we discuss the special characteristics of mass communication, that human communication is not restricted to any single mode (such as written language) or to any one channel (such as auditory) of symbolic exchange. On this point, see Ray L. Birdwhistell, "Communication," in the *International Encyclopedia of the Social Sciences* (New York: Macmillan, 1968), vol. 3, pp. 24–29; and *Kinesics and Context* (Philadelphia: University of Pennsylvania Press, 1970).

the environment, and (3) transmission of the social heritage from one generation to the next.[4] Modifying Lasswell's categories somewhat and adding a fourth, entertainment, gives us the classification of the major communication activities with which we will be concerned in this book.

Surveillance refers to the collection and distribution of information concerning events in the environment, both within a particular society and outside it. Coverage of events during a presidential election campaign is an example. To some extent, surveillance corresponds to what is commonly thought of as the handling of news. The news process, however, as we shall see later involves much more than "collecting" and distributing "facts" about self-evident events. There is a complex social process that produces what is accepted as news in a society.

Correlation includes interpretation of the information presented about the environment, prescriptions about what to do about it, and attempts to influence such interpretations, attitudes, and conduct. These operations are usually seen as editorial activity, propaganda, or attempts at persuasion.

Although it is useful here to distinguish surveillance from correlation, in practice this may be difficult to do. Surveillance itself incorporates editorial judgments that determine what items qualify as news or information to be disbursed. Interpretation and value judgments are often implicit, sometimes explicit, in the "news" that is reported by mass media and by word of mouth. Linda Lannus, for example, reports that surveillance and correlation activities tended to be indistinguishable to the reporters, editors, and readers of two daily metropolitan newspapers that she studied in 1977.[5] True, the newspapers had special sections regarded as mainly editorial, such as the editorial page and signed columns of opinion or commentary. But the news people found it difficult and unrealistic to separate certain kinds of editorial judgments, such as the significance of an event and how much coverage to give it, from the surveillance process. Nevertheless, the distinction between surveillance and correlation is useful to our discussion—and easier to see in certain kinds of communication ventures, such as propaganda campaigns and mass persuasion. So we will keep it.

The third communication activity, transmission of the social heritage, focuses on the assimilation of people into society. It concerns the communicative processes by which society's store (or part of its store) of values, social norms, knowledge, and other cultural components is made known to and instilled in members and potential members. Our meaning goes beyond Lasswell's specification of transmission of the social heritage from one generation to the next and includes concern with communication relevant to the assimilation of children and adults into various social roles, immigrants into a new (new to them, that is) society, and related matters. This activity sometimes is called education or *socialization,* the term we will use.

[4] Harold D. Lasswell, "The Structure and Function of Communication in Society," in Lyman Bryson, ed., *The Communication of Ideas* (New York: Harper & Brothers, 1948), pp. 37–51. Lasswell calls these operations "functions," a term we reserve for a different meaning later in this chapter.

[5] Linda Rush Lannus, "The News Organization and News Operations of the Urban Press: A Sociological Analysis Based on Two Case Studies" (Ph. D. dissertation, University of Pennsylvania, 1977).

4.   Finally, _entertainment_ refers here to communication activities primarily (even if arbitrarily) considered as amusement, irrespective of any other features they may seem to have. A television situation comedy, for example, may be regarded as an entertainment activity, even though it may contain some information.

It is good to remember that our four major communication activities are abstractions, useful for purposes of discussion and analysis. Clearly any specific case may be seen in terms of any or all four activities. A television news story, for example, may play a part in surveillance of events (A hurricane is coming this way!), evaluation of what to do (board up the windows), reflect social norms (people are responsible for protecting themselves and their property), and still be entertaining (It's a thrilling drama of humanity versus the elements!). Or a choice piece of gossip passed along to a friend may be informative, judgmental, reinforcing of some shared values, and titillating. (That's what makes gossip so much fun!) People may use the same materials in different ways—for entertainment or instruction. Life doesn't follow theory. Nonetheless our distinctions serve a useful purpose so long as we treat them as abstractions—convenient ways of looking at certain aspects of communication.

At this point the reader might properly ask: What has become of the promised focus on *mass* communication? Surely the four activities described above were carried on long before the invention of modern mass media. This observation is not only correct but to the point. What are the consequences of conducting each of these four activities through *mass communication*, in addition to (or sometimes instead of) interpersonal communication? Before proceeding to consider this question, however, it is necessary to clarify what we mean by mass communication.

To start, we need a working definition. One purpose of a definition is to inform the reader of the sense in which a word that may have several meanings is to be used as a term for purposes of the discussion that follows. Such a term should be regarded as a working concept rather than as a definitive statement about reality. We aim to specify the main characteristics by which we distinguish mass communication from other forms of human communication.

WHAT IS MASS COMMUNICATION?

In popular usage, the term *mass communication* is a synonym for *mass media*. It brings to mind television, radio, motion pictures, and so on—ordinarily our means of contact with mass communication. But the mass media and their technology are only instruments (albeit important, even essential ones) in mass communication; they are not the process of mass communication that concerns us here. The presence of modern communication technology need not signify mass communication. The nationwide telecast of a political convention is an instance of mass communication; the closed-circuit television system over which the convention delegates' hotel security is monitored is not. A Hollywood motion picture shown in a theater is another instance of mass communication; a home movie of vacation scenes is not. It is not the technical apparatus of the mass media that distinguish mass communication. Therefore, as used in this book, mass communication is not merely a synonym for the mass media or for modern communication technology. Rather, it is a special kind of social communication involving distinctive characteristics of the audience, the communication experience, and the communicator.

Nature of the Audience

Mass communication is directed toward a relatively large, heterogeneous, and anonymous audience. Messages addressed to specific persons are not usually considered mass communication. Therefore we exclude letters, telephone calls, telegrams, and the like from our working definition. This does not deny that the postal and telecommunications systems play an important role in the communication network of any society. Most certainly they do. In some instances they are directly linked to the mass media and perform vital tasks in the overall system of communication. They may help, for example, in carrying information to places and people not reached by the mass media. But we reserve the term mass communication for other activities.

Each of our criteria for a mass audience is relative and needs further specification. For example, what size audience is "large"? Extreme cases are easily classified: a television audience of millions is large; a lecture audience of a few dozen is small. But what about an audience of a thousand or so people at a political rally? Obviously the cutoff point, if there need be one, must be arbitrary and tailored to the purposes at hand. We consider as "large" an audience composed of too many people for the communicator to interact with personally during a reasonable period of time.

The second criterion is that the mass audience is relatively heterogeneous in socially significant ways. Thus mass communication usually does not involve only a narrow, exclusive audience that is mainly homogeneous in its social characteristics. It involves audiences whose members occupy a variety of positions within a society—persons from many walks of life, different generations, various geographic spots, and so on. Obviously heterogeneity is another relative criterion. Only an audience of clones would be completely homogeneous. It is helpful to think of a continuum. An audience for a college alumni magazine, for example, is more homogeneous in educational background than the general population, but at the same time may consist of a heterogeneous mix of adult men and women of all ages, widely dispersed in cities, towns, and rural areas, single and married, with and without children, and so on. It is, however, likely to have a narrower mixture of occupations and economic characteristics than the typical audience for mass communication.

Finally, the criterion of relative anonymity means that most—perhaps nearly all—of the particular individuals in the audience are personally unknown to the communicator. This does not mean that they are socially anonymous or isolated. People's exposure to mass-communicated news and entertainment often takes place within small social groups where they are known to others; and even when an audience member is physically isolated from others, he or she is linked to them through previous and anticipated social interaction as a member of primary or secondary groups. These interactions give a person a social identity and affect his or her actions. Still, to the communicator and to the audience, mass communication seems to be addressed "to whom it may concern."

Nature of the Communication Experience

Mass communication can be characterized as public, rapid, and transient. It is public, not private, communication. Messages are addressed to no one in particular; their content is open for public oversight. Members of the audience are aware of the public character of what they are seeing or hearing, of the fact that other people—perhaps anyone who so desires—are witnessing the same mass-communicated stuff. Mass communication is rapid in the sense that the content is intended to reach large audiences within a relatively short time, even simultaneously—unlike, for example, works of fine art that may be examined at leisure and build audiences over centuries. By transient we mean that mass-communicated content is usually made to be consumed immediately. Sometimes it may end up in more enduring form, in television news archives, film libraries, radio transcriptions, and videotape recordings; but usually the output of the mass media is far from timeless and often ephemeral.

These features of mass communication can have important social consequences. For example, its public nature makes it a target for community censorship and legislative control or other expressions of public opinion. Its rapidity—the ability to reach large audiences in a brief time span—suggests its potential social power. The transient character of its content—here today, gone tomorrow—might encourage superficiality, sensationalism, and an undue emphasis on timeliness.

Nature of the Communicator

Mass communication is organized communication. Unlike the romantic image of the lone artist or writer, the communicator in mass communication works through a complex organization in which there is an extensive division of labor and a lot of expense. Think of the vast organizational structure surrounding the production of a Hollywood film, or the bureaucratic complexity of television networks. They hardly resemble even a modern romantic image of the writer at a typewriter (or word processor), an artist with a camera (or video camera), let alone notions of the independent communicator.

Mass communication is also expensive. Commercial television in the United States provides some dramatic examples. The television program "The Winds of War" (1983) is reported to have cost $38 million to produce and another $20 million to promote. Advertisers reportedly paid $175,000 for each of some 200 or so commercial "spots" for their messages during the 18 hours of telecasting.[6] A 30-second spot commercial during the ABC telecast of the 1984 Summer

[6] *Broadcasting*, January 31, 1983, p. 73.

Olympic Games cost the advertiser $250,000.[7] In order to reach an estimated nightly audience of 80 million viewers in the United States, ABC paid $225 million in fees and another $100 million in production costs. It telecast 180 hours of the games. (In 1960 it cost CBS a fee of $394,000 to telecast 20 hours of the Olympic Games from Rome; in 1980 NBC paid $87 million in anticipation of telecasting the Olympics from Moscow, which it did not broadcast because the United States boycotted the Olympics that year.)[8] A minute of commercial advertising during the 1985 ABC telecast of Super Bowl XIX cost one million dollars.

Of course not all media costs are as high as these. But the costs for production and distribution of news and entertainment through mass communication are far from small, and someone has to pay for them in noncommercial as well as commercial communication media systems. It takes more than a sheet of paper and a ballpoint pen to "communicate" in this way. (In fact, it is reported that the Los Angeles Olympic Organizing Committee ordered 90 million sheets of paper for journalists covering the Olympics to use.)

These organizational and financial features of production and distribution are not merely academic distinctions useful for defining mass communication. They seriously affect the nature of the communicator in mass communication and suggest issues of public concern. The complexity of the production and distribution process makes the creative artist just one player in the construction of the mass-communicated news and entertainment that finally reaches the public.[9] Indeed, as we will see in Chapter 3, it is often impossible to say just who is responsible for what is presented on television or by the other mass media. The mass media organization itself seems to be the communicator in some instances, although that impression deserves closer examination. In any case, it is argued that the creative artist or writer working in these organizational contexts loses some individual control over a project. And the high costs of production and distribution make it difficult—even impossible—for some individuals and groups to use the mass media at all for producing and distributing their messages to the public. Access to mass communication facilities is therefore limited.

The development of mass media has therefore led to a new form of social communication—mass communication. This new form can be distinguished from other types by the following characteristics: It involves relatively large, heterogeneous, and anonymous audiences; messages are transmitted publicly, often timed to reach most audience members simultaneously, and are transient in character; the communicator tends to be a complex organization, or to work within one, in an industry where expenses are great.

[7] Gail Shister, *Philadelphia Inquirer*, August 4, 1983, p. 9D.

[8] Kathy Rebello, "It's the 1984 Media Olympics," *USA Today*, July 31, 1984, pp. B1–2; and Lee Winfrey, "Olympics' Popularity as a TV Attraction Continues Unabated," *Philadelphia Inquirer*, August 3, 1984, p. 4E.

[9] For a good example, see "The Product Image: The Fate of Creativity in Country Music Songwriting," by John Ryan and Richard A. Peterson, in *Individuals in Mass Media Organizations*, eds. James S. Ettema and D. Charles Whitney (Beverly Hills, CA: Sage Publications, 1982), *Sage Annual Reviews of Communication Research*, vol. 10, pp. 11–32.

TOWARD A WORKING CONCEPT OF MASS COMMUNICATION

Our working concept specifies the components that we would include if we constructed a theoretically "perfect" example of mass communication. It provides a set of criteria against which any specific case can be examined and, if you like, compared with others. It thereby avoids possibly unproductive arguments about whether some particular case (such as communication through a college student newspaper) is "really" mass communication or not. It is far more useful to examine each case and to ask: In what respect does this communication resemble our concept of mass communication, and in what ways does it not? Then we can go on to ask what is the significance of apparent similarities and differences—that is, what are some of their implications for individuals and for society?

To illustrate our point, communication by campus newspaper might have certain characteristics of mass communication but not others. Campus publications usually involve moderate-sized audiences of people who are more homogeneous than the general population in age and in some other characteristics. These deviations from the full model of mass communication may have significance for the role of the campus newspaper; it may provide, for example, specialized surveillance and correlation about matters of particular interest to students and perhaps give them a temporary sense of common identification and interests that set them apart from students elsewhere or from the local community. A campus FM radio station, by contrast, may reach a larger, more heterogeneous audience, including many people who are not students and who live in the local community. These circumstances, in turn, may have important implications for the station's communication activities and their social consequences.

With a little imagination, we should be able to think of types of social communication other than mass communication. The nearly polar opposite is easy to specify—communication involving only a few people, often similar to one another in important respects, known to a communicator whose messages are addressed to them privately and are constructed and conveyed directly rather than through the complex formal organizations of mass media. An instructor speaking to students is a good example. The term *interpersonal communication* or *person-to-person communication* is the closest alternative to mass communication that I've been able to use productively. The problems come with forms of communication that fall somewhere in between mass and interpersonal communication, as so defined.

Ronald Rice and Frederick Williams, for example, use the term *new media* to refer to recently developed electronic communication technologies that allow computer interactivity among users. They suggest that the new media create a continuum between interpersonal and mass-mediated communication.[10] Herbert Menzel proposes the concept of *quasi-mass communication* to cover certain

---

[10] Ronald E. Rice and Frederick Williams, "Theories Old and New: The Study of New Media," in Ronald E. Rice et al., *The New Media: Communication, Research, and Technology* (Beverly Hills, CA: Sage Publications, 1984).

types of communication, such as streetcorner orators, speakers who take part in election campaigns, and missionaries preaching in foreign societies. These are institutionally arranged and recognized forms of communication that reach an audience somewhat larger than that in face-to-face, pinpointed communication, but far smaller than that in mass communication. Menzel suggests that such quasi-mass communication may have special functions related to certain social processes, such as the diffusion of innovations in a society.[11] And Herbert H. Hyman proposes distinguishing between large-scale and small-scale forms of mass communication, such as television broadcasting and popular books, in considering their contributions to socialization in society.[12]

Our concept of mass communication captures the major general distinctive qualities that specific cases of such communication share in varying degrees. Having presented it, we now are able to return to the question raised earlier in the chapter: Since our four communication activities (surveillance, correlation, socialization, and entertainment) can be carried out in many ways, what are some of the consequences of handling them as mass communication?

We become more sensitive to this issue whenever something intended to be communicated in another context becomes a subject of mass communication. The entire nature and meaning of the communication seem to change because the social conditions under which it originated (and had one meaning) are now violated and replaced by those of mass communication. A message whispered to a friend is not the same message when publicly broadcast over the radio. What was private communication has been made public; what was understood in one social context sounds different, and is different, in another.

There are ample examples from recent history. The Pentagon Papers, documents intended for limited communication within the U.S. government, took on different significance when published in the public press. Things said in the presidential Oval Office during conversations that were presumed to be private sounded different when secretly made tape recordings of them were broadcast to the public or read from the newspaper. Anyone who saw the televised Abscam tapes, showing political figures apparently taking bribes and making deals in motel rooms, can appreciate the changes that take place when private communication gets mass-communicated. Sometimes the vulgarity, profanity, and crudeness of private conversations by elected officials, when replayed in another context, shocks the public perhaps as much as some of the deals that apparently are being made. Some communications, it seems, just don't transform well into mass communication.

Our sociological interest is in what happens when these basic communication activities are performed through mass communication on a regular basis, as a socially institutionalized form of communication, not just occasionally (although we have some interest in the occasional case too). The consequences of

[11] Herbert Menzel, "Quasi-Mass Communication: A Neglected Area," *Public Opinion Quarterly*, 35, 3 (Fall 1971), pp. 406–409.

[12] Herbert H. Hyman, "Mass Communication and Socialization," in W. Phillips Davison and Frederick T. C. Yu, *Mass Communication Research: Major Issues and Future Directions* (New York: Praeger, 1974), pp. 36–65.

regularized social activity have long attracted the attention of social scientists concerned with *functional analysis.* Some of the concepts developed by these theorists are especially useful for the present discussion. We draw in particular upon concepts suggested by Robert K. Merton, the contemporary sociologist most widely identified with functional interpretation of sociological data.[13]

SOME FUNCTIONS OF MASS COMMUNICATION: AN OVERVIEW

The first lesson we can learn from functional theory is not to infer the social consequences of mass communication from its apparent or stated purposes. Merton stresses the need to distinguish between the significant consequences (functions) of a social activity and the apparent goals or aims given for it. The two matters need not be, and often are not, identical. This means that the functions of mass communication are not necessarily what is intended by the communicators.

Public health programs, for example, sometimes use mass communication in order to persuade people to get physical checkups, to get immunization shots against the flu, to stop smoking, and so on. This is the explicit purpose of regular local health campaigns. In pursuing these goals, the campaigns also may have important side effects. For example, as some research suggests, they could improve the social prestige and the morale of local public health workers, whose formerly unrecognized work now receives attention from the mass media and hence from the public. If this improvement in prestige and boost in morale leads to better community cooperation in public health efforts, that would be an important, but unexpected, consequence of the mass communication campaigns.

Merton labels significant intended consequences *manifest* and those that are unintended *latent.* Functional interpretation also distinguishes between those consequences that seem significantly useful to the maintenance and well-being of a system and those that seem harmful to it. Positive consequences are called *functions* and negative ones *dysfunctions.* (Those that seem irrelevant to the system under study are considered nonfunctions.) Any regular social activity, such as mass communication campaigns, can be analyzed in terms of what seem to be manifest or latent functions and dysfunctions for the society, its members, or its culture.

To return to our example of public health campaigns, we might look for such manifest functions as reductions in the risk of an epidemic, and for latent functions such as the boosts in prestige given to public health workers (thereby improving their occupational effectiveness in the community). We also might look for possible dysfunctions, such as frightening away potential health clients who fear they may learn that they have some incurable disease. Clearly the in-

[13] See Robert K. Merton, *On Theoretical Sociology: Five Essays, Old and New* (New York: Free Press, 1967), chap. 3, "Manifest and Latent Functions," pp. 73–138.

terpretation of social consequences as functional or dysfunctional involves judgment by the researcher. Are there some guidelines?

It seems important, to me, to avoid two problems if possible.[14] First, we should avoid trying to classify *every* possible effect of mass communication as functional or dysfunctional. It is more useful to limit functional analysis to those consequences that seem important to the maintenance and/or change of society, its members, or culture. For example, movie or television stories set in contemporary places might lead some viewers to learn a few new facts about the story's locale, such as some street names. But unless we can see how that minor effect is significant for the maintenance or change of society, its members, or culture, then simply calling it functional or dysfunctional does not increase our understanding of mass communication. Suppose, on the other hand, that movie and television settings influenced viewers' ideas about how attractive (or unattractive) a place is and thereby affected how many people sought to migrate to it. That could be a matter of considerable social significance and a potential topic for functional interpretation.

Second, it is important to avoid equating the terms functional and dysfunctional with our personal ideas of good and bad. We need not personally approve of some aspect of mass communication that we interpret as functional for a society. It does not have to fit our ideological preference. To call it functional means only that the practice seems to contribute to the strength and continuing operation of the society under study.

If we keep these two cautions in mind, we can use a functional framework to good advantage in reviewing some of the possible consequences of mass communication.

By combining Merton's specification of consequences with the four major communication activities, we arrive at a functional framework that serves to guide the inquiry.[15] Thus schematized, the basic comprehensive question becomes:

	(1) manifest	(3) functions
What are the	and	and of
	(2) latent	(4) dysfunctions
mass-communicated	(5) surveillance (news)	
	(6) correlation (editing/persuasion)	
	(7) socialization (cultural transmission)	
	(8) entertainment	
for the	(9) society	
	(10) individual members	
	(11) subgroups	
	(12) cultural systems?	

[14] For a further brief discussion of these problems and other experiences in applying functional analysis to mass communication, see my "Commentary" on functional analysis in *The New Communications*, ed. Frederick Williams (Belmont, CA: Wadsworth, 1983), pp. 89–90.

[15] The discussion and functional inventory chart draw heavily and in places directly on some of my earlier writings. The functional inventory is adapted from my article "Functional Analysis and Mass Communication," *Public Opinion Quarterly*, 24 (Winter 1960), pp. 605–620, and is used here by permission of the publisher. Further discussion of research strategies and additional exam-

The twelve elements in the schema can be transformed into categories in a master inventory chart that organizes many of the alleged, hypothesized, and empirically illustrated "effects" of mass communication. The essential framework is illustrated in Table 1, into which some hypothetical examples of mass communication effects have been inserted. We use the term "effects" here and throughout the book mainly for literary convenience, and more or less as a synonym for "consequences," without necessarily implying a direct causal relationship. (In later chapters we discuss some studies of media effects that employ a more literal meaning of cause and effect than we do here.)

In the following sections the analytical approach will be illustrated without undertaking a full explication of the chart. The topic of social consequences of mass-communicated surveillance, correlation, socialization, and entertainment will be discussed further in later chapters, where we will examine some research findings about them.

Surveillance by Mass Communication

Consider what it means to a society for its members to have a constant stream of public information about events in the world. One positive consequence (function) of such surveillance is that it provides warnings about imminent threats of danger—a hurricane, earthquake, or military attack. Forewarned, the population can mobilize and protect itself from destruction. Furthermore, insofar as the information is available to all, rather than to a select few, warnings through mass communication may have the additional function of supporting feelings of egalitarianism within the society—everyone has had fair warning to escape from danger.[16] Such warnings also can be interpreted as functional for individual members of the society (second column in the chart) insofar as personal (and family) safety is at stake.

A second social consequence of such communication is that it contributes to the everyday institutional operations of the society: it is instrumental in stock market activities, sales, navigation, and recreation plans. The instrumental functions of news also apply to the individual. For instance, a group of social scientists took advantage of a local newspaper strike in New York City to study what people "missed" when they did not receive their regular newspaper. One clearly identifiable role of the newspaper for these urbanites was providing information about routine events: local radio programs and movie schedules, sales by local stores, weather forecasts, and so on. When people "missed" their daily newspapers, they were missing a multipurpose tool for daily living.[17]

ples of functional analyses of mass communication are presented in "Functional Analysis and Mass Communication Revisited," in *The Uses of Mass Communications: Current Perspectives on Gratification Research*, ed. Jay Blumler and Elihu Katz. *Sage Annual Review of Communication Research*, vol. 3, 1975, pp. 197–212.

[16] I am indebted to Herbert H. Hyman for this suggestion.

[17] Bernard Berelson, "What 'Missing the Newspaper' Means," in *Communications Research 1948–1949*, eds. Paul F. Lazarsfeld and Frank Stanton (New York: Harper & Brothers, 1949), pp. 111–129.

Table 1 Partial Functional Inventory for Hypothetical Effects of Mass Communication, by System (Manifest and Latent Functions and Dysfunctions)

| | MASS-COMMUNICATED ACTIVITY: SURVEILLANCE (NEWS) | | | |
	Society	Individual	Specific Subgroups	Culture
Functions	Warning: Natural dangers; attack; war Egalitarian feelings Instrumental: News essential to the economy and other institutions Ethicizing Status conferral on social issues Agenda-setting	Warning Instrumental Adds to prestige: Opinion leadership Status conferral Agenda-setting	Instrumental: Information useful to power, agenda-building Detects: Knowledge of subversive and deviant behavior Manages public opinion: monitors; controls Legitimizes power; status conferral	Aids cultural contact Aids cultural growth
Dysfunctions	Threatens domestic stability: News of "better" societies Risks panic Widens knowlege gap between social strata	Anxiety: privatization; apathy; narcotization	Threatens power: News of reality; "enemy" propaganda; exposés	Permits cultural invasion

Table 1 Continued

MASS-COMMUNICATED ACTIVITY: CORRELATION (EDITORIAL SELECTION, INTERPRETATION, AND PRESCRIPTION)

	Society	*Individual*	*Specific Subgroups*	*Culture*
Functions	Aids mobilization Impedes threats to social stability Helps prevent possible panic Agenda-setting	Provides efficiency: Assimilating news Impedes: Overstimulation: anxiety; apathy; privatization Agenda-setting	Helps preserve power Increases responsibility	Impedes cultural invasion Maintains cultural consensus Impedes cultural growth
Dysfunctions	Increases social conformism: Impedes social change if social criticism is avoided; fosters spiral of silence	Weakens critical faculties Increases passivity		

MASS-COMMUNICATED ACTIVITY: SOCIALIZATION

	Society	*Individual*	*Specific Subgroups*	*Culture*
Functions	Increases social cohesion: Widens base of common norms, experiences, and so on Reduces anomie Continues socialization: Reaches adults even after they have left such institutions as school	Aids integration: Exposure to common norms Reduces idiosyncrasy Reduces anomie	Extends power: Another agency for socialization	Standardizes Maintains cultural consensus
Dysfunctions	Augments "mass" society	Depersonalizes acts of socialization		Reduces variety of subcultures

Table 1 Continued

| | MASS-COMMUNICATED ACTIVITY: ENTERTAINMENT | | |
	Society	Individual	Specific Subgroups	Culture
Functions	Respite for masses	Respite	Extends power: Control over another area of life	
Dysfunctions	Diverts public: Avoids social action Cultivates mass conformity	Increases passivity Lowers "tastes" Permits escapism		Weakens esthetics: "Popular culture" Cultural "pollution"

Two important functions of mass-communicated news, suggested by sociologists Paul Lazarsfeld and Robert Merton, are (1) status conferral and (2) ethicizing or the enforcement of social norms.[18] *Status conferral* means that news reports about persons, groups, or social issues increase their importance in the public's view by the very fact that they receive such attention. Presumably this is beneficial to society, in the case of certain social issues which thereby get put on the public agenda for consideration, discussion, and social action. Status conferral also benefits individuals and groups who receive the media's attention, since it certifies their importance and even may legitimize their real or aspired status as celebrities, leaders, and spokespersons for particular groups or about certain topics.

Mass-communicated news has an *ethicizing* effect when it strengthens social control by exposing deviant behavior to public view and possible censure. Newspaper crusades, for instance, publicize wrongdoings that might already have been known about privately by some people and silently borne, if not condoned, by them. Public disclosure of these wrongdoings makes them now a matter of public, not private, knowledge. Under these conditions, most people are obliged to condemn the misbehavior and to support public standards of morality. In this way, mass-communicated news strengthens social control, complementing other formal and informal methods for community detection and control of deviant behavior.

Mass-communicated surveillance can be dysfunctional for society and its members in a variety of ways. For example, the flow of world news could threaten the stability of a particular society or nation. Information about better living conditions elsewhere or about different ideologies might lead to invidious contrasts with conditions at home and to pressures for social change. Or, as another example, some people fear that mass-communicated news about impending danger, broadcast to the general public without local mediation and interpretation by someone, may lead to widespread panic (although contemporary sociological and social psychological research on disasters suggests that mass panic such as this rarely, if ever, happens.)[19]

Mass-communicated news may heighten an individual's anxieties, some say, especially concerning dangerous conditions in the world. What used to be called "war nerves" is an example. Perhaps "nuclear nerves" is the contemporary equivalent. Too much news—an information overload, as some call it—may lead to privatization. The individual, overwhelmed by matters brought to his or her attention by mass communication, escapes to private concerns over which there seems to be more control—family or hobbies, cultivating one's own gar-

---

[18] Several ideas about the functions of mass communication that we discuss here stem from this classic essay. Paul F. Lazarsfeld and Robert K. Merton, "Mass Communication, Popular Taste and Organized Social Action," in Bryson, *The Communication of Ideas*, pp. 95–118.

[19] For a classic study, see Hadley Cantril, Hazel Gaudet, and Herta Herzog, *Invasion from Mars* (Princeton, NJ: Princeton University Press, 1940). For discussions of current research that questions earlier interpretations, see John F. Lofland, "Collective Behavior," in Morris Rosenberg and Ralph Turner, eds., *Social Psychology: Sociological Perspectives* (New York: Basic Books, 1981), and Joseph B. Perry, Jr., and Meredith D. Pugh, *Collective Behavior: Response to Social Stress* (St. Paul, MN: West Publishing, 1978).

den, so to speak. Mass-communicated news may lead to individual apathy about civic activity, it is said, because people spend so much time following the news that they have little time or energy left to try to solve social problems. They become so intent on keeping informed, mesmerized by the newscasts and newspapers, that they equate being an informed citizen with being an active citizen.

Lazarsfeld and Merton call this *narcotization.* Thus, for example, the person—feeling compelled to watch an hour or more of daily news (network or local) on television, read through the newspaper (maybe also the Sunday edition), several newsmagazines—ends up so numbed or self-satisfied by it all that he or she misses the local township meeting for public action to clean up toxic waste dumps in the neighborhood!

One also can analyze functions and dysfunctions of mass-communicated news for specific populations or subgroups, such as ethnic groups, minorities, workers, children, elderly people, or political elites. To illustrate (third column in the chart), news attention given to political leaders can confer status on them and legitimize their position. Mass-communicated news also may be instrumental for them by providing information that is useful for governance, by exposing subversive activities, and by gauging public opinion. On the other hand, one can think of some dysfunctions too. Uncensored mass-communicated news can threaten the political elite's power by presenting news that contradicts the leaders' claims about some situation (wartime victories, economic prosperity), or allows opponents (domestic or foreign) to present their message, or exposes wrongdoings (taking bribes).

Finally, one can consider possible consequences of mass communication surveillance for a society's cultural system—its body of social values, norms, folkways, beliefs, and other cultural features. Mass-communicated news and information about other societies and their cultures might enrich and add variety to one's own culture, and encourage cultural growth and adaptability. On the other hand, some people fear that the host culture will lose some or all its distinctiveness and integrity as a result of such open cultural "invasion."

Correlation by Mass Communication

Many of the functions of the correlation activity in mass communication seem to prevent or limit some of the undesirable consequences of the mass communication of news. Correlation—including the selection, evaluation, and interpretation of events—imposes order on the surveillance activity and signifies the relative importance of what is reported. This helps to prevent an even greater flood of mass-communicated news than we already have, one that could overwhelm and confuse the public. Editorial activity also packages the news into categories (international news, sports, business) and signals a story's importance through the conventions of headlines, placement in the paper or newscast, and other devices.

We become more aware of such taken-for-granted management of the news when it is not provided. For example, in the study of what "missing" the newspaper means to readers, people said that they not only missed information about events, but also the evaluation and interpretation that the papers ordinarily provided. Some journalists believe it is their responsibility to evaluate and interpret events for the reader or listener—that is, to set events within their larger historical and social context, to evaluate the sources from which the "facts" came, and to suggest what the reader or listener may make of the facts reported. This could have the function, for example, of preventing undue public anxiety about news of impending danger.

One possible dysfunction of editorial-type activities through mass communication is that needed social changes may not get media support while social conformism does. Because of the public nature of mass communication, communicators risk sanctions if they publicly express social criticism or take an unpopular stand on issues. There may be political sanctions, economic ones, consumer boycotts, or other repercussions. Discretion may lead some mass communicators to avoid controversial topics and social criticism.[20] Certain practices associated with news reporting and interpretation may also work against social change, as for example when the mass media heavily rely on government, business, or other institutional sources for interpretations of events.

Another possible dysfunction would be the weakening of peoples' critical ability to find, sift, sort, interpret, and evaluate news for themselves. It can be argued that dependence on mass-communicated, prepackaged news, ideas, opinions, and views lessens people's effectiveness as citizens and makes them less capable of thinking for themselves. (It should be noted here, however, that people rarely, if ever, depend solely on mass communication, and frequently talk with one another in forming their opinions.)[21]

The mode of analysis outlined in the chart should be clear by now, and there is no need to belabor it. We will simply give a few examples for our two remaining communications activities: socialization and entertainment.

Socialization

In this section we simply note some possible functions and dysfunctions of handling socialization activities by mass communication. Such activities may help unify the society and increase social cohesion by providing a broad base of common social norms, values, and collective experiences to be shared by its members. That would be functional. Individuals too might be helped in their integration into the society through exposure to common social norms and other cultural matters. That could be especially functional for immigrants or other socially mobile persons. Mass communication also may contribute to the socialization of adults into new social values and changing social norms.

[20] On the other hand, playing down socially divisive news and criticism may be interpreted as functional for keeping the society together. For an example, see Warren Breed, "Mass Communication and Socio-cultural Integration," *Social Forces* 37 (1958), pp. 109–116.

[21] For a recently articulated theory of mass media dependency on the individual level, some of the conditions leading to it, and some functional and dysfunctional consequences, see Sandra J. Ball-Rokeach and Melvin De Fleur, "A Dependency Model of Mass Media Effects," *Communication Research*, 3 (1976), pp. 3–21. Also see *Theories of Mass Communication*, 4th ed., by De Fleur and Ball-Rokeach (New York: Longman, 1982), pp. 236–251.

On the other hand, the presentation of a more or less standardized view of culture through mass communication could result in a loss of regional, ethnic, and other subcultural variety and could discourage cultural diversity and creativity. That would be dysfunctional. It can also be argued that mass communication makes the process of socialization seem less humane in some respects. David Riesman, for example, suggests that the moral lessons of tales told by mass media cannot be tailored to fit the capacity of the individual child hearing or seeing the story, as they might have been in traditional face-to-face storytelling. Hence some children might make unduly harsh demands on themselves if they try to internalize cultural lessons from movies, television, and other mass media.[22] (But as we will see in Chapter 9, such a process may be less common than was once thought, since parents and others play an active role in interpreting these "media lessons" for children.)

Entertainment

Mass entertainment offers some diversion and amusement for everybody, and relaxation and respite can be functional for people and beneficial to society. But too much escapism, too many TV circuses at one's fingertips, may distract people from important social issues and divert them from useful social participation and action. That would be dysfunctional. It would also be dysfunctional if people became so dependent on mass communication for entertainment that they no longer were able to entertain themselves and became permanent mass media spectators.

Some critics suggest that entertainment changes its nature and quality when mass-communicated. Mass entertainment, it is argued, lowers, or at least fails to raise, public taste to the level that might be achieved by less extensive forms of entertainment such as the theater, books, or opera.[23] There also may be significant changes in the social institutions of entertainment. Change in organized sports provides a case in point.

Mass communication, if nothing else, has vastly increased the number of people who witness a sports event (or, more accurately, the version of the event as presented by television, radio, or some other medium). Some 105 million television viewers saw the 1984 Super Bowl XVIII football game.[24] By comparison, personal attendance at professional football games usually averages in the thousands. Television, perhaps more than any other mass medium of communication, has affected this area of popular entertainment and its institutions.

Sociologists John Talamini and Charles Page remark that "the most spectacular rise of sport as mass entertainment, a post World War II development, has

---

[22] David Riesman et al., *The Lonely Crowd* (Garden City, NY: Doubleday, 1953), chap. 4.

[23] For an examination of the mass culture critique and an alternative to it presenting a sociological analysis of the qualities of mass entertainment, see Herbert J. Gans, *Popular Culture and High Culture* (New York: Basic Books, 1974). For a sociological analysis of mass entertainment and its functions, see Harold Mendelsohn's *Mass Entertainment* (New Haven, CT: College and University Press, 1966), especially chapter II; and Harold Mendelsohn and H. T. Spetnagel, "Entertainment as a Sociological Enterprise," in *The Entertainment Functions of Television*, ed. Percy H. Tannenbaum (Hillsdale, NJ: Lawrence Erlbaum, 1980), pp. 13–29.

[24] *Broadcasting*, January 14, 1985, p. 70.

been largely the product of ... television."[25] Commenting on the functional and dysfunctional results of the increasing dependence of organized sports on the technology of television and on advertising funds, Talamini and Page see these consequences as including

> ... on the one hand, higher salaries and pensions for professional athletes, geographical expansion, dividends for spectators such as instant replay and visibility of errors by officials, and improved quality of play; and, on the other hand, ruthless schedule manipulation, the conversion of athletes into ad men and salesman, and, in boxing and baseball, the undermining of local clubs and minor league teams—with tragic effects for apprentice players and journeyman fighters.[26]

These observations illustrate some of the potential consequences of mass-communicated sports for the sport itself as well as for individuals and society. How socially significant these effects seem depends on one's viewpoint. Certainly they are important to those directly involved (professional athletes, businessmen, amateurs).

The symbolic value of mass-communicated sports also should not be overlooked. For example, consider the political significance of the Olympics, which are televised throughout the world. The study of these and other social implications of mass-communicated sports presents a relatively unexplored but interesting area for research in the sociology of mass communication.

Interconnection of Mass Communication Activities

Thus far we have treated each communication activity—surveillance, correlation, socialization, and entertainment—as if it existed separately from the others. Obviously it does not. The performance of one activity can have consequences for the others. Our concluding suggestion is that some of the functions of one mass-communicated activity are the products of steps to minimize dysfunctions of another mass communication activity. Some of the functions of mass-communicated correlation, for example, counteract certain dysfunctions of conducting surveillance by mass communication. In this regard, a pattern of interconnection between mass communication activities (including the practice of using the same mass medium for a variety of communication activities, such as for both news and entertainment) can be seen as a *social mechanism* for curbing possible disturbances brought on by mass communication. An example should make this clearer.

Let us accept, for the sake of illustration, the presupposition that modern societies must depend on mass-communicated surveillance for a significant part of the information their members need. In this sense, mass-communicated surveillance or news is functional; people cannot depend solely on personal experiences and conversations with others, although both of these are important sources of information. At the same time, mass-communicated surveillance risks

---

[25] John T. Talamini and Charles H. Page, *Sport and Society: An Anthology* (Boston: Little, Brown, 1973), p. 417.

[26] Ibid., p. 418.

specific dysfunctions. Large amounts of unevaluated news, for example, may overwhelm people, or lead to widespread anxiety, apathy, or other reactions that prevent people from further following the news. The public (or segments of it) is in danger of being out of touch with important information about social, political, and other events.

This risk to the social system is reduced by the practice of mass-communicated correlation. As we have noted earlier, there is a regular process of selection, editing, and interpretation of the accounts of events that appear as news, often accompanied by suggestions or prescriptions as to what people should do about these events. These practices make the news seem more manageable to the public.

But the public may even avoid following edited news if it is too much to bear. A steady diet of bad news, anxiety-provoking news, or just plain unpleasant news is too much to take. At this point the interconnection with mass-communicated entertainment becomes relevant. Mass entertainment items may be interspersed with or woven into the news itself, in such forms as human interest stories, oddities in the news, scandal, gossip, details of private lives, cartoons, comic strips, or television "happy talk."[27] One function of such mass-communicated entertainment carried by the same medium that is presenting news is to hold people's attention. It provides ready respite, relief, and immediate gratification, and thus makes it easier for people to be available for mass-communicated news, interpretation, and public orientation.

This example is conjectural, intended only to illustrate a general point. That functional connections between news and entertainment might happen occasionally is of less significance for analysis than that they occur regularly and are built into the mass communication process in a society. Functional analysis is less concerned with an isolated communication practice than with general, standardized, patterned, repetitive, or otherwise regular features of mass communication.

SOME OTHER THEORETICAL ORIENTATIONS

Functional analysis, as used here, provides a conceptual framework that is useful for thinking about the social consequences of mass communication. But it is by no means the only theoretical approach used in the sociological perspective presented in this book.

There are many conceptual approaches to the sociological study of mass communication, each of which reflects different ways of thinking about and analyzing the complex array of phenomena and issues concerning mass communication and society. Each approach has its own merit in calling attention to one

---

[27] For an early discussion of the functions of human interest stories, see Helen MacGill Hughes, "Human Interest Stories and Democracy," *Public Opinion Quarterly*, 1 (April 1937), pp. 73–83. For a more recent discussion of the entertainment aspects of televised news, see Leo Bogart, "Television News as Entertainment," in Tannenbaum, *The Entertainment Functions of Television*, pp. 209–249.

problem or another in the field and illuminating it in some way. Fortunately, therefore, no one theoretical orientation is definitive or totally accepted by everyone. This plurality of viewpoints keeps the field lively and ensures that no single theoretical paradigm dominates it to the exclusion of all others. The reader can find discussions of other theoretical orientations in several sources.[28]

Rather than undertake an abstract discussion and comparison of various theories about mass communication (which is not our purpose in this book), I have chosen to present and illustrate a sociological approach that has been helpful to my own understanding of mass communication as a social phenomenon and that provides the student with ideas for future research on these topics. The result is a perspective that gives emphasis to what I regard as an important array of problems. This perspective is not idiosyncratic, however: It draws from major theoretical outlooks in sociology and sociological social psychology and applies them to the field of mass communications study.

Each theoretical approach looks at a range of problems from a special viewpoint and gives emphasis to one rather than another feature of mass communication. Functional theory, as we have noted, focuses on the processes that contribute to social order, to the maintenance and stability of societies. It also considers the unplanned, and sometimes unanticipated, developments in social structure and processes that more or less constantly press toward social change. We examine the consequences of mass communication for society and its members mainly from this perspective.

Social conflict theory, by contrast, stresses the dynamics of struggle between segments of the population (such as social classes) and gives emphasis to the dynamics of social change. In mass communications study, an orientation called *critical theory* reflects some of these concerns.

Critical theory draws attention to the differential distribution of power in and among societies. It is critical of what it regards as the subordination of mass communication to the needs of the established power structure within and between societies. Critical theory is likely to focus on the dysfunctions of mass communication as organized and operated in the world today. It raises, among other issues, a concern over possible cultural pollution, cultural invasion and cultural dominance of Third World countries by Western nations who dominate the world's mass media technology and content. Herbert Shiller's research, discussed briefly in Chapter 8, is an example.[29]

While we do not take critical theory (or social conflict theory) as our sociological perspective, our functional approach also permits hypotheses about dysfunctional consequences of mass communication, without necessarily linking them to the so-called media imperialism of Western nations. It suggests we consider the possibility that cultural pollution, cultural invasion, and the like are so-

[28] See, as examples, De Fleur and Ball-Rokeach, *Theories of Mass Communication; Ferment in the Field: Communications Scholars Address Critical Issues and Research Tasks of the Discipline*, a symposium issue of the *Journal of Communication*, 33, 3 (Summer 1983).

[29] For one critique of the critical approach, see Kurt Lang and Gladys Engel Lang, "The 'New' Rhetoric of Mass Communication Research: A Longer View," *Journal of Communication*, 33, 3 (Summer 1983), pp. 128–140.

cial consequences of international mass communication whatever the ideology of the communication source—capitalistic or communistic, democratic or authoritarian.

Another orientation related to critical theory is *cultural studies*. This approach regards societies as "threaded throughout, held in . . . complex unity, by culture: by the production and reproduction of systems of symbols and messages," according to one proponent, James W. Carey. Carey also reminds us that the mass media "must be considered in relation to everything else," rather than studied "in relation to this or that isolated problem . . . or institution . . . or practice. . . ."[30]

The structural and functional perspectives used in this book also consider the nature of the society within which mass media are organized and operate, as noted in Chapter 2. Several social theories of mass communication are discussed there, along with comparative descriptions of some alternative mass media systems in different kinds of societies. These features of mass media systems, and perhaps the systems themselves, can sometimes be interpreted as functional for the established societies within which they have developed historically and whose structural and ideological purposes they seem to serve.

Our discussion of the sociology of the communicator (Chapter 3) draws upon sociological theory used in organizational studies and the sociology of occupations and work. From these theoretical approaches, we stress the usefulness of the comparative analysis of occupational roles within complex organizations, thus linking the formation of mass communication content to the social processes of production, distribution, and exhibition. In this treatment we also draw upon the *production of culture* approach to the study of mass communication, which as one of its proponents, Richard Peterson, reminds us, "takes as its point of departure the observation that the nature and content of symbolic products are shaped by the social, legal and economic milieus in which they are produced."[31]

Our approach to the sociology of the audience gives special emphasis to interpersonal communication and its link to mass communication through examination of the theoretical concept of *opinion leadership* as a social role and the related theoretical image of a *multistep flow of communication* throughout society. Our discussion of audiences is also informed by concepts commonly used in the sociological study of *social differentiation* (such as social stratification by economic class, occupation, and age), as these characteristics relate to people's communication behavior. Certain other theoretical concepts from social psychology are also discussed in the chapter.

Another widely cited theoretical orientation, the *uses and gratifications* approach to the study of audiences and communication effects, also informs our discussion. This approach addresses questions about what people do with mass

---

[30] James W. Carey, "The Origins of the Radical Discourse on Cultural Studies in the United States," *Journal of Communication*, 33, 3 (Summer 1983), pp. 311–313.

[31] Richard A. Peterson, "Five Constraints on the Production of Culture: Law, Technology, Market, Organizational Structure and Occupational Careers," *Journal of Popular Culture*, 16, 2 (Fall 1982), pp. 143–153.

media, rather than what the media do to people. For example, it considers the uses people make of mass communication and the gratifications they say they get from this behavior. This orientation is related to functional theory, which asks: What are the social consequences of people using mass communication (rather than, say, face-to-face communication) for such purposes?[32]

Dependency theory is a sociological approach that tries to account for the social conditions under which people become increasingly dependent on mass communication for their ties to necessary social knowledge and their concepts of social reality. Dependency theory stresses the current increasing interdependence of mass media systems and other social systems. These interdependencies among systems, in turn, affect what appears in mass communication and hence influence people's dependence on them. People become more dependent on mass media as these media provide important (and even minor) communication services, such as news and entertainment. Moreover, such media dependency, it is argued, increases during times of social conflict and social change. One predicted consequence of dependency is that those who are more media-dependent will also be more susceptible to mass communication's effects on their belief systems, sentiments, and behavior. They become, for example, more vulnerable to influence by mass communication campaigns. This theory informs one of the major case studies on mass persuasion that we present in Chapter 7.[33]

Cultivation theory, which relates specific mass communication content to its possible effects on individuals and on society, is touched upon in Chapter 6, on content analysis, and later in Chapter 8 on the effects of mass entertainment. It is consistent with an overall functional framework that invites consideration of both positive and negative consequences of mass communication. It also suggests ways by which some of these consequences might come about.[34]

Symbolic interactionism provides a perspective on the processes by which people develop their concepts of self and of the world, through their social interaction with others sharing a system of significant symbols. This social psychological orientation, strongly identified with the works of George Herbert Mead, has several contemporary versions, too complex for review here. They stress the active part that people play in giving meaning to physical and social situations, including their own identities, through communication with others. The relevance of symbolic interactionism to a sociological perspective on mass communication is implicitly evident, for example, in our treatment of socialization (Chapter 9) and in our concern for examining the role of interpersonal as well as mass communication in people's construction of the meaning of mass-communicated news and entertainment.[35]

---

[32] Charles R. Wright, "Functional Analysis and Mass Communication Revisited," in Blumler and Katz, *The Uses of Mass Communications*, pp. 197–212.

[33] For a fuller presentation of this theory, see De Fleur and Ball-Rokeach, *Theories of Mass Communication*, pp. 236–251.

[34] See citations in Chapters 5 and 7, below.

[35] For discussions of the varieties of approaches to symbolic interactionism, see Sheldon Stryker, "Symbolic interactionism: themes and variations," in Morris Rosenberg and Ralph H. Turner, *Social Psychology: Sociological Perspectives* (New York: Basic Books, 1981), pp. 3–29, and Bernard

Technological determinism gives emphasis to the dominant communication mode and technology of the times (oral, print, electric) as it affects society. This approach is best represented in the historical-sociological analyses of Harold Innes and in the more widely known formulations by Marshall McLuhan, whose phrase "The medium is the message" became so popular.[36] Although this theoretical orientation is not taken in our sociological perspective, it nonetheless reminds us of the significance of available technology and modes of communication for society and for social change.

The social implications of changes in communication technology, such as the increasing intrusion of electronic techniques into traditional print media, and the linkage of computers to cable television or to one another through networks, have led some theorists to suggest that we are entering an era of the *new media*, which will bridge the prior dichotomy between mass and personal communication. This, it is argued, will blur the distinctions between modes of communication, cause the transformation of mass communication, and lead to a reduction in its importance, and even to the disappearance of mass communication as we know it today. We discuss some of the social implications of the new communication technology in our final chapter, returning again to our argument that one needs to be sensitive to both functions and dysfunctions in anticipating or analyzing social consequences.[37]

We have occasionally borrowed ideas from some other theoretical approaches when they expand our analysis or are useful for illustration. But our general theoretical orientation stems from sociology and social psychology, as will become apparent in more detail in the following chapters.

N. Meltzer, John W. Petras, and Larry T. Reynolds, *Symbolic Interactionism: Genesis, Varieties and Criticism* (London and Boston: Routledge & Kegan Paul, 1975). For Mead's views on communication, see George Herbert Mead, *Mind, Self and Society: From the Standpoint of a Social Behaviorist*, edited by Charles W. Morris (Chicago: University of Chicago Press, 1934), especially pp. 253–260.

[36] For examples, see Harold A. Innis, *Empire and Communications* (Toronto: University of Toronto Press, 1972) and *The Bias of Communication* (Toronto: University of Toronto Press, 1951); Marshall McLuhan, *Understanding Media: The Extensions of Man* (New York: McGraw-Hill, 1965), esp. chap. 1, "The Medium Is the Message";·and James W. Carey, "Harold Adams Innis, and Marshall McLuhan," *Antioch Review*, 27 (1967), pp. 5–39.

[37] Rice et al., *The New Media*.

CHAPTER 2

Mass Communications as Social Institutions

OVERVIEW

Mass communication is one way in which social communication has become institutionalized and organized. Our society expects, for example, that certain news will be routinely handled through mass communication so as to reach large numbers of people, from all walks of life, quickly and publicly. Social communication can be institutionalized in other ways; for example, a society may expect that personal news about family matters will be transmitted privately and kept within the family circle. A sociological approach to the study of mass communication is concerned with the institutionalized forms of social communication and with the patterns of social organization through which mass communication occurs. It seeks to describe and understand the regular and patterned features of mass communication as part of a society.

Institutional analysis of mass communication is concerned with the detection, description, and analysis of the social norms and expectations about its production, content, distribution, exhibition, reception, and use. Sociologists look for the cultural prescriptions as to who may or may not and who should or should not engage in the production, distribution, exhibition, and reception of mass communication; how these activities should be performed; and what ought or ought not to be mass-communicated, according to the norms of a particular society.

Who *may* participate in these mass communication activities is sometimes formally specified and prescribed by law or by some other formal agreements such as union contracts or guild regulations. The question of who *should* participate is less a matter of law than of public sentiment, beliefs, and mores. For example, although it might be perfectly legal for a group of Communists to publish a community newspaper in the United States, many local residents might feel that they should not.

Analysis of the organizational dimension of mass communication considers who can (or cannot) and who does (or does not) engage in the production, distribution, exhibition, and reception of mass communication. Who *can* do these things, among those who are allowed, may depend upon economic and other resources. Who actually *does* them is yet another question. Thus sociologists study, among other things, the observed division of labor involved in carrying out mass communication tasks.

In both normative and organizational analyses, sociology tries to go beyond the description of which specific individuals or groups conduct these communication tasks and seeks to characterize participation in terms of broader social categories. For example, are both men and women legally permitted to own and operate a television station? Foreigners or only citizens? Children or only adults? *role→structure* People of any political persuasion, or only members of approved political parties? Organizational analysis is also guided by theoretical concepts. For example, what are the patterns of authority, responsibility, accountability, and information flow? Investigations consider both the formal relations among participants in media production (or other tasks) and relevant informal ones, such as friendships. Both normative and organizational analyses are enriched through considering links between these mass communication operations, such as between production and distribution, and between the mass communication system and *linkage* other social institutions—government, family, the economy. Much can be learned too from comparisons with accounts of how mass communication is institutionalized in other societies.

All this is a vast order and serves more as a overview of the kinds of questions that can be raised rather than an account of what has been accomplished through research to date. Nevertheless, sociological studies have made valuable contributions that help fill in pieces of the overall picture.

Although the analytical distinction between social institutions and social organization is important, it is usually difficult to distinguish the two in a descriptive account of a specific group or organization involved in the mass communication process—say a television network, a broadcasting station, or a daily newspaper—or in a descriptive account of a society's total mass communications arrangement—referred to collectively as "the mass media." Such case studies generally gloss over the distinction between the institutional and organizational features of mass communication and treat the medium (or set of media) under analysis as a social system, combining both normative and organizational elements in the description.

Some order can be introduced if there is a good way to make comparisons among mass communication systems. The difficulty is, as aptly stated by W. Phillips Davison and his colleagues, that "there are as many media systems as there are countries." Every country, they maintain, "has the media system it has earned. The structure of a system is dictated by politics and economics and, to a certain extent, shaped by geographical, linguistic, and cultural forces."[1] Is there a useful way (or several useful ways) to classify these many systems for comparative purposes?

Typologies of communication systems can be useful if one keeps in mind *Typologies* some of their underlying assumptions and limitations. Each typology reflects its creator's judgments about which organizational and normative criteria are important, such as whether the media are state or privately owned, and the norm of freedom of communication. The use of different criteria leads to a variety of classification schemes and typologies of mass communication systems.[2]

---

[1] W. Phillips Davison, James Boylan, and Frederick T. C. Yu, *Mass Media: Systems and Effects*, 2nd ed. (New York: Holt, Rinehart and Winston, 1982), p. 42.

[2] For examples, see Davison et al., *Mass Media*, pp. 40–62; Frederick W. Frey, "Communication and Development," in *Handbook of Communications*, ed. I. de Sola Pool et al. (Chicago: Rand McNally, 1973); George Gerbner, "Institutional Pressures upon Mass Communicators," *Sociolog-*

Matters are further complicated by the fact that the "types" of systems proposed in a typology are not always mutually exclusive and hence, as Davison and others point out, "It is not always easy to fit a country into one of the theories or groups." For example, Davison classifies communication systems into three categories, "those of democracies, communist states, and developing nations," but notes that this typology poses difficulties, since "many countries are both communist and developing."[3] A recent study of world media systems groups them into three types for comparison: Western, Communist, and Third World.[4]

The usefulness of such broad typologies lies in pointing out, in a more or less systematic fashion, important similarities and differences in how mass communication is institutionalized throughout the world. They bring some order into the picture. To that end they can be helpful guides, especially if we do not take them too literally.

Currently most comparative descriptions of mass communication systems classify them according to type of media ownership and control and how the media "fit" into the society. Attempts have been made to develop broad typologies of mass media systems that reflect each particular society's "philosophy of social communication" (the normative element, at least as expressed through ideology) and the organizational conditions of media ownership, access, and control, whether by government, private individuals, public bodies, or other entities.

One example of a broad typology of mass communication systems that has become well known among theorists was proposed in *Four Theories of the Press*, by Fred Siebert, Theodore Peterson, and Wilbur Schramm.[5] It views the communication systems of the world as operating, more or less precisely, under four major theories:

1. Soviet-Communist
2. Libertarian
3. Social responsibility
4. Authoritarian

Under the first theory, Soviet-Communist, may be grouped most of the communications systems of Communist countries, including those of the Soviet Union itself. In these countries the mass media—press, broadcasting, film—have clear and explicit mandates from the Party and the government as to their primary objectives. Above all, they are to carry Communist theory and policy to the masses, rallying support for Party and government and raising the general cultural level of the people. To achieve these aims, the Party and the government exercise relatively strict control over the media and their operation.

The libertarian theory dominates the Anglo-American and many other Western countries. Emphasis is upon the freedom of the media, especially from

ical Review Monograph, 13 (1969), pp. 205–248; and L. John Martin and A. G. Chaudhary, eds., *Comparative Mass Media Systems* (New York: Longman, 1983).

[3] Davison et al., *Mass Media*, p. 43.

[4] Martin and Chaudhary, *Comparative Mass Media Systems*.

[5] Fred Siebert, Theodore Peterson, and Wilbur Schramm, *Four Theories of the Press* (Urbana: University of Illinois Press, 1963).

government control, although some government regulation, restriction, and operation may be found. The third theory, social responsibility, is also in the Anglo-American tradition. This theory emphasizes the moral and social responsibilities of the persons and institutions that operate the mass media. Among these responsibilities are the obligations to provide the public with information and discussion on important social issues and to avoid activities harmful to the public welfare. Often the mass media in Western countries seem to operate under a mixture of these two theories, although some writers contend that there is a trend toward the social responsibility concept.

The last theory, authoritarian, was characteristic of European systems in the sixteenth and seventeenth centuries, but also describes communication systems in some countries in modern times. Under this theory, the media, private or public, are clearly subordinate to the state and are restrained from expressing major criticism of the government or its officials or both. Such restraint may be achieved through a variety of methods, such as relatively strict government procedures of licensing and censorship.

ALTERNATIVE SYSTEMS OF MASS COMMUNICATION

In the balance of this chapter we examine some features of several different systems of mass communication. Our cases have been selected for their intrinsic interest and for their sociological value as examples of the variety of ways in which mass communication is organized and institutionalized in different societies, both now and in the past.

We do not attempt to describe the organization and operation of all mass media in each society examined; that is too great a task for our purposes. Rather, our treatment is selective (fuller accounts can be obtained from sources cited in the references). Our examples are drawn mainly from the field of broadcasting and occasionally from other media. While the general descriptions are as current as possible, some things will have changed by now, especially details and statistics. Perhaps it is fitting that we must depend on the mass media themselves for up-to-the-minute news about the mass media! On occasion we cite examples of sociologically interesting features of a communication system, valid in their day but now passed into history. We can learn from them too.

Each of these systems can be seen as dependent upon, yet itself a part of, the social system within which it is found. It is interrelated with the governmental, political, economic, and other institutions which characterize that society. From the perspective of functional analysis, the reader may conclude that some of the features of mass communication systems described here seem to be useful to the particular society where they operate; other features, even the same ones, may appear to be dysfunctional from another point of view. There may be a number of features of the systems we are about to describe that go against our personal values. It may be good to remember, as pointed out in Chapter 1, that to interpret something as functional is not the same as saying that one likes it or approves of it.

When looking at any mass media system, it is useful to keep in mind too that each society is subject to international influences. Mass communication crosses international boundaries, and this passage raises important policy issues for each nation: concern about cultural invasion, free flow of information, cultural values, access to and control over media resources. But our chief focus here is on the mass media system within a particular society.

We consider first the Soviet system, and then the Communist Chinese system. Next we discuss some aspects of the British, Canadian, and American systems, especially broadcasting. Finally, we discuss briefly some points about communication patterns in nonindustrial countries. We hope that comparative information about a variety of communication systems will provide a broader framework within which to view and understand the more familiar American arrangements for mass communication. These set the stage for much of the sociological research on communications discussed in the remainder of the book.

CASE 1:   Mass Communication in the Soviet Union

Of all the mass communication systems in the world, one of the most intriguing for American readers, because it contrasts so sharply with their own, is the Soviet Union's. The major outlines of this system have been described and analyzed by several researchers in the past and in recent years.[6] These works are the major sources for our presentation here. We consider, first, the Soviet systems of television and radio broadcasting and then the Soviet press.

Broadcasting

Television, the ubiquitous mass medium, has found its way into the Soviet household as it has into the American. By the early 1980s there were an estimated 80 million television sets (approximately one for every three persons) in the Soviet Union, many capable of receiving color broadcasts.[7]

In 1970 all television and radio transmissions were placed under the centralized direction of the Union-Republic State Committee for Radio and Television under the Council of Ministries of the USSR. In the late 1970s television

[6] Alex Inkeles, *Public Opinion in Soviet Russia: A Study in Mass Persuasion* (Cambridge, MA: Harvard University Press, 1951) and *Social Change in Soviet Russia* (Cambridge, MA: Harvard University Press, 1968); James W. Markham, *Voices of the Red Giants* (Ames: Iowa State University Press, 1967); Walter B. Emery, *National and International Systems of Broadcasting* (East Lansing: Michigan State University Press, 1969), chap. 22; Gayle D. Hollander, *Soviet Political Indoctrination: Developments in Mass Media and Propaganda since Stalin* (New York: Praeger, 1972); Ellen P. Mickiewicz, *Media and the Russian Public* (New York: Praeger, 1981); John J. Karch, "USSR," in *World Press Encyclopedia*, ed. George Thomas Kurian (New York: Facts on File, Inc., 1982); Thomas Remington, "The Mass Media and Public Communication in the USSR," *The Journal of Politics*, 43 (1981), pp. 803–817; Ellen Mickiewicz, "Feedback, Surveys, and Soviet Communication Theory," *Journal of Communication*, 33, 2 (Spring 1983), pp. 97–110. See also *World Communications* (Paris: UNESCO, 1975), and UNESCO's *Statistical Yearbooks*, various dates. Since our presentation draws on many of these works and attempts a synthesis, it is not possible to cite each source used on every point. I will give major references wherever possible.

[7] UNESCO, *Statistical Yearbook, 1982.*

programs were broadcast through telecenters organized at different administrative levels and spread widely, although not evenly, throughout the Soviet Union. They served its population of approximately 265 million people, whose cultures contain more than 200 languages and dialects, settled throughout an area of 8.65 million square miles.[8]

National-level telecasts originate in Moscow; there also is a second level of broadcasting with a major telecenter in each of the republics in the Soviet Union; then there are stations in a number of large cities and in various provincial capitals. National-level programs, in Russian, are retransmitted by stations at lower levels, which also broadcast programs of local origin, often in a local language or dialect. Initial physical limitations on the reception of national-level broadcasts have been greatly reduced, it is reported, by the introduction of space satellites, which allow direct transmission in Russian to various telecenters many miles apart, which then transmit them locally.[9]

The glamour of television may have overshadowed radio in recent years. Nevertheless, radio continues to be important in the Soviet Union, especially in rural areas.[10] In 1982 there were an estimated 130 million radio receivers in the Soviet Union. In the past, Soviet radio presented a dramatic contrast with American radio because of its extensive system of wired radio diffusion. This early system persisted at least into the early 1970s and may play some role today. A brief description of it is of interest here because of its unique place in the early development of mass communication in the Soviet Union and its apparent functional compatibility with the Soviet philosophy of communication and the needs of Soviet society at that time.

Three administrative levels of radio broadcasting—central, local, and lower—provide a network of radio service that transmits in more than eighty-five languages and dialects and reaches citizens widely spread across the Soviet Union. Central broadcasting comes from Moscow. It consists primarily of all-union programs—that is, broadcasts directed to all citizens in the Soviet Union, plus special programs for selected audiences, outlying areas, and so on. Local broadcasting refers to the network of regional stations that supply radio service within the several territories and republics of the Soviet Union. Local stations may create their own programs. For a sizable portion of their broadcast time, however, they rebroadcast programs originating at the central level.

Mickiewicz, commenting on this in 1981, says that certain local radio stations and telecenters rarely supplement the central or national broadcasts. ("Thus," she points out, when one speaks of the public's "choices between local and national media, it is really only the local press that is competitive.")[11] The third level of radio broadcasting, the lower level, is made up of radio-diffusion

[8] Karch, "USSR."

[9] Mickiewicz, *Media and the Russian Public,* especially pp. 18–19.

[10] Mickiewicz remarks that "Domestic radio listening is a leisure-time activity that has been radically altered by the introduction of television into Russian households," but that it remains more popular and relevant in rural than in urban areas. She also presents some rare data on Soviet audiences based on previously unpublished sociological surveys by Vladimir Shlapentokh in the first survey of the readership of *Pravda* in 1968. Ibid., pp. 138–139.

[11] Ibid., pp. 47–48.

exchanges which, for the most part, distribute central and local programs to listeners through a network of wires and wired receivers, in some ways like cable TV. Emery estimated that about half of the radio receivers in the USSR in the late 1960s resembled the radios familiar to us—that is, sets capable of receiving broadcasts directly from the air. The others were wired sets, comparable to loudspeakers, that receive only programs distributed through a radio-diffusion exchange.[12]

The wired sets and public address systems were often located in public places—recreation halls, factories, collective farms, reading rooms—and radio listening thus became a group experience. In such public settings, it is possible for local representatives of the Communist Party to "agitate" the audience by interpreting and commenting upon the broadcast and by leading group discussions.[13] But Karch notes that by 1980, the dramatic expansion of both radio and television may have changed things, because increased "possession of radios and TV sets dilutes the 'collective' idea as it increases private listening and viewing."[14] He also reports in 1980 that out of 115 million radio sets, 45 million are shortwave sets, capable of receiving foreign broadcasts.

Each of the three organizational levels of broadcasting is ultimately responsible to the Union-Republic State Committee for Radio and Television under the Council of Ministers of the USSR. The overall structure of radio broadcasting is highly centralized, with maximum authority located in the state committee, lesser authority and responsibility held by the various local committees, and the least authority exercised by the radio-diffusion exchanges that supply the local listener.

Inkeles's analysis of the radio broadcasting system in the 1950s and 1960s describes how broadcasting was effectively controlled by the Communist Party through a combination of indirect and direct mechanisms.[15] Consider, for example, the Party's three chief methods of guiding central broadcasting. First, the Party issued decisions criticizing the work of the state (then, all-union) committee and directing its future activity. Such directives were customarily issued by the Party's central committee, through its propaganda department. Second, the Party placed trusted officials in positions of responsibility and control on the broadcasting committee. Third, the rank-and-file employees of the communication system included a large number of Party members, who took care that the system operated in line with the Party's directives and who reported any deviations to their Party cells. On the local and lower levels of broadcasting, similar controls existed. The local radio committees were supervised by local Party organizations, and the "editors" of lower radio-diffusion exchanges were supervised by such local Party organs as the local trade union committees. How many of these control mechanisms persist in the 1980s and what, if any, new procedures have been introduced, we do not know.

[12] Emery, *National and International Systems*, p. 386.

[13] See Alex Inkeles, *Public Opinion in Soviet Russia*, for a discussion of how this worked.

[14] Karch, "USSR," pp. 906, 918.

[15] Inkeles, *Public Opinion in Soviet Russia*.

How did the wired diffusion arrangement come about? What are its functions and dysfunctions for Soviet society? Inkeles summarizes four arguments that are commonly given to support the arrangement and that also provide clues as to its origin and current functions. Initially, the system provided an economical solution to the problem of communicating over a large land area to a population with limited financial and technical resources. The cost to install and operate a simple wired speaker was less than one-tenth that of a regular receiver. In addition, the supply of parts required was much less.[16] At the same time, the wired system provided higher-quality reception than regular sets because the single lower-level receiver that served many wired speakers was of higher quality than the usual private set. Furthermore, it was argued that the wired network facilitated local communications and permitted such communication to continue without enemy detection during war. Finally, the restriction of listeners to one program or at best a few programs offered on their sets strengthened the control and propaganda power of the system, virtually eliminating the reception of outside propaganda.

The major features of early Soviet radio broadcasting—wired speakers in radio-diffusion exchanges, levels of broadcasting, collective radio listening, public address systems—may be regarded as products of the social history of broadcasting in that society. That is, they represent a functional organizational pattern (not necessarily the only possible pattern) that developed historically to meet the particular technical, economic, social, and political conditions of the moment: "the great distances to be covered in the Soviet Union, the limited number of broadcasting stations available, and the difficulties of producing a sufficient number of regular radio sets to meet the needs of the population."[17] Furthermore, the pattern is highly compatible with the social and political ideology that directs all mass communication in the Soviet Union to aid the Communist Party in its education of the masses in bolshevism, a concept emphasized by Lenin. According to Leninist philosophy, the Party has, among other objectives, the clear duty to lead the proletariat—to raise their general cultural level and to guide them toward their social, economic, and political destiny. Under this philosophy, the radio and other mass media are regarded primarily as instruments for achieving the Party's goals.[18]

[16] See Inkeles, *Public Opinion in Soviet Russia*, pp. 243–244. Data on the initial cost of receivers is provided in an earlier essay by Inkeles, "Domestic Broadcasting in the U.S.S.R.," in *Communications Research 1948–1949*, ed. Paul Lazarsfeld and Frank Stanton (New York: Harper & Brothers, 1949), pp. 223–293. Emery has pointed out, however, that because maintenance of wired systems is becoming increasingly expensive and because the reception quality of wired loudspeakers is low, future development of facilities will probably concentrate on multiple-channel broadcasting and on improved radio sets. This new emphasis can be seen in the changing proportion of radio sets to wired loudspeakers from 1958 to the present time. In 1958 there was approximately one private radio set to every three loudspeakers. By the end of the 1960s, there was a little over one private set for every loudspeaker, and over one-half of these private radio sets were equipped for shortwave reception. See Emery, *National and International Systems*, p. 386. For details of an attempt to intensify wired broadcasting in the late 1960s, see Hollander, *Soviet Political Indoctrination*, pp. 101–102.

[17] Inkeles, "Domestic Broadcasting in the U.S.S.R.," p. 256.

[18] For a discussion of the impact of Lenin's theories on mass communication, see Inkeles, *Public Opinion in Soviet Russia*, especially chaps. 1 and 2.

The Soviet Press

No newspapers in the Soviet Union are privately owned. They are published by the Communist Party, the government, or such public associations as trade union organizations, sports clubs, youth organizations, factory groups, and collective farms. In general, the press consists of papers published at various "levels" that correspond to the major administrative-territorial divisions within the Soviet Union. The press is also specialized along a number of lines. Geographically, the levels of the press include the central all-union press, which circulates throughout the Soviet Union; the provincial press, including the republican, territorial, and regional papers; the local press, including the district, city, and lower (primary) press; and single-copy typewritten or handwritten "wall" newspapers tacked on bulletin boards in factories, farm buildings, and the like. The number of papers published increases as you move from the level of the all-union papers, through the provincial sector, through the local sector, to the several hundred thousand wall newspapers.[19] Daily newspapers totaled nearly 700 in 1978, with a circulation of nearly 104 million.[20]

As described by Inkeles and others, each sector of the Soviet press has special roles. The all-union press carries the message of the central authorities, publishes the Party line, and generally provides the pattern and main source of material for all newspapers of a similar functional type in the provincial and local sectors. The provincial press translates these materials for a particular region, clarifies and discusses regional economic and political problems, and propagandizes for the Party. The local press is charged with teaching the masses and translating Party directives into daily life; but it may not discuss Party theory or other top-level matters.

Within each of the three main sectors of the Soviet press there are papers designed specifically to treat a particular subject matter or to reach a special audience. Major examples include *Pravda*, the official newspaper of the Central Committee of the Communist Party, with an estimated readership of 50 million people and the largest circulation in the world (11 million). Some others are *Izvestiya* of the Supreme Soviets, *Red Star* and *Soviet Fleet* of the military services, and *Trud*, the publication of the All-Union Trade Union Council. There are also special papers for youth, such as *Komsomolskaya Pravda*, which had a circulation of 10 million in 1978.[21]

Ultimately each level of the press is subject to the direction, inspection, and control of the Central Committee of the Communist Party of the Soviet Union.[22] Earlier descriptions by Inkeles and other report that the central committee is responsible for the central, provincial, and local presses. Each level is

[19] In 1961, for example, there were 25 all-union papers with an estimated circulation of 24 million, about 580 provincial papers with more than 26 million circulation, and about 9,000 local-sector papers with a circulation of more than 18 million. See Markham, *Voices of the Red Giants*, p. 112. Inkeles reports that by 1964–1965 there were 7,700 newspapers in the Soviet Union (including collective farm papers) due to cutbacks in direct newspaper publication as a result of the 1962 party reorganization. See Inkeles, *Social Change in Soviet Russia*, p. 277.

[20] Karch, "USSR," p. 901.

[21] Ibid., p. 905.

[22] According to Karch's account, the Central Committee since 1978 has exercised its control through two departments: the International Information Department (IID) and the Propaganda

also subject to control by the press sector of the propaganda and agitation department of the Communist Party committee that operates on that level of administration. This sector nominates the editors for its level, supervises the press in that area, and reviews and criticizes the press in the next lower level. Thus the press sector of the Communist Party committee in each republic would nominate the editor in that republic and supervise the press there, while reviewing and criticizing the district or city papers in its area.

Each lower committee of the Communist Party is ultimately responsible to the central committee. Each paper is also subject to review and criticism: The lower press may be criticized by the district paper, the district by the regional, the regional by the central all-union paper. The content of each newspaper is subject to censorship by its "responsible secretary" and by its censor, who approve what is to be printed and released. Finally, cutting across all levels, is the power of the chief official agency of censorship, the Main Administration for Safeguarding State Secrets in the Press (formerly *Glavlit*).

Every publication must give special attention to letters written by readers stating complaints about such matters as consumer goods, repair and maintenance of housing, and public facilities. This system of *samokritika*, "self-criticism," provides the Soviet citizen with opportunities to criticize the bureaucracy, although Mickiewicz reports that it has been limited mainly "to certain kinds of criticisms, primarily at the local level, which do not call into question the basic policies, leading personnel, or legitimacy of the political system."[23] The disproportionately large staff working in departments of letters suggests the great attention given to this system by Soviet newspapers.[24] Party leaders, through the institution of *samokritika*, thus allow the population to participate in the process of social control.

Summary

The Soviet system of mass communication has the following characteristics: (1) It is a planned system, in both formal organization and communication content. Newspapers, radio transmitters, diffusion networks, and other media can be altered to fit the changing needs of the society by expanding or contracting, by focusing on a special segment of the audience, and so on. (2) The media are operated under a philosophy strongly committed to the Communist Party line and the achievement of Soviet goals. (3) There is a high degree of review and control of communication content. (4) There is a high degree of specialization, especially with respect to the level or type of audience toward which each medium is directed. (5) The Soviet system maximizes opportunities for audience

Department. The IID has the responsibility for Tass, the Soviet news agency, and also for Novosti (another information agency), *Pravda, Izvestia,* Radio Moscow, and "the information concerns of the embassies." The Propaganda Department controls, among other communication outlets, journals and newspapers (p. 913).

[23] Mickiewicz, *Media and the Russian Public,* p. 50.

[24] Mickiewicz reports that in 1967 *Izvestia* received about 487,000 letters to the editor, and that *Pravda* employs 45 people in its letter department (Ibid., pp. 67–68). Research by George Gerbner in the 1960s reports that at that time *Izvestia* employed nearly one-half of its entire headquarters staff in its department of letters. See Gerbner, "Institutional Pressures upon Mass Communicators," p. 231–238.

exposure in a group context, such as listening to the radio in public halls, reading news while gathered before the wall newspapers, and visiting reading rooms at collective farms and other places. But this last feature may be changing rapidly, according to Karch, who says that in recent years people's use of the mass media has changed to mainly individual and private exposure.[25]

At the risk of oversimplification, the four major communications activities that concerned us in Chapter 1 may be ranked as follows in the Soviet system. (1) The Soviet system gives priority to the interpretation of events and to prescriptions for conduct in the audience. The concept of "news" in the Soviet press does not mean the rapid reporting of current events out of their historical context. Rather, the Soviet editor is responsible for selecting from the events of past and recent history those incidents which illustrate or document the ongoing social processes, especially the process of Socialist construction. Furthermore, a large portion of the daily press is often devoted to suggestions and instructions (in short, prescriptions) for the conduct of local Party officials, workers, and others. (2) High priority is given also to the transmission of Soviet culture, including culture in the broader sense of the basic values and norms of the civilization as well as in the sense of artistic and intellectual materials. Thus many radio broadcasts consist of music, much of it classical. (3) Entertainment receives less emphasis, except for those forms of entertainment that show maximum promise of improving the audience's taste or of contributing to its political or cultural education. (4) Surveillance or reporting of news events, as we know it, plays a less important part in the Soviet system. The mass media have not been obliged, in the past, to transmit information about current events to the audience rapidly, although there are indications that this is changing with the spread of television.[26]

Mass communication comprises a system within the Soviet society—a system that is highly controlled and planned, but that nevertheless must adapt to new conditions and to the needs of the society as perceived by those in power.

CASE 2:   Mass Communication in the People's Republic of China

The mass communication system in Communist China has many institutional and organizational features that are similar to those found in the Soviet system but some that seem interestingly different. In both systems the mass media serve

[25] Karch, "USSR," p. 901. Our discussion has not covered movies in the Soviet Union. For a recent analysis, see Mickiewicz, *Media and the Russian Public*, chap. 6. She reports that, in general, television has decreased the audiences for movie theaters.

[26] Gayle Hollander reports that developments in Soviet radio and television news reporting had produced certain changes in the practice of mass communications in the USSR by the mid-1960s. Among these changes are an increase in the role of radio and television in the rapid transmission of information; and an increase in the variety of news presentations, including information about accidents and other socially undesirable events previously reported chiefly through foreign radio or by word of mouth. Gayle Hollander, "Developments in Soviet Radio and Television News Reporting," *Public Opinion Quarterly* 31 (1967), pp. 359–365. But Mickiewicz reports that many kinds of stories are considered inappropriate for the Soviet press and that only a relatively small percentage of newspaper stories are about events that had occurred the day before publication. *Media and the Russian Public*, p. 53.

as major instruments for implementing the government's social and political policies and goals. The media are organized, operated, and controlled to this end. Furthermore, mass media messages often are followed by face-to-face communication in organized forums, thereby linking the mass media and personal communication into a system.[27]

Writing in 1984, after having recently returned from China where he observed the uses of the mass media to promote national goals, Robert Terrell reports that, "Each of China's mass communications systems is operated as a government agency [and] . . . used to promote the [Communist] Party's objectives." These goals include a national commitment to modernization by the end of the century.

Terrell reports that workers in the mass media are assigned their positions by party officials and that their behavior is subject to party review. Each communications agency is a work unit with powerful authority over the lives of its employees. For example, "If an employee wants to travel from one city to another; return to school for further study; have a baby; get married or purchase a bicycle, his or her work unit must provide formal approval." As responsible government employees, mass media workers are expected to support the party's objectives and to conduct themselves properly both on and off the job.[28]

Radio broadcasting in Communist China, as in the Soviet Union, combines over-the-air stations and wired-diffusion networks. Wireless broadcasts originate in the Central People's Broadcasting Station (Peking) or in any of several provincial and municipal stations. These programs can be received directly by individuals with access to radio receivers. In addition, a third level of broadcasting through wired-diffusion networks operates in the counties and communes. These local stations diffuse the central, provincial, or municipal broadcasts through wires to individual sets and public loudspeaker systems in factories, fields, streets, parks, and other public places.

"It is through these loudspeakers," writes Howkins in 1980, "which are counted in the tens of millions, that the real nature of Chinese radio is most readily apparent."[29] He estimates that 90 percent of the households have a loudspeaker in or near their place of work. Wired diffusion is especially widespread in the rural areas. M. Chen and J. Chu commented in 1982 that, although there is no shortage of regular radio receivers in China today, 95 percent of local com-

---

[27] The major structural and organizational features of the communications system have been described by several scholars, upon whom we rely for the following discussion. See Emery, *National and International Systems;* Alan P. L. Liu, *Communications and National Integration in Communist China* (Berkeley: University of California Press, 1971); Markham, *Voices of the Red Giants;* Dallas W. Smythe, "Mass Communications and Cultural Revolution: The Experience of China," in *Communications Technology and Social Policy,* ed. George Gerbner et al. (New York: Wiley, 1973); Frederick T. C. Yu, *Mass Persuasion in Communist China* (New York: Praeger, 1964); Godwin C. Chu, *Popular Media in China: Shaping New Cultural Patterns* (Honolulu: The University Press of Hawaii, 1978); John Howkins, *The Media in China* (London: Nord Media, 1980); and Min Chen and James Chu, "People's Republic of China," in *World Press Encyclopedia* (1982), pp. 219–231. The quotations from Smythe are reprinted by permission of John Wiley and Sons Inc., and the quotations from Yu, by permission of Praeger Publishers, Inc.

[28] Robert L. Terrell, "Modernization and the Media in China," *Gazette* 33 (1984), pp. 143–154. Quotations are from p. 147.

[29] Howkins, *The Media in China,* p. 67.

munes are hooked into the wired system.[30] Radio sets capable of receiving over-the-air broadcasts have become widely available in the urban areas. As early as 1972, Dallas Smythe estimated that between 80 and 90 percent of the households in Kwangchow and Wuhan had such receivers, and in Shanghai radio sets were generally available for purchase, many of them containing shortwave bands.[31] The place of radio broadcasting—and especially wired diffusion—may be in for some changes with the spread of television broadcasting and the further development of transmission from broadcast satellites capable of sending programs direct to receivers across the land.[32]

Regular television broadcasting in China began in 1958. Early reports indicated that the majority of television receivers were purchased by such collective associations as people's communes.[33] By 1980 there were an estimated 4 million television sets in China. These numbers suggest that television is diffusing throughout the population as well as being located in most factories, schools, government offices, and in other public places.[34]

Television broadcasting is organized into two main levels: national and regional (including municipalities, provinces, and republics). There were 47 television stations in the early 1980s. The Central Television Station (in Peking) broadcasts in a common language; others may use local dialects. According to Emery, television developed with goals similar to those for radio broadcasting—that is, emphasizing education and indoctrination.[35] Hawkins describes, as an example, one day's national telecasts by the Central Television Station as consisting of a morning of TV university, a late afternoon educational program for middle school children, national and international news beginning at 7 P.M., followed by an evening program on science, technology, sports, or some other cultural feature. The station broadcast for about 10 hours per day. CTS has bought the rights to show some foreign entertainment programs, such as *David Copperfield* and *The Man from Atlantis*. In 1979, a very limited amount of commercial advertising was introduced into television and radio broadcasting (and into some print media).[36]

In broad outline, the press in Communist China appears to be organized like that in the Soviet Union. There is differentiation along administrative or geographical lines and by various specialized functions. There are national, provincial, and district (including town and county) newspapers. At each of these levels there may also be papers managed by or directed toward specialized groups such as farmers, youth, and workers. Two features of the Chinese system are of special sociological interest: the important role of *tatzepao* at the local level and the expansive network of grassroots "correspondents" for the press.

Tatzepao are large sheets of paper on which a slogan or message has been

[30] Chen and Chu, "People's Republic of China," p. 227.

[31] Smythe, "Mass Communications and Cultural Revolution," p. 459.

[32] Howkins, *The Media in China*, p. 126; UNESCO *Statistical Yearbook*, 1982.

[33] Emery, *National and International Systems* p. 476.

[34] Chen and Chu, "People's Republic of China."

[35] Emery, *National and International Systems*, pp. 477–478.

[36] Howkins, *The Media in China;* also Chen and Chu, "People's Republic of China."

handwritten in large or bold characters and then posted in some public place.[37] These posters have become a major medium of mass communication, specializing in criticism and self-criticism. They are hung by the hundreds, thousands, and even hundreds of thousands on the walls and in the corridors of factories, universities, government buildings, and other public places. Yu reports that there is no set form or style for *tatzepao*, which may contain slogans, cartoons, accusation letters, or songs. David Poon, based on his observations, classifies *tatzepao* into three categories of content: news reports; directives, orders, and proposals; and criticisms.

Poon recounts the history of *tatzepao* in China and its uses, especially during political purges. Even during ordinary times, *tatzepao* have been used effectively to criticize in public some specific person or persons for their ideological positions or their behavior. Frederick Yu explains:

> That *tatzepao* should be unusually effective as a means of persuasive communications is easy to understand. In the first place, it is written by and about people whom all the readers know. In the second place, it cannot be ignored or dismissed, for it may appear on the wall of one's office or at the door of one's house.[38]

Further, "Virtually everyone in China is within the reach of a *tatzepao*. Its ideological assault is at once personal and direct, and the accused must react not only correctly but also immediately. Almost everyone in Communist China today is in one way or another involved in this particular form of persuasion."[39] The production or distribution of most *tatzepao* is seldom individual and spontaneous. Both Poon and Yu point out that it is likely to be a form of mass communication organized and executed under Communist Party direction and in some cases may be a "formalized affair run almost like a newspaper."[40]

A second feature of interest is the widespread involvement of nonprofessionals as newspaper correspondents, supplementing the work of journalists. Yu observed in the 1960s that "A correspondent is any man or woman, in factory or field, who writes to newspapers about his work, his economic life, his experience in political study, and the accomplishments or failures of those around him."[41]

In 1982 Chen and Chu stated that professional staff reporters "spend most of their time helping amateur correspondents—government employees, workers, teachers, soldiers, peasants—write articles for the paper," and investigating events reported by these correspondents. The amateurs are believed to know the local situation best and to be able to supply leads not readily available to professional reporters.[42]

---

[37] See Yu, *Mass Persuasion in Communist China*, pp. 137–142, and David Jim-tat Poon, "*Tatzepao*: Its History and Significance as a Communication Medium," in Godwin Chu, *Popular Media in China*, pp. 184–221.

[38] Yu, *Mass Persuasion in Communist China*, p. 141. This and excerpts from pp. 142 and 106 are reprinted by permission of Holt, Rinehart and Winston, CBS College Publishing. Copyright 1964 by Frederick A. Praeger, Inc.

[39] Ibid., p. 142.

[40] See Poon, "*Tatzepao*," p. 202.

[41] Yu, *Mass Persuasion in Communist China*, p. 106.

[42] Chen and Chu, "People's Republic of China."

The participation of amateur correspondents in news work does not imply that professional journalism is not taken seriously in China. It is. Accredited courses and journalism programs are offered in major universities and other opportunities are provided for journalistic training. But local, unpaid amateur correspondents are numerous and probably explain some newspapers' counts of hundreds or thousands of correspondents. For example, Smythe reports in 1972 that the *People's Daily* had approximately 300 correspondents in one county alone, and he estimated that there were as many as a quarter to a half million such nonprofessional correspondents throughout China, who supplied some 500 to 600 articles and reports daily to that newspaper, some at the writer's initiative, others by invitation. Smythe asserts:

> The tactical policy is everywhere to seek out outstanding examples of socialist construction and get amateur correspondents (who are workers or peasants) to write them. The editorial function is to select from this vast flood of reports those appropriate to the short-term strategic line of the propaganda plan. . . . Finally, individual articles are selected by the editors on the basis of their profundity, vividness, and inspirational and educational quality.[43]

(It should be noted that for more than fifty years the Soviet press also has utilized volunteer worker-peasant correspondents, in addition to its professional journalists.)

CASE 3: British Broadcasting

Great Britain's mass communication system operates under a philosophy quite different from those of Soviet Russia and Communist China. Media ownership and control are not centralized in a state apparatus. Newspapers, magazines, and films are produced and distributed as private, commercial ventures, as in the United States. Radio and television broadcasting, once operated as monopolies under a public corporation, now are a mixture of public and commercial operations.

Great Britain has been said by some observers to have a predominantly national audience for its mass media because of its comparatively small geographic area and the concentration of population around major cities such as London and Manchester. "The average Briton," writes Winston Fletcher, "gets his news from a national newspaper, his entertainment from nationallly networked television programs; his wife listens to national radio . . . and reads nationally published women's magazines. When they both go out to the cinema . . . they see a nationally distributed film."[44]

Ten of Britain's major daily newspapers in the early 1980s were nationally circulated on the day of issue. Six have been described as the "popular" press

---

[43] Smythe, "Mass Communications and Cultural Revolution," p. 455.

[44] Winston Fletcher, "Britain's National Media Pattern," in *Media Sociology: A Reader*, ed. Jeremy Tunstall (Urbana: University of Illinois, 1970), p. 79.

(usually tabloids): the *Daily Express, Daily Mail, Daily Mirror, Daily Star, Morning Star,* and *The Sun.* Four have been called the "qualities": the *Daily Telegraph, Financial Times, The Guardian,* and *The Times.* Audiences are large. For example, the *Daily Express* has an average circulation of a little more than 2.4 million; the *Daily Telegraph,* not quite 1.5 million. In addition to the national newspapers, there are nearly another hundred or so daily newspapers and more than a thousand nondailies distributed throughout the United Kingdom. Total average daily circulation exceeds 23 million copies (about one copy for every four people).[45]

But Great Britain's unique broadcasting institutions are our main concern here, so we will limit the remainder of our discussion to a brief overview of this system.[46]

Radio broadcasting in Great Britain, following a brief early period of commercial operation, was placed in the hands of a public corporation, the British Broadcasting Corporation (BBC), created by a royal charter in 1927. It remained a monopoly of the BBC from 1927 to 1972, when the Sound Broadcasting Act authorized the establishment of commercial radio stations as well. Television broadcasting was also a monopoly of the BBC until 1954, but now there is commercial television in addition to the BBC broadcasts. The Independent Broadcasting Authority, under license from the government, is responsible for both Independent Television (ITV) and Independent Local Radio (ILR).

As a public corporation, the BBC has certain obligations. The government may, for example, require it to broadcast certain announcements considered important to the public. But the BBC is not owned, controlled, or operated by the government. Formally, it is headed by a board of governors, appointed by the queen in council, and is operated under a director-general and a professional staff. Its charter was renewed in 1981 for another fifteen years. Broadcast operations are financed in part by licensing fees from owners of receivers and in part through other revenues. BBC transmitters supply four national radio networks (BBC Radio 1, 2, 3 and 4), some radio stations, and two national color television services (BBC-1 and BBC-2).

Limited broadcast frequencies played an important part in shaping the initial character of British broadcasting. Because of Britain's proximity to the Continent, the British had to reach an international agreement concerning which radio broadcast frequencies they alone could use without interference from broadcasters abroad. Initially only two frequencies were available for stations having sufficient power to reach the entire nation. The license to use these two airways therefore became a matter of public concern, with important political, social, and economic consequences. It was decided that these frequencies should

[45] James Welke, "United Kingdom," in *World Press Encyclopedia,* vol. 2, pp. 923–943.

[46] British broadcasting has been described and analyzed by a number of authors. We draw primarily upon the following works: Emery, *National and International Systems,* chap. 5; James D. Halloran and Paul Croll, "Television Programs in Great Britain: Content and Control," in *Television and Social Behavior,* Reports and Papers, Vol. 1: Media Content and Control, ed. George Comstock and Eli Rubinstein (Washington, D.C.: U.S. Government Printing Office, 1972); Charles Siepmann, *Radio, Television and Society* (New York: Oxford University Press, 1950), Chap. 7; James W. Welke, "United Kingdom."

be entrusted to a public corporation rather than being placed in private hands (as, indeed, British broadcasting once had been).

But technical constraints alone do not account for the unique system of British broadcasting. It also reflects an ideological commitment made early in its history, under which broadcasting was regarded as an opportunity for the cultural improvement of a mass audience. The BBC was committed to a policy of balanced program service designed to help the listener grow. The three sets of radio programs provided after World War II—Light, Home, and Third—originally represented three levels in a hierarchy of taste or cultural quality. It was hoped that listeners who were initially attracted to radio by the entertainment provided over the Light broadcasts would, in time, sample the more serious programs of the Home Service, and eventually expand their tastes to include the literary, musical, and artistic level of the Third Program. Furthermore, it was planned to have each level of programming raise its own standards as time went by. BBC's monopoly over broadcasting was to be used for this great "cultural experiment." The policy had its advocates and its critics, as one can imagine. How well it might have worked in the long run is unknown, since circumstances changed with the spread of television in the 1950s.

BBC's monopoly on broadcasting ended, and hence the total system of British broadcasting changed shape, when the government authorized a competitive, commercially financed television system in 1954 and commercially financed local radio in 1972.

BBC Radio 1, which is reported to be the most popular radio station in Britain, features mainly music—rock and pop. Radio 2 features sports, music, and light entertainment. Radio 3 has classical music, drama, and public affairs. Radio 4 broadcasts a mixture of unusual drama programs (such as a 26-part adaptation of Tolkein's *Lord of the Rings;* 26 episodes of a documentary on the British seafarer; Dickens's *Bleak House*), lectures, news, and information.[47] The content of Independent Local Radio programming, it is said, "varies widely according to the station, from all news and features to combinations of music, news, public affairs, education, sport, talk and children's programs."[48]

The BBC's television network (BBC-1 and BBC-2) provides a wide range of programs to the nation's viewers. One estimate reports that about 18 percent of these programs are about current affairs, features, or documentaries; 14 percent cover sports; 14 percent, Open University; 14 percent, films and foreign imports; and the rest spread over a variety of categories such as children's programs, light entertainment, drama, education, news, and music. Among BBC-TV's most popular programs are light entertainment such as the situation comedy "To the Manor Born" (16.5 million viewers) and American imports such as "Dallas" (13 million). BBC-1 offers a mixture of light entertainment, sports, drama, news, and documentaries, children's programs ("Dr. Who") and other fare. BBC-2 offers another range of culture, information, and entertainment broadcasts, including news and information programs, comedy and sketches, and cultural broadcasts such as a series on one hundred great painters, and on the architecture of English towns. It is estimated that, on an average day, at least 80 percent

[47] *BBC Annual Report and Handbook 1983* (London: BBC, 1983).

[48] Welke, "United Kingdom," p. 939.

of the British population watch something on BBC-1 and at least 33 percent watch BBC-2. (During a week's time, more than 90 percent watch BBC-1 and more than 75 percent, BBC-2.) Around 39 million people viewed the wedding of Prince Charles and Lady Diana Spencer, 25 million watching it on BBC-TV.[49]

Independent television, as noted, is under the control of the Independent Broadcasting Authority, which owns and operates its transmitters, and supervises programming and advertising. Actual program production is by a number of independent television programming companies (and, for radio, independent local radio contractors). There also is an Independent Television News company (ITN) that supplies news to ITV stations. About 30 percent of ITV's programs are reported as plays, dramas, or movies; 13 percent, current affairs; 12 percent, entertainment and music; 11 percent, news; 11 percent, sports; 10 percent, children's programs; and the rest in education, religion and other categories.[50]

In 1980 the British Government authorized the establishment of a second commercial television channel, Channel Four. Channel Four is intended to complement ITV-1 by providing programs for audiences with special interests as well as for larger general audiences. The Channel Four Television Company, Ltd. is a subsidiary of the Independent Broadcasting Authority. Its national service should reach about 80 percent of the United Kingdom. Controversy arose in Wales, however, where there was public sentiment favoring use of the Fourth Channel for a television service in the Welsh language. In time this was settled through establishing a new television authority in Wales, the Welsh Fourth Channel Authority. Both BBC and ITV supply television programs in the Welsh language to the Welsh Fourth Channel, which also carries other non-Welsh Channel Four programs for its viewers.[51]

Independent television in Great Britain has been described by Halloran and Croll as "a federal system made up of a nonprogramming Authority and fifteen program-producing companies." They comment further that:

> We have seen that the BBC is a public service institution. Independent Television would claim to be both public service and commercial. . . . It is said by those in the system that an outside investigator would be struck, not so much by the commercial character of ITV, but by the extensive powers and duties of the public authority under which it operates. The Authority is meant to be more than a watchdog; it is required to be involved in the positive processes of program planning and the formulation of program policy. . . . It has certain duties and obligations which the law spells out quite clearly. These legal provisions have the general effect of making the Authority answerable to the public and Parliament for the content and nature of all the programs transmitted by Independent Television, no matter who produces them.[52]

[49] *BBC Annual Report*, pp. 38–39.

[50] Welke, "United Kingdom," p. 939.

[51] Welke, "United Kingdom"; W. J. Howell, Jr., "Britain's Fourth Television Channel and the Welsh Language Controversy," *Journal of Broadcasting*, Spring 1981, pp. 123–157; *BBC Annual Report and Handbook, 1982*, pp. 86–90; *World Radio TV Handbook*, 37th edition, 1983 (London: Billboard Limited, 1983).

[52] Halloran and Croll, "Television Programs in Great Britain," pp. 418–419.

The British system of broadcasting is thus a combination of public and commercial organization and is heavily influenced by national norms stressing the broadcasters' public responsibility and accountability for the nature and quality of the broadcasts. This system developed historically without producing the high degree of political centralization and control apparent in the Communist systems described above. It differs, too, in many ways from the more commercially dominated system of American broadcasting.

CASE 4: Canadian Broadcasting

Canadian radio and television broadcasting is a combination of public and private station operations, financed through public funds and commercial advertising. In this respect it may appear to resemble the British system. But the Canadians have developed their own distinctive national system of broadcasting in response to their country's particular physical, economic, political, social, and cultural circumstances.[53]

Canadians face the problem of providing broadcast services over a vast territory, larger than the United States and more than forty times the size of Great Britain. Much of this territory is sparsely populated; most of the population is concentrated in densely settled areas along its southern border and coastal strips. A national commitment to serve its population in all regions, plus the realization that it would not be economically practical for such service to be carried into remote and thinly populated regions if financed only by private broadcasters, has contributed to the development of dual sectors of public and private broadcasting.

A second significant feature of Canadian broadcasting is its commitment to provide regular services to both of the country's major language groups, English-speaking and French-speaking Canadians. This concern has led to the development of a dual system of English-language and French-language television and radio broadcasts and networks. In addition, Canadian broadcasting has attempted to meet the tastes and needs of its varied regional and other subcultural groups.

Third, the Canadian government is concerned with developing and maintaining Canadian program content and production talent in the face of the constant threat of cultural invasion by programs from the United States. Most Canadians live within a few hundred miles of the United States border, well within the reach of American radio and television broadcasts (the latter some-

---

[53] For accounts of these early developments, see Siepmann, *Radio, Television and Society*; Emery, *National and International Systems*, chap. 4; and E. Austin Weir, *The Struggle for National Broadcasting in Canada* (Toronto: McClelland and Stewart, 1965). For recent descriptions and information, see Carman Cumming, Peter Johansen, W. H. Kesterton, Allan Morantz, and Robert Rupert, "Canada," in *World Press Encyclopedia*, pp. 181–201; and Canadian Radio-Television and Telecommunications Commission, *Annual Report 1983–1984* (Ottawa: CRTC Information Services, 1984).

times extended in coverage by cable television systems). Videotape and film provide additional means by which American programs can be imported.

Faced with these circumstances, among others, many Canadian government and broadcast leaders have publicly expressed the philosophy that Canadian broadcasting should be distinctively Canadian in ownership, control, and content. Another publicly expressed view is the idea that Canadian broadcasting should be one national system, serving the needs of its society, whether it operates through public or privately owned stations, or both.[54]

Radio broadcasting in Canada was through privately owned radio stations until 1932, when the government established the Canadian Radio Broadcasting Commission (CRBC). The CRBC started several new stations of its own and joined them with established private stations to form a network of regularly scheduled national broadcasting. The commission was relatively short-lived, being replaced in 1936 by the Canadian Broadcasting Corporation (CBC).

CBC was established by an act of Parliament as a public corporation responsible to a board of governors. CBC owned or leased its broadcast facilities and used them, together with privately owned stations, as outlets for its network programs. Broadcasting facilities expanded greatly over the following years, especially after World War II, so that by now most of the Canadian population is covered by radio service. By 1981 CBC's English-language AM network covered 97 percent of the population, and its French-language AM network reached 91 percent of the population. Canadians are also served by CBC FM radio broadcasts and by private AM and FM stations.[55]

Canadian television, originally established in 1952, has expanded rapidly in the past two decades. At the outset television broadcasting was a national system, with CBC responsible for production, and private stations, as well as a limited number of CBC stations, licensed as outlets. An independent commercially operated television network, CTV, was authorized in 1960. By the early 1980s there were some 11 million television receivers in Canadian homes, servicing nearly the entire Canadian population. In 1981, the CBC's English-language television network covered 96 percent of the Canadian population, while its French network covered 84 percent of the population. Cable television reached 35 to 84 percent of the population in various provinces by 1984. Private English-language and French-language stations provided additional coverage.[56]

The organizational structure for control of both radio and television broadcasting has changed considerably over the years. Initially, the CBC, in addition to conducting its own network and station operations, served as the official regulatory agency for broadcasting, recommending licenses for the private stations, and so on. By clearly subordinating private stations to the CBC, this arrange-

[54] See, as examples, *Report on the Committee on Broadcasting, 1965* (Ottawa: Queen's Printer, 1965); Report of the Special Senate Committee on Mass Media, Vol. 1, *The Uncertain Mirror* (Ottawa: Information Canada, 1970); and Canadian Radio-Television Commission, *Annual Report 1972–1973* (Ottawa: Information Canada, 1973), and the CRTC *Annual Report 1982–1983, 1983–1984.*

[55] Canadian Radio-Television and Telecommunications Commission, *Annual Report 1980–81*, p. 36.

[56] UNESCO *Statistical Yearbook*, 1982; CRTC, *Annual Report 1980–81, 1983–1984.*

ment, according to its supporters, helped to achieve the national goal of maintaining Canadian culture and supplying programs for minorities. Stations were thus prevented from disregarding the CBC network programs and from carrying so many shows from the United States as to permit cultural invasion.

In 1958, a national political change led to the establishment of a new structure for control of broadcasting, the Board of Broadcast Governors, to regulate both public and private stations and networks. The CBC was reconstituted as a separate body under its own board of directors. Still later, in 1968, new legislation established the Canadian Radio-Television Commission, replacing the Board of Broadcast Governors and strengthening the single control over both the CBC and private broadcast operations. Its responsibilities were enlarged in 1976 to include regulating telecommunications carriers, and its name was changed to the Canadian Radio-Television and Telecommunications Commission. These changes are in keeping with the concept of Canadian broadcasting as a single national system—a concept that has persisted over the years.

> In its annual report for 1970–1971 the Commission asserted that: Broadcasting is not an end in itself. It is subject to higher and more general imperatives of national development and survival. Thus broadcasting is an integral part of the larger constitutional domain; a national priority itself, it may at certain times be subject to realignment with other national priorities, be they economic, social, political or cultural.[57]

Among these national priorities have been, as mentioned above, the extension of quality radio and television coverage to remote areas of the provinces as well as to people in the metropolises, bilingual broadcasting, and barriers against cultural invasion from the United States. Efforts to cultivate and preserve Canadian cultural content have included limitations on the ownership of broadcasting facilities by foreigners, specifications for the minimum amount of broadcast content that must be Canadian programming (including Canadian music), and regulations limiting the amount of programming that comes from any one foreign country. For example, 60 percent of all programs broadcast on each television station must be Canadian and, between 6 P.M. and midnight, 60 percent of CBC and 50 percent of private station programs must be Canadian. This may be calculated on an annual basis, or perhaps, as was proposed by CRTC in 1983, on a semi-annual basis, and calculated through a weighted points system—so many points for Canadian directors, writers, composers.[58] Through such efforts, the Canadian system strives to maintain a national cultural integrity in the face of unusual, if not unique, geographical, technical, social, and economic circumstances. It thus provides an important sociological case study in the adaption of broadcasting to a social system.

[57] Canadian Radio-Television Commission, *Annual Report 1970–71* (Ottawa: Information Canada, 1971), p. 3.
[58] CRTC, *Annual Report 1982–1983*, pp. 18–19.

CASE 5:   American Broadcasting

No other country in the world is as permeated by mass media as the United States. Each day over 62 million newspapers are circulated—about one copy for every three or four people. Over 477 million radios are available—more than two per person. Approximately 142 million television sets are available, about one for every two people; many households have two or more sets. And millions of magazines and comic books circulate every month.[59]

For the most part, the American media are privately owned and operated as profit-making organizations. But they are subject to some governmental regulation, especially when their operations require the use of public resources or touch upon matters of public welfare. Hence radio and television broadcasting, which make use of public airwaves, must be licensed by the federal government; laws prohibit the transmission of material considered libelous; censorship has been employed in time of war; and so on. Aside from such specific situational regulations, however, the American media operate chiefly as business enterprises, under a philosophy of minimum governmental restriction.

The legal roots of the American approach toward mass communication can be found in the First Amendment to the Constitution, which guarantees freedom of speech and press. Each of the mass media at various times in its history has defended itself from what it regarded as excessive government control by recourse to this amendment.[60] This legal protection of the media has been substantially supported by American public opinion. For example, national polls have shown that at least 95 percent of the public say that they believe in freedom of speech.

Nevertheless, neither the law nor public opinion endorses *unlimited* freedom of expression. The norm of freedom of expression becomes qualified when it appears to conflict with certain other social values and institutions. The courts have held that freedom of the press does not extend to the publication of obscene material or writing that constitutes a clear and present danger to the nation. Public sentiment also qualifies its approval of the mass media's freedom when other values are at stake. National opinion surveys taken at various times during the past fifty years indicate that, at best, public opinion is split 50–50 over whether the mass media should have the absolute right to publish or broadcast anything they choose, excluding libelous matter, even during peacetime.[61]

[59] See George Kurian and Aviam Soifer, "United States," in *World Press Encyclopedia,* pp. 945–1021; see also UNESCO *Statistical Yearbook,* 1982. For more recent figures, consult the latest edition of *Statistical Abstracts* (Washington, DC: U.S. Government Printing Office), and occasional publications of the U.S. Census Bureau.

[60] Government officials have been very critical of the mass media at times and have attempted to restrict press and broadcast activities through appeals to public opinion and by legislation, court rulings, and other means. Discussions of current developments can be found in such specialized publications as the *Columbia Journalism Review.*

[61] See, for example, Hadley Cantril, ed., *Public Opinion 1935–1946* (Princeton, NJ: Princeton University Press, 1951), pp. 244, 416–418; Robert Chandler, *Public Opinion: Changing Attitudes on Contemporary Political and Social Issues* (New York: Bowker, 1972), p. 7. See also Hazel Ers-

Opinions get more restrictive when military activities or matters of national security seem to be involved. For example, a Harris survey in 1983 reports that 53 percent of a national sample of adults said that our country is better off because of the mass media's extensive coverage of the Vietnam war, but 36 percent said we were worse off, and most of the others were not sure. The public's answers to several questions about our country's banning of media coverage during the invasion of the Caribbean island of Grenada indicate that the majority of people believe the press should have the basic freedom to know what is going on during a military action; 65 percent agreed that, all in all, a small group of reporters should have been allowed into Grenada with the troops. But on the other hand, 54 percent agreed that the president and the military were right to keep the media out in this instance.[62] Thus we see how, at times, the value of freedom of the press is qualified by circumstances.

The following paragraphs examine, very briefly, the organization of broadcasting in America, touching on the changing role of the government and some of the historic steps in the development of the present organizational structure.[63]

Current Structure of the Radio and Television Industry

Anyone who intends to transmit radio or television signals within the United States must first obtain the permission of the federal government through the Federal Communications Commission (FCC), an independent government agency established by Congress in 1934. The FCC is, in its own words,

> charged with regulating interstate and foreign communications by radio, television, wire and cable. It is also responsible for orderly development and operation of broadcast services, and for rapid, efficient, nationwide and worldwide telephone and telegraph service at reasonable rates. Other functions include the protection of life and property through radio, and the use of radio and television facilities to strengthen national defenses. The Commission's jurisdiction covers the fifty States, Guam, Puerto Rico and the Virgin Islands.[64]

Thus the FCC is empowered, among its other charges, to issue, review, and renew licenses for broadcasting. The licenses stipulate the frequency on which broadcasters must remain, the power and times of their transmissions, and other terms of operation.

Since technical conditions limit the number of frequencies available for

kine, "The Polls: Opinion of the News Media," *Public Opinion Quarterly*, 34 (Winter 1970–1971), pp. 630–643.

[62] Louis Harris survey, December 26, 1983.

[63] There are a number of available accounts of American broadcasting. See, as examples, Sydney W. Head, with Christopher H. Sterling, *Broadcasting in America*, 4th ed. (Boston: Houghton Mifflin, 1982); Llewellyn White, *The American Radio* (Chicago: University of Chicago Press, 1947); George Gerbner, "The Structure and Process of Television Program Content Regulation in the United States," in *Television and Social Behavior*, vol. 1, pp. 386–414; and Muriel G. Cantor, *Prime-Time Television: Content and Control* (Beverly Hills, Calif.: Sage, 1980). For a detailed history, see Erik Barnouw, *A History of Broadcasting in the United States*, vols. I–III (New York: Oxford University Press, 1966, 1968, 1970).

[64] Federal Communications Commission, *37th Annual Report/Fiscal Year 1971* (Washington, DC: U.S. Government Printing Office, 1971), p. xi.

radio or television broadcasting, not every applicant can obtain a license. Some criteria of priority had to be developed, and a certain amount of sharing of frequencies is necessary to maximize the service provided by the available frequencies. Some radio stations can operate only during certain hours of the day, for example, when there is little chance that their signals will interfere with those of other nearby or distant stations. Other stations are given priority to operate with stronger signals and at different times in order to reach parts of the country that might not otherwise be serviced. Maximizing the public service performed by radio and television broadcasting is a major concern of the federal government.

Because of its privileged use of a scarce public resource—that is, the airwaves—commercial broadcasting, although a business, has been regarded as a business with a public interest. It has, as a consequence, been subject to more direct regulation by the national government than most of the other American media. Still, this control tends to be more regulatory than restrictive in its intent and effects. The FCC is forbidden by law, for example, to censor programs. But it was charged with the responsibility for determining that each broadcast station operated "in the public interest, convenience, and necessity."

The American system of governmental regulation of broadcasting is a complicated one of interaction among three groups: a regulative agency that has been sorely understaffed since its creation; commercial broadcast interests that, from the time of their initial role in helping to create the regulatory agency, have striven to maintain sufficient independence to protect their huge financial investment and ability to make money; and politicians, interest groups, and various other advocates for the public interest. Neither space nor available data permit the full exploration of this drama here, but some of these components can be touched upon briefly in order to illustrate the complexity of the system at work and to provide some information about how it came about.

The Shaping of the American System

During the early years, radio was controlled under the Radio Act of 1912, which empowered the secretary of commerce to issue licenses specifying frequency of operation. Prior to 1922, licensees were primarily maritime stations and a few amateurs, but when broadcasting "arrived," the number of applicants increased greatly. The courts held that the secretary of commerce and labor was required to issue licenses and to assign frequencies to all applicants. But as the transmitters increased in number, they began to interfere with one another—some stations drifted from their assigned frequencies, more powerful stations blanked out weaker ones, and portable transmitters added to the confusion.

Hopes for self-regulation within the industry were not realized, and members began to look to the federal government for relief. In 1927 a new Radio Act was passed, asserting the federal government's right to regulate all forms of radio communication within the United States through a system of licensing to be administered by a Federal Radio Commission. This authority became the FCC under the Communications Act of 1934.

The financial resources of the FCC and the size of its staff are small, considering the magnitude of the public charge. The task of overseeing broadcast activities (let alone the additional responsibilities of the FCC mentioned above) is formidable. For example, in 1983 there were 10,714 broadcasting stations on the air. These included 8,216 commercial and 1,104 educational radio stations, 870 commercial, 279 educational, and 245 low-power television stations. Commercial broadcasting constitutes the bulk of the stations, although public and educational broadcasts have increased since the enactment of the Public Broadcasting Act of 1967 and the establishment of the Corporation for Public Broadcasting in 1969.

To carry out its many tasks, the FCC, which consists of seven members appointed by the president and confirmed by the Senate, has a staff of approximately 1,900 employees. Only a few hundred staff members concentrate on problems of broadcasting, implementing the FCC's regulatory program, processing applications, and handling complaints and investigations. In 1983, the FCC received more than 3,200 applications for broadcast license renewals. In addition, there were requests for transfers of licenses, and other broadcasting operations needing approval. The FCC also processed more than 667,000 complaints.[65]

"The relative scarcity of FCC resources and manpower," in the judgment of communications economist William Melody, has

> acted to inhibit the aggressiveness of Commission action. Monitoring functions could not be as thorough as desired; industry performance and compliance with regulatory law had to be carried out largely on the honor system, and the Commission usually awaited initiation of a complaint from other quarters before taking action. In addition, priorities had to be set in which long-range planning functions were subordinated to day-to-day administrative procedures. Policy therefore came to be formulated on an ad hoc, case-by-case basis, rather than on long-range policy goals and programs of action.[66]

Melody also notes limitations imposed by the fact that the FCC cannot directly regulate the broadcast networks; that it has a wide range of administrative responsibilities in addition to those dealing directly with broadcasting; and that the broadcast industry has taken an active role in making its own interests and desires known.

During the late 1970s and early 1980s there was movement toward active "deregulation" of some aspects of broadcasting, less emphasis on broadcasters' having to demonstrate service in the public interest, and consideration of longer-term (even indefinite) licenses. Congress extended radio broadcasting licenses to seven-year terms; television, to five. The courts, and later the FCC, greatly deregulated cable television. In 1981 the FCC also reduced some of its requirements of radio broadcasters. Reflecting on the meaning of these FCC moves, Head and Sterling conclude: "Deletion of these items had little substantive effect on radio regulation; their significance lay more in their symbolic role,

---

[65] These data were computed from information contained in the Federal Communications Commission, *49th Annual Report/Fiscal Year 1983* (Washington, DC: U.S. Government Printing Office).

[66] William Melody, *Children's Television: The Economics of Exploitation* (New Haven, CT: Yale University Press, 1973), p. 103. By permission of the publisher.

signaling the culmination of a long-term trend in FCC thinking about its regulatory function . . . in the direction of self-regulation through market competition."[67]

Historically, the broadcasting industry itself has used voluntary self-regulation, as demonstrated in the codes of ethics for radio and television adopted by the National Association of Broadcasters. These codes not only assert the freedom of broadcasters, but also underscore their responsibility to the public. Enforcement of both federal and self-imposed norms in broadcasting is complicated, however, by the structure of the industry, in which the power of program construction is sometimes assigned not only to the individual station owner-operator, but also to networks, production companies, and advertising agencies.[68]

Each radio or television station is responsible for selecting the material it broadcasts. The station originates some of this material, but many stations also carry programs distributed through one or another of the regional or national networks with which a station becomes affiliated. The networks own a few important stations of their own, primarily in the major metropolitan centers, but the affiliated stations supply their greatest number of outlets. An affiliated station agrees to put aside certain broadcast hours, for which the network supplies programs. The local station may make additional hours available to the network in return for further programming. The stations in the network thus created may, in fact, vary from time to time and from program to program, as each of the potential members decides whether or not to hook in. Networks need no license, except for the stations they own and operate themselves. But networks have provided important support for codes of self-regulation within the industry.

Its revenues make the broadcasting industry a big business. In 1980 television revenues, net, were $8.8 billion, and radio revenues, net, were more than $3 billion.[69] Most of the money for stations comes through the sale of time to advertisers. On the local level, a potential sponsor may deal directly with the station. On the national level, however, most advertisers deal with the networks through an advertising agency. Either directly or through an agency, advertisers usually buy time for brief spot announcements about their products or (more rarely) sponsor particular programs. Some of these programs are created and controlled by the station itself, and some are created by the networks, by independent producers, or (in the case of commercials) by advertising agencies.

Broadcasting is big business in an organizational sense too, as conglomerate ownership links stations and networks to other media, such as newspapers, and to large, diversified corporations. A brief history of one such corporation will illustrate the phenomenon.

The initial period in the history of radio has been characterized by historians

[67] Head and Sterling, *Broadcasting in America*, p. 574. The authors present a review and discussion of these and other developments in the history of the regulation and deregulation of broadcasting.

[68] For analyses of the codes and how they work in practice, see Gerbner, "The Structure and Process of Television Program Content Regulation in the United States"; Head and Sterling, *Broadcasting in America*, pp. 507–512; and Cantor, *Prime-Time Television*, pp. 63–80.

[69] Federal Communications Commission, *47th Annual Report, 1981.*

as one of great amateur inventiveness, experimentation, and unregulated growth. Then, with the promise of commercial advantages, a continuing struggle for power and control of the industry developed. Legal battles over patents for the technical components and processes necessary for radio communication became "patent wars," from which a few large-scale organizations emerged to dominate the industry. In time, some of these giants formed combinations either within one branch of the industry (for example, manufacturing), between several branches of the industry (for example, manufacturing and broadcasting), or between several different mass media industries (for example, joint ownership of newspapers and radio). Occasionally, communications empires resulted, within which broadcasting was only a part. One such empire is the RCA Corporation, formerly the Radio Corporation of America.[70]

RCA was formed in 1919 to purchase the radio rights and assets of the American Marconi Company (then controlled by British Marconi). At that time, commercial radio broadcasting had not yet begun, but it was subsequently developed by several organizations, including RCA. Competition became especially keen between the American Telephone and Telegraph Company and RCA. Each organization built a network of affiliated radio stations that centered around its major station in the New York City area, WEAF and WJZ, respectively. In 1926, after an agreement was concluded between RCA, AT&T, and others, RCA emerged as the major broadcaster. RCA developed commercial broadcasting through a subsidiary organization, the National Broadcasting Company (NBC), which was later reorganized as two semi-independent networks. These were the Blue Network, centering on the old RCA network of stations affiliated with WJZ (later sold by NBC), and the Red Network, the stations affiliated with WEAF (which AT&T had sold to RCA).

Within a few decades of its founding, RCA extended its operations to include many diverse communications activities. It established two subsidiaries to handle the old Marconi business—the Radiomarine Corporation of America and RCA Communications. It obtained control of the Victor Talking Machine Company and a number of other companies, permitting it eventually to expand its manufacture of radio receivers, phonograph recordings, and electronic parts and equipment through the RCA Victor Division. Other subsidiaries were developed for servicing electronic equipment (RCA Service), for research (RCA Laboratories), for training (RCA Institute), and for the distribution of products (RCA International Division).

The organizational scope, structure, and composition of RCA have continued to change with time (once it included Random House, Inc., but no longer). By 1982, RCA's revenues from its service businesses made up 52.8 percent of its total revenues of $8.2 billion; the rest came from its manufacturing operations. Its service activities included the National Broadcasting Company, satellite communications, and Hertz car rentals, among others; manufacturing included consumer, commercial, and defense electronics.[71]

[70] For more detailed accounts, see White, *The American Radio*, chaps. 2 and 3; Head and Sterling, *Broadcasting in America*, especially chaps. 5 to 9; and *Who Owns the Media*, ed. B. M. Compaine (New York: Harmony Books, 1979).

[71] See *Fortune*, May 2, 1983, p. 258.

Network broadcasting, the initial function of NBC, became part of a vast communications organization involved in manufacturing, distribution, sales, service, telecommunications, recording, broadcasting, training, publishing, and research. In this, NBC is not unique. Other broadcast networks, notably ABC and CBS, also have organizational connections with nonbroadcasting activities.

As noted above, organizational linkages between television, broadcasting, newspapers, magazines, radio, book publishing, and other mass media are common today. So are connections between mass media organizations and other industrial corporations, through ownership, common membership in a conglomerate, interlocking directorates, or other links. Ben Bagdikian concludes that fifty corporations own our major mass media and thus "control," in varying degrees, what we see and hear through them.[72] For example, a parent corporation usually appoints media leaders who are at least sympathetic to its views and not likely unnecessarily to print or broadcast stories or other matter that will harm it.

Big business and government regulation, then, are two of the forces shaping the American system of broadcasting. Despite the limited resources available to the FCC, and given the economic power of the industry it is required to regulate, the FCC has made a number of historic decisions and regulations that have affected the structure of the broadcasting industry and the content of its programming. Certain of these decisions appear to have been inspired by complaints or requests from nonbroadcasting groups and organizations and other advocates for the public interest. A review of these developments is not possible here.

Cable Television and Direct-Broadcast Satellites

One increasingly important mode of mass communication is cable television or cablevision. In 1984 there were nearly 33 million basic subscribers to cable television in the United States, representing nearly two out of every five households that have television sets. It is estimated that by 1990 more than half of America's television households will subscribe to cablevision, with total subscriptions of more than 50 million.[73]

Cablevision provides several kinds of programming services that it sends over wires into subscribers' houses. The basic service, obtained for a monthly fee, normally provides the subscriber with all television programs being broadcast over-the-air by local broadcasting stations and any other station significantly viewed in the area. It also may provide community programs, produced by the local cable station or simply diffused over its channels. Some cable channels may carry television programs received from communication satellites. In addition to these basic services, cablevision may provide particular program services for additional fees. The viewer can subscribe to one or several channels carrying these services and thus have available all the programs which a particular service supplies, such as movies or sports. Another arrangement is pay-per-view (PPV). The consumer pays for each specific program that he or she selects from among those available on the channel by using a special selector device included in a two-way

---

[72] Ben H. Bagdikian, *The Media Monopoly* (Boston: Beacon Press, 1983).

[73] *Cable Vision*, January 21, 1985, p. 44.

or "interactive" cable system or by telephoning an order to the cable station. Finally, some cable channels are used for special interactive communication (usually nonentertainment), such as banking, shopping, videotext, or teletext.[74]

The number of subscribers to a local cable system may range from more than 200,000 (as in San Diego, California, for example) to nearly 50,000 (as in Moline, Illinois) among the top 100 individual cable systems. Furthermore, one cable company may operate several systems located in different cities or markets. Tele-communications Inc., for example, the largest multiple system operator in America in 1985, services more than 3,300,000 basic subscribers. And the smallest of the top 100 MSOs services more than 26,000 subscribers.[75] The potential audience for the programming services that are satellite-fed to the cable systems and delivered by them to their basic subscribers numbers in the millions. Cable News Network (CNN), for example, can reach more than 30 million viewers; Music Television (MTV), more than 24 million, as of the beginning of 1985. The audiences for pay services also is large. More than 13 million subscribers paid for Home Box Office (HBO) service, for example, in 1984. Thus cablevision has become a significant part of our mass communication scene.[76]

One feature of cablevision that seems different from over-the-air television is that some channels or program services specialize in specific types of programming, such as movies, news, public affairs, or sports. Some authors believe that this differentiation of the audience into smaller special interest publics will significantly change the character of mass communication. Perhaps. But nonetheless the number of viewers who watch cablevision is quite large and comes closer to our concept of a mass audience than a small, private one. For example, a national survey of subscribers to C-SPAN, a cable programming service that specializes in public affairs programming, reported in 1985 that more than 7 million American homes tune it in each month—representing a potential monthly audience of more than 20 million viewers. (Ninety-three percent of those surveyed said that they had voted in the 1984 national elections, thus suggesting an audience with higher than average political interest and participation.)[77]

Cablevision also is a big business and the norms specifying its conditions of operation and its relations to the broadcast media and other parties are still being worked out. In 1984 the U.S. Congress passed legislation to establish a federal cable policy, to provide cable with its own set of regulatory guidelines. Many issues still remain to be settled and one can be certain that new ones will arise as the industry grows. Among these are matters of copyright; what royalties a cable system must pay for carrying signals from television stations ouside its local market; the relations between telephone and cable companies in the trans-

[74] For further details see Nancy Jesuale and Ralph Lee Smith, *CTIC Cablebooks*, Vol. 1: *The Community Medium* (Arlington, Va.: The Cable Industry Information Center, 1982).

[75] *Cable Vision*, January 21, 1985, p. 45.

[76] *Cable Vision*, December 31, 1984, p. 36.

[77] *Cable Vision*, January 14, 1985, p. 12.

mission of data, and federal and local regulations over this activity; relations with local governments, including terms of local franchises; and rights to cable system ownership and television station ownership.[78]

Economic concerns may affect future developments in the cable business as in other mass media. As an example, pay-per-view cable television is seen by some analysts as a potentially expanding business that will meet the challenge to Hollywood of the video-cassettes which, once sold, bring no further revenue to the studio. With pay-per-view, the studio can receive an accounting of the number of subscribers to a cablecast film and can receive a share of the income. The money involved can be significant. As an example, according to one report, theatrical showings of a motion picture usually earn the studio about $1.50 per viewer per run of the film; the studio may earn 5 cents per viewer for a network television showing; 25 cents per viewer on a pay television channel. In 1984 Paramount is said to have earned about $25 per video cassette sold for its film *Terms of Endearment.* It sold about 200,000 videocassettes to the 13 million owners of video-recorders, for a net profit, after costs and royalties, of $1 million. At the same time, a pay-per-view release of the film was made available to 1.3 million cablevision households. It earned $1 million in revenues, from which Paramount netted a half-million dollars. Projections from this latter experience lead some analysts to predict that pay-per-view cablecasts will become increasingly important as major outlets for movies and other entertainment programs in the future.[79]

Another mode of televised communication that has been heralded by some as the wave-of-the-future is a direct-broadcast satellite system (DBS). DBS broadcasts signals from communication satellites in space directly into residences or other places of reception having "dish" antennae. Since it could be received directly in this manner, DBS shares many of the characteristics of our familiar over-the-air public television except that special equipment is needed. Also, since some of the programming is meant for use only by subscribers, there are questions about who should be allowed to receive broadcasts. Some satellite transmissions are "scrambled" or coded in such a way that only persons authorized to receive them (i.e. paying subscribers) can do so. The first company applying for DBS in the United States was the Satellite Television Corporation, a subsidiary of the Communications Satellite Corporation (Comsat). Seven others also were authorized in 1982 by the FCC. However none were in full operation by 1985 and several had dropped out of the field. (But four more have been authorized.)[80] Some of the current unresolved issues are reported to center on the power levels for transmission and their relation to the size of the dish antenna required for direct reception, spectrum use, market viability, and system costs, which appear to be greater than originally estimated. By the mid-1980s, then, DBS was far less developed than cable television. According to one assessment,

[78] *Cable Vision,* November 26, 1984, pp. 46–55.

[79] Eric Taub, "Home Movies: Will PPV cure the VCR blues?" *Cable Vision,* October 22, 1984, pp. 32–39.

[80] Ron Wolf, "Direct-broadcast TV is still not turned on," *The Philadephia Inquirer,* January 20, 1985, C1,6.

"the prospects for DBS are cloudy, as a number of political, economic and technical uncertainties remain."[81]

Conclusion

Clearly the full story of the social, economic, political, and other forces that have shaped the structure of American mass media is complex and yet to be told. But the many recently published detailed accounts of events involving one or another of these media—including journalistic, autobiographical, historical, sociological, and other contributions—provide much useful information for scholars in the future who wish to work toward a social history and sociological analysis of American media systems.

CASE 6: Communications in Nonindustrial Countries

Today many of the predominantly agricultural, less industrially developed countries have relatively limited systems of mass media compared with more industrially developed countries. Accurate current accounts of these systems are difficult to obtain, and available statistics are sometimes of dubious quality and soon out of date. UNESCO reports published in 1982, however, indicate that while developing countries had a ratio of 817 radio receivers for each 1,000 inhabitants, the average ratio in developing countries was only 98 sets for each 1,000 inhabitants. Comparative figures for television sets were 393 per 1,000 inhabitants in developed countries and 30 per 1,000 in developing countries. Developed countries had an average daily newspaper circulation of 324 per 1,000; developing countries, 35 per 1,000.[82]

However shaky some of these statistics may be, it remains apparent that by Western standards, most of the developing nations have media systems with a very low ratio of personal mass media receivers to total population. Still, by the mid-1970s, as Elihu Katz and his colleagues point out in a study of broadcasting in the Third World, "The majority of people in the world live within reach of a domestic radio signal, however poor the quality of the signal in many areas, however remote the language."[83] Television is less available, but it is spreading too.

[81] *The 1984 Satellite Directory* (Bethesda, Md.: Phillips, 1984), p. 60.

[82] UNESCO, *Statistical Yearbook, 1982.* Some other useful sources of media data are *World Press Encyclopedia*; Emery, *National and International Systems*; UNESCO, *World Communications: Press, Radio, Television, Film* (New York: UNESCO, 1975); and Wilbur Schramm, Philip H. Coombs, Friedrich Kahnert, and Jack Lyle, *The New Media* (Paris: UNESCO, 1967). See also the three volumes entitled *New Educational Media in Action: Case Studies for Planners* (Paris: UNESCO, 1967); Wilbur Schramm, *Mass Media and National Development* (Stanford, CA: Stanford University Press, 1964). For research and policy discussions, see George Gerbner and Marsha Siefert, eds., *World Communications: A Handbook* (New York: Longman's, 1984).

[83] Elihu Katz and George Wedell, with Michael Pilsworth and Dov Shinar, *Broadcasting in the Third World: Promise and Performance* (Cambridge, MA: Harvard University Press, 1977), p. v. Their analyses are based on intensive case studies, including interviews with key officials and broadcasters, in Algeria, Brazil, Cyprus, Indonesia, Iran, Nigeria, Peru, Senegal, Singapore, Tanzania, and Thailand, between September 1973 and April 1975.

The new media of mass communication, especially television, are not indigenous to these societies, but have been imported, usually from Western countries. They have been introduced by national governments, international agencies, business enterprises, and others to facilitate and stimulate political, economic, social, and cultural change in these countries. The mass media, however, have not proved to be automatic, autonomous forces for social change. Communications researcher Robert Hornik argues, for example, that "Communication technology works best as a complement—to a commitment to social change, to changing resources, to good instructional design, to other channels of communication, and to detailed knowledge about its users."[84]

The newly introduced mass media's character and influence have been shaped by the social structure and the political, economic, cultural, and other features of the recipient society. As Katz and his colleagues observe: "The polity is there to receive the electronic media when they arrive at the dock, its leaders and rulers are careful to put them under tight security. That social integration may be enhanced thereby or that the basis of social solidarity may be affected is the point of our story. . . ."[85]

In many developing countries, the mass media systems eventually come under the control of the immediate ruling powers, be they military, civilian, religious, or some other group. Then the media usually operate under what has been called an "authoritarian" philosophy, which holds that the primary function of the mass media is "to support and advance the policies of the government in power; and to service the state."[86] Katz and his associates comment that the most striking fact in their study "is the virtual abandonment, throughout the developing world, of Western patterns of broadcasting in which, however defined, the broadcasting system has some element of autonomy from the government of the day."[87] The state, then, exercises strong control over the mass media through censorship, restrictive licenses, and so on, even though the media need not be government-owned.

Limitations of space prevent detailed accounts of the media systems in various developing countries. We will, instead, point out two phenomena that are highlighted in nonindustrial countries, although they also are important—if less readily observed—in industrial societies. They are, first, widespread group exposure to mass media, and second, the importance of personal networks of word-of-mouth communication that are often linked to the mass media, extending as well as modifying their influence.

Even though individual, private access to the mass media may be less common in developing countries, the "reach" of mass communication is extended

---

[84] See a review of recent research findings and a thoughtful discussion of the issues in Robert Hornik, "Communication as Complement in Development," *Journal of Communication*, 30, 2 (Spring 1980), pp. 10–24.

[85] Katz et al., *Broadcasting in the Third World*, pp. 183–184.

[86] Siebert, Peterson, and Schramm, *Four Theories of the Press*, p. 7.

[87] Katz et al., *Broadcasting in the Third World*, p. 212. As an example that postdates that study, in Iran the Ayatollah Khomeini is reported to have ordered non-Muslims purged from Iran's state-operated broadcasting. "Radio," he is reported to have said, "must be a tool to disseminate Islamic ideas and teachings." *Philadelphia Inquirer*, date unknown.

through group, often public, exposure to radio, television, newspapers, and other mass media. Through such group listening, viewing, or reading aloud, several persons, even an entire village, may make use of a television receiver or copy of a newspaper, thus multiplying its reach. Years ago this was demonstrated for countries in the Middle East, where researchers found that many villagers listened to the radio outside their homes—in local coffeehouses, in the houses of friends or neighbors, in schools and clubs, at work, and elsewhere. More recently, Katz and his colleagues comment on the potential power of community television viewing for effecting social change. "Community viewing centers," they write, "besides enabling people in rural areas to gain access to television, are often good reinforcers of [a program's] messages. As meeting places they become, in effect, group learning centers that . . . are often more effective than addressing people as isolated individuals. Traditional gathering places, such as marketplaces, teahouses, pubs, tavernas, and coffeehouses, serve all societies as crucibles for the formation of public opinion. The presence of television sets in such situations enlarges the range of subjects for discussion and informal learning. . . ."[88]

A second especially interesting feature of communication systems in developing countries is the important role of informal, interpersonal communication, especially word of mouth. In developing countries, even persons who regularly listen to the radio or read newspapers seem likely to rely heavily on word-of-mouth communication for certain kinds of news, and they are likely to tell others about what they have learned from the mass media. To some extent we have found this to be true in industrialized societies too, as noted in Chapter 4. But it may be even more pronounced in developing countries, where it seems to fit in with traditional oral modes of communication. In any event, face-to-face communication joins with mass communication in a society's total communication system in both developing and modern societies.

[88] Katz et al., *Broadcasting in the Third World*, p. 187.

CHAPTER 3

Sociology of the Mass Communicator

Who is the communicator in mass communication? The answer is "no one." The question itself is, in fact, speciously formulated, because we tend to think about mass communication in terms taken from a popular model of human communication. Reduced to its minimum elements, this model instructs us that in order to have communication, there must be a communicator, a message, some medium of transmission, and a receiver. A simple example would be a speaker, words, a telephone connection, and a listener. But, as noted earlier, the production of mass communication is an organized social activity, rarely the direct handiwork of a single creative artist. The content of mass communication is manufactured through the organized efforts of many participants, and then mass-produced and mass-distributed. To search for "the" communicator in such a complex operation is like looking for "the" maker of an automobile. It is tempting, especially when dissatisfied with the product, to think of personal responsibility, or at least of corporate locus: If a car is faulty, blame Detroit designers; if television programming is bad, blame the Hollywood producer or the television network executives in New York. But such personalizing of the mass communicator cannot be taken literally. And it provides no base for the systematic sociological analysis of mass communicators.

The sociological study of mass communicators, once neglected by comparison with research on communication content, audiences, and inferred effects, has received more attention lately. Some important studies also were conducted earlier in the century. These studies of mass communicators link mass communication research to long-standing sociological interests in status and role, occupations and professions, analyses of complex organizations, and the sociology of work—to mention but a few connections.[1]

Studies of mass communicators employ a variety of research strategies. One is to identify the key occupations involved in mass media production and to study these occupational categories in terms of such questions as: Who gets into them? What kinds of training do these people have? What are their occupa-

---

[1] For some recent examples of sociological analyses of mass communicators, see Josephine R. Holz and Charles R. Wright, "Sociology of Mass Communications," *Annual Review of Sociology*, 5 (1979), pp. 193–217; Paul M. Hirsch, Peter V. Miller, and F. Gerald Kline, eds., *Strategies for Communication Research, Sage Annual Reviews of Communication Research*, vol. 6, 1977, Part I, pp. 13–91; James S. Ettema and D. Charles Whitney, eds., *Individuals in Mass Media Organizations: Creativity and Constraint, Sage Annual Reviews of Communication Research*, vol. 10, 1982. Other examples will be cited throughout this chapter.

tional values and norms? What do they do? These accounts may use role theory to focus attention on how communicators are involved with others while doing their jobs; organizational theory to raise questions about the kinds of organizations within which communicators work; and ideas from the sociology of work to guide questions about the conditions under which communicators work (deadlines) and peoples' relevant behavior on and off the job.

Sociologists are likely to combine several of these perspectives, and others, while studying particular kinds of mass communicators. We will select a few research cases to illustrate the approach and to serve as the bases for our discussion in this chapter. We begin with a study of the kinds of people who work as American journalists. Then we look at a study of how several kinds of people holding the same job title, television producer, carry out their occupational roles in somewhat different ways. Next we single out some observations about communicators made by researchers with an eye on journalists' day-to-day work experiences. Finally we look at two studies of the social production of America's national news and discuss parts of them in terms of role theory.

OCCUPATIONS IN COMMUNICATIONS

CASE 1:   The News People

Who goes into news reporting as a job? The most comprehensive sociological study of practicing American journalists to date is *The News People*, by John Johnstone, Edward Slawski, and William Bowman.[2] It reports on interviews with more than 1,300 working men and women in the news field, a national sample of "all salaried full-time editorial personnel working in daily and weekly newspapers, magazines, and periodicals concerned with news and public affairs, the wire services, and the news departments of broadcast media."[3] The study examines, among other matters, the news peoples' social origins, education and recruitment, career histories, professional values and beliefs, work tasks, and working conditions. It thereby provides us with a rich social profile of America's news personnel in the early 1970s, as we were about to start our third century as a nation. The sociological issues it addresses and the analyses it presents are as timely today as they were then.

Where do you suppose most news people, as defined above, work? Broadcasting, I'd have guessed, but this is dead wrong. Fully 75 percent of them worked for newspapers or news magazines at that time, only 20 percent for television or radio, and the remaining 5 percent worked for the news services. While there may have been some increase in the proportion working in news broad-

[2] John W. C. Johnstone, Edward J. Slawski, and William W. Bowman, *The News People: A Sociological Portrait of American Journalists and Their Work* (Urbana: University of Illinois Press, 1976). For a study of specialist correspondents in the British national news media, see Jeremy Tunstall, *Journalists at Work* (London: Constable, 1971).

[3] Johnstone et al. *The News People*, p. 6. This excerpt, and those from pp. 32, 131, 186, and 182 are reprinted by permission of the University of Illinois Press. ©1976 by the Board of Trustees of the University of Illinois.

casting since the 1970s, the majority of practicing journalists most likely still work for the press.

Journalists tend to be young. About a third of them were in their twenties, nearly 80 percent were less than age fifty. The majority are men (8 out of every 10 in the study) and few are black (4 percent of the journalists surveyed). The majority of the men seem to have been brought up in urban, middle- or upper-middle-class families, judging from the reported occupations of their fathers. No more than 1 in 10 had a father who had worked in mass communication. News people are highly educated formally—86 percent attended college, nearly 3 out of 5 are college graduates, and 1 in 5 went beyond college to graduate study or professional school. The data also suggest "that the average educational attainment of journalists has been increasing steadily over recent decades."[4]

What did journalists study while in college? Quite a diversity of subjects, it seems. Most of their majors were in the liberal arts and sciences, chiefly English and the humanities (especially prior to World War II). Next frequent are majors in journalism or some other communication field (especially since World War II). Few journalists majored in the physical or biological sciences, agriculture, or business. The percentage of journalists who majored in government and political science has increased over the years, but majors in the other sciences remained relatively few.

These data suggest to me—and here I go beyond inferences drawn by the researchers in their book—that most news people start their careers as well-educated persons, but without a great deal of formal training in certain areas (science, medicine, business, economics, agriculture) which they might have to cover someday in news stories. Some examples are the nuclear accident at Three Mile Island, economic recessions, toxic wastes and other environmental problems, food production and distribution, national budgets, and health problems—to mention but a few. This situation, in turn, may help account for the relative importance given to presumably reliable, authoritative, and trustworthy experts, officials, and other responsible news sources during reporting and interpreting such unforeseen and complex events. Journalists, especially those assigned to some specialty beat, such as medical news or investigating a topic in some depth, may develop substantive expertise on the job that supplements their formal training.

Most of the people surveyed started their first job directly in the news media; others entered journalism from other jobs, usually white collar. They did not, perhaps contrary to popular stereotypes, move around a lot from paper to paper or station to station. They had, on average, worked for their current employer for nine to ten years.

News work involves a variety of duties, and most news people perform several of them. As examples, nearly 4 out of 5 journalists were directly engaged in reporting, news gathering, and news writing; 7 out of 10 edited or processed other peoples' work; and 4 out of 10 had managerial and supervisory duties. The proportion who do news reporting regularly tends to decrease with years of expe-

[4] Ibid., p. 32.

rience in the media; the proportion doing editing increases. Managerial responsibilities also tend to increase—as seems to happen among some other professionals working in complex organizations.

Johnstone and his colleagues studied the professional values about journalism in the following way. First, they asked journalists to rate the importance of each of several news activities. As examples, 76 percent of the respondents said that it was extremely important for the news media to investigate claims and statements by the government; 61 percent said it is extremely important to provide analysis and interpretation of complex problems (what we've called correlation activities); but only 16 percent regarded entertainment as an extremely important task of the news media.

The researchers regarded opinions about each of these activities as indicators of either of two underlying views about journalism reflecting "neutral" versus "participant" professional values. The "neutral" value orientation stresses, for example, the importance of verifying information and then getting it to the public quickly, concentrating on news which is of interest to the widest possible public, and providing entertainment and relaxation. The "participants" value orientation stresses investigative, analytical, and interpretive reporting and discussion of national policy while it is being developed. Journalists were given scores on their "participant" and "neutral" conceptions of the press according to their ratings of each of the several activities mentioned and their replies to some other questions.

The researchers then examined the statistical associations between scores on the two value scales and certain of the respondents' social characteristics, such as formal schooling, age, gender, work duties, and work setting. They report that although the statistical associations are small, certain relationships seem worth noting. Participant journalism appears to be statistically associated with more formal schooling, youth, more reportorial and less supervisory duties, working in a large city, and being integrated into an informal social network of colleagues. Neutral or libertarian professional values were associated with less higher education (but perhaps more apprentice experience), middle age, administrative career paths, working in a middle-sized and smaller town, and being socially integrated into that community.

The authors argue that there is a value cleavage within contemporary journalism involving familiar issues of subjectivity versus objectivity, advocacy versus detachment, and others. They assert that "While most practicing newsmen subscribe to elements of both viewpoints, these two segments are visible as pure ideological types among practicing newsmen."[5] They interpret the statistical association between journalists' amount of formal schooling and their scores on neutral and participant values as showing "that the type of training that journalists get has a lasting impact on the perspectives they bring to their work."[6] And they suggest that this possible source of differentiation will be reduced in a few decades as more and more journalists will have gone to college.

[5] Ibid., p. 131.
[6] Ibid., p. 186.

In a concluding note to their study, the authors note "how very much modern newswork is a collective enterprise, and how very intricate is the process by which occurrences in the real world come to be translated into news stories." It is important, they point out, "to know that so many journalists devote the major share of their time and energy to processing and transmitting information structured by others; awareness of this fact should better enable us to evaluate the information the media provide. Mass news is very much an organizational phenomenon. . . ."[7] This is a point we will return to later in the chapter.

Other Issues

Research on the kinds of people who go into occupations in communications also bears directly on questions of social equality, representation of viewpoints in the media, and perhaps on the content of what is produced. Social concern about occupational and economic opportunity makes it important to have information about such questions as whether black people are as likely to be employed in certain communications jobs as are white people, women as likely as men, and so on.

Sometimes it is assumed or argued that the social background of mass communicators has consequences for the range and substance of content produced, such as news coverage, dramatic themes, portrayal of minorities in television stories, and the like. This assumption seems apparent, to cite an early example, in one of the major recommendations to improve mass media coverage of urban affairs that was set forth by the National Advisory Commission on Civil Disorders in 1968.[8] The commission, in relating the media's reportage of urban civil disorders to the background of the normal news coverage of race relations in America, expressed the view that the mass media fail to report adequately on race relations and ghetto problems and that one means for correcting this oversight is to bring more blacks into journalism and other new organizations. The commission expressed the belief that increased employment of blacks in communications occupations would have an impact on news coverage of black activities, among other topics.

A similar belief that greater access to occupations in the communications field would increase the presence of minority ideas, tastes, and values in media content has been expressed by women and by various minority groups. Much may depend on how important these occupations turn out to be.

Some studies of mass communicators narrow an occupational category down to what are believed to be key positions that carry power to influence communication content significantly. An example is a very early study of the editors of what the researchers called the "prestige papers." These newspapers are seen as "institutions which function to express the views of significant segments of the elite and to disseminate to the elite at home and abroad information and judg-

---

[7] Ibid., p. 182.
[8] See *Report of the National Advisory Commission on Civil Disorders* (New York: Bantam, 1968), esp. p. 385.

ments needed by them to function as an elite in a great society. . . ."[9] Examples are the *New York Times* and the Soviet *Izvestia.*

The researchers studied the social backgrounds and career histories of these editors in order to see where they fit in society. The study concludes that, in general, the social background of the editors reflects the characteristics of the larger social structure. The editors come from the same social circles as other members of the elite, have similar educational and other experiences, have careers parallel to those of the elite, maintain close connections with the government, and achieve considerable prestige and many honors. The researchers summarize:

> In all respects, then, the editors conform to those patterns of life which we would predict for the heads of one of the key institutions in the social structure. They fit into the type of pattern we would predict for the heads of national churches, or the heads of governments. They provide evidence in their careers for our assumption that the prestige paper has become the same kind of central social institution. The social structure of such institutions tends to reflect, each in its own way, the social structure of the society as a whole.[10]

Editors of prestige papers constitute a singular, albeit an important, occupational role in mass communication. Our knowledge about the relations between mass communicators and social structure would be greatly increased through studies of other key occupations, especially research that sheds light on the relative power of the holders of such occupations to influence mass media content. It seems reasonable to assume that editors in chief, television producers, and others in presumably key positions in the mass communication industries have some influence over content. But how much? Of what kind? And in what ways does it work? These are questions in need of further research.

THE COMMUNICATOR IN ORGANIZATIONAL CONTEXT

Faced with the task of analyzing the complex organizational structure of a communication medium, sociologists must choose what seem to them strategic occupations and work from there. The editor in chief in newspaper publishing is an example of such a selection. We turn now to television—another medium of communication—and a sociological examination of one key occupational role: the Hollywood television producer.

[9] Ithiel de Sola Pool et al., *The Prestige Papers* (Stanford, CA: Stanford University Press, 1952), p. 120. This and the following quotation are by permission of the publisher.

[10] Ibid., p. 140.

CASE 2:   The Hollywood Television Producer

The television film producer has been described as one of the most powerful forces in television, from both a creative and an executive standpoint.[11] He—or she, in a very few cases—has overall authority for major decisions in the production of dramatic television series that reach millions of American viewers during evening prime-time broadcast hours. Certainly, this is a key occupation to study if one wishes to unravel some of the sociological forces at work in determining the content of a major genre of popular culture. It is precisely for this reason that the sociologist Muriel G. Cantor selected this group for intensive study.

Cantor interviewed nearly all the male "on-the-line," or working, producers of Hollywood-filmed television dramatic series during the 1967–1968 season.[12] She supplemented these interview data with information obtained through examination of various records (such as scripts) and through direct personal observation in the studios. The main focuses of the inquiry were the organizational, professional, occupational, and personal factors that influence the producer's selection of stories and other major decisions affecting television content, according to his own account.

Few occupational titles fully connote the actual social roles the jobs involve. Even formal job descriptions do not convey the reality of the complex activities and interactions involved in everyday job performance. Some titles are labels without significant tasks or duties attached; more generally, certain occupational titles are so broad that they actually cover a variety of jobs having few if any identifiable, significant activities in common. (The label "scientist," widely used as a job classification, is a title of the latter sort.) A sociological analysis of the television producer cannot take for granted that such a title even denotes a specific social role. Therefore, Cantor took care to let the respondents describe, in their own words, what it is that they do as "producers"—their specific responsibilities, duties, authority, tasks.

As each producer described what he did, a common pattern emerged that outlines in broad terms the actual functions of an on-the-line producer of television drama series. The producer is in charge of story selection, both theme and content; hires the cast, directors, and writers; serves as coordinator between the film company and the television networks; has final authority for cutting and editing the filmed show; and is generally in charge of major aspects of production.

Given the roles the producer plays, it should not be surprising that this title is regarded as one of key importance and great power in the industry. But, as Cantor demonstrates, even though the producer holds a position of relative power, he does not have autonomy:

[11] Frank La Tourette, in a foreword to Muriel G. Cantor, *The Hollywood TV Producer: His Work and His Audience* (New York: Basic Books, 1971), p. vii.

[12] These were supplemented by interviews with a sample of producers of television shows for children for the 1970–71 season. The main analysis presented here, however, is based primarily on the interviews with producers of prime-time adult drama series.

[B]ecause the producer is a part of a large, complex bureaucratic organization, he does not have complete control. He is a working producer—a man in the middle between those above him in the networks and production companies and those he supervises in the production crew. As a representative of management, he must fulfill the goals of the organization. Ideally, the producer has responsibility for the creative aspects of the show, but this is always delegated authority because even when a man owns, creates, and produces his own show, the network retains the right to *final* approval of scripts, casts, and other creative and administrative matters.[13]

Just how the producer's control over television content is moderated by himself and others during the course of daily work is skillfully illuminated throughout the study.

For analytical purposes, an occupational role, like any other social role, can be dissected into its many component activities. Of particular concern are activities central to the major tasks of the role and involving social interaction with other persons playing roles relevant to those tasks—that is, members of one's *role set.*[14] Cantor divides the producer's activities into two major categories: (1) business operations and decisions, and (2) actual filmmaking with the production company or crew. She then details the key role partners with whom the producer must deal in each of these broad areas and whose own role performances set demands, constraints, expectations, or rewards or otherwise influence the producer's performance and ultimately the content and quality of the film that is telecast. The business activities require the producer to interact with or otherwise take into consideration, among others, various executives and representatives of the television networks, sponsors, and advertising agencies. During the actual filming of a show, the producer's key role partners—key in the sense that they are especially important in the producer's decisions about story selection and the creative process—include writers, directors, and actors.

Sometimes the producer interacted directly with these role partners; at other times he kept them in mind as reference groups whose values, wishes, expectations, and other considerations were relevant to his own performance. Cantor's findings strongly suggest that producers are as concerned with reactions of the "secondary" audience for their shows—which includes the network and studio executives and the production group, especially writers, directors, and actors—as they are with the reactions of the primary audience of television viewers.

Direct contact with representative members of the viewing audience rarely or never occurs. Nevertheless, most producers have created for themselves an image of what kind of audience views their shows (or, more likely, will view their shows, since the logistics of production require that a number of episodes of a series be completed long before they are broadcast, and therefore before any direct measures of national audience response). Although the producers' views of their audiences were often limited to stereotypes of broad social characteristics and often did not match the actual composition subsequently revealed by audience research, many producers said that they consider the viewing audience

[13] Cantor, *The Hollywood TV Producer*, pp. 8–9. By permission of Basic Books, Inc.

[14] For an instructive discussion of role sets and related concepts, see Robert K. Merton, *Social Theory and Social Structure*, rev. ed. (Glencoe, IL: Free Press, 1957), pp. 368–386.

when making decisions about the shows they produce. In practice, however, some producers appear to project their own tastes or those of their families or acquaintances as being representative of those of "the audience."

Working producers are likely to have direct contact with representatives of their "other" major audience—that is, the television network representatives—and these contacts, together with the producers' use of the network officials as a reference group, may lead to conflicts over the artistic and substantive content of the shows. Cantor notes that network controls can operate in a variety of ways. For example, a network liaison person may attend the story conference where ideas for new shows are presented and explored; the network censor must approve all scripts; and the network has final power to decide whether a show is aired through its facilities. Most producers reported that they had some conflicts with the networks about content, and more than half said that they had experienced network attempts at "interference" with story selection or content, or both, during the production of their current shows. But more than a third of the producers said they had not experienced such pressures.

Of interest is Cantor's analysis of why some producers seem to be pressured and others not, and of why some comply readily with network suggestions and directives, whereas others "seem to try to thwart the network directives at every opportunity and therefore are under constant pressure."[15] This analysis shows that despite the broad similarity in official and unofficial duties among producers and in general norms prescribing the conduct of this role, there is considerable latitude in how the role relationships are carried out. To be sure, some of the variation in performance may be attributed to the personality and idiosyncracies of the individual playing the role. But certain regular variations in role performance emerge when one further specifies the role of producer into several types of television producers. Cantor presents a typology of producers based upon combinations of their personal backgrounds and histories in the industry and their occupational goals and values. Three major types identified are *filmmakers*, *writer-producers*, and *old-line producers.*

The filmmakers are usually college graduates who have studied in a university communications media program; they went to work in television and eventually came up through the ranks of a major studio. They regard their main task as coordinating the various parts of the process of filmmaking; and they hope, upon mastering these skills and acquiring sufficient economic means, to make films to be shown in motion picture theaters. To achieve these personal goals, filmmakers believe that they are "using the system," rather than vice versa.

Writer-producers are also likely to have attended college, perhaps majoring in English or journalism; most had been freelance scriptwriters, and many had worked in mass media other than television. They became producers in the hope of having more control of their own creative products and stories than they had been able to have when they were only writers. The old-line producers are less likely to have had college training directly relevant to media production; they had varied experience in other mass media, and they are the most successful

---

[15] Cantor, *The Hollywood TV Producer*, p. 132.

producers in terms of income and the ability to get their ideas and pilot shows made into television series. Continued opportunity to produce shows that are successful in attracting large mass audiences is an important, although by no means the sole, goal of the old-line producers.

Cantor reports that the filmmakers are the least likely of the three types of producers to have conflicts with the networks over the artistic, political, or social content of their shows. Filmmakers are oriented toward learning all that they can about production, are willing to postpone expression of their own creative talents until they can start new careers as independent movie makers, and are likely to share the network officials' views that television is essentially an entertainment medium which should give the mass public "what it wants."

Both the writer-producers and the old-line producers experience more conflicts with the networks. The former feel strongly that they should have control over story content, especially as it is used to express political and social objectives. Writer-producers often engage in covert struggles with the networks, striving to maximize their control over content without directly displeasing the networks to the degree that they would risk either cancellation of the series or their removal as producer. The old-line producers are likely to have direct conflicts with network officials, especially concerning what is likely to be successful with the audience—the story idea, for example, or the character of the hero or heroine—or over the choices of cast and director.

Cantor also reports on differences in role conflicts between each of these three types of producers and their role partners within the production crew: writers, directors, and actors.

Cantor's subsequent work on the content and control of prime-time television again concludes that most creative artists in television (producers, writers, directors, and actors) are relatively powerless to determine the final content of the show on which they are working. There are exceptions.[16] Some on-the-line producers and star actors "have some power to fight for their ideas." But "most of those in the ranks must suppress controversial political and artistic values in order to work in the television industry. The way films for television are made ensures bureaucratic control and necessitates organizational compliance from those working as writers, directors, and actors."[17]

This situation, however, is not seen as peculiar to American commercial television. Rather, Cantor (and some others) regard it as a general sociological phenomenon of mass communication production through bureaucratic organizations. Cantor puts the issue in broader perspective in her report for the 1982 update of the NIMH report on *Television and Behavior*, as follows:

> Whether ownership of the means of mass communications rests directly with the government, as in many socialist and third world countries, or with individuals and corporations that privately own the various media as in western democracies, mass

[16] For a different viewpoint, see Horace Newcomb and Robert S. Alley, *The Producer's Medium: Conversations with Creators of American TV* (New York: Oxford University Press, 1983). This study is based on personal interviews with a number of major television producers whom the authors regard as self-conscious, creative producers responsible for the "creative vision of the projects they control" (p. xiii).

[17] Muriel G. Cantor, *Prime-Time Television: Content and Control.* Sage COMMTEXT Series, vol. 3 (Beverly Hills, CA: Sage Publications, 1980), p. 95.

communications are organized activities. The work of creating content is never completed by one artist, but rather by groups, most of them having a bureaucratic form of organization. In most bureaucracies, ultimate decisionmaking power over what is broadcast or printed rests with just a few people, and the creative people working in these contexts become employees subject to the power of those few individuals having the power to hire and fire."[18]

One can appreciate the importance of the power to hire and fire, for example, in the light of Cantor and Peters' observation that at any one time 85 percent of the membership of the Screen Actors' Guild is likely to be unemployed. (Further, about half of those members who worked as actors in 1974 earned less than $1,000 during the year. We tend to be aware of the stars, but less than 1 percent of the Guild members earned $100,000 or more in 1974.)[19]

Another—not necessarily contradictory—view of the occupational world of television production is presented in Todd Gitlin's detailed account of behind-the-scenes activities, *Inside Prime Time*. Gitlin examined the process of television production through personal on-the-set observations and interviews with more than 200 television producers, network executives, writers, actors, and agents in the 1980s. He discusses how television shows are affected by interpersonal, economic, political, and other considerations.

Gitlin says that television production takes place in a widespread climate of uncertainty—uncertainty about which particular programs will be accepted or rejected by broadcasters, which will receive high audience ratings, which will prove financially successful, and which will fail. He interprets many of the work practices in the industry as strategies to cope with uncertainty and to minimize professional and financial risks. With so much at risk—money, jobs, reputations, for example—people in the industry, especially those who make key decisions about production, prefer to deal with others whose work they know and whom they consider good and reliable. Thus, for example, television network executives come to depend upon a relatively small group of reliable suppliers of television programs and of creative and performing talent. The "inside track" in this small world is held by a New York–Hollywood network of persons in the industry, known to one another personally or by reputation, many of whom have been in the industry a long time.

It is likely, as Gitlin says, that everyone in the industry "knows" that "the advertisers set the terms, the networks order up the shows, the producers produce to order, and audiences play their part by accepting the results." But his study goes beyond this general set of beliefs and supplies specific details and analysis of how this overall process looks at the level of day-to-day working activities.[20]

Sociologists and mass communication researchers have studied the process

[18] Muriel G. Cantor, "The Organization and Production of Prime Time Television," NIMH *Television and Behavior*, 1982, pp. 349–362; quotation, p. 351.

[19] Muriel G. Cantor and Anne K. Peters, "The Employment and Unemployment of Screen Actors in the United States," in W. S. Hendon, J. L. Shanahan, and A. J. MacDonald, eds., *Economic Policy for the Arts* (Cambridge, MA: Abt Books, 1980), pp. 210–217; A. Peters and M. Cantor, "Screen Acting as Work," in Ettema and Whitney, *Individuals in Mass Media Organizations*, pp. 53–68.

[20] Todd Gitlin, *Inside Prime Time* (New York: Pantheon, 1983); quotations are from p. 272.

of the production of popular culture in a variety of fields in addition to television.[21] To mention but one example here, John Ryan and Richard Peterson describe and analyze the organized work processes in the production of country music records. The songwriter, they suggest, is but the first link in a long organizational chain of distinct tasks leading to record promotion, and perhaps to a popular "hit" record. Each task in the production chain is performed by "specialists who do their part and pass the work to the next stage. What is more, no one specialist has artistic responsibility for or financial control over all the stages."[22] At each stage the product is shaped by a "product image" in expectation of what will be acceptable to the decision-makers or specialists at the next link in the production chain. What is being manufactured, then, may not be regarded by these participants as "communication" at all, but rather as a popular cultural product for sale.

Ryan and Peterson's study, along with those of researchers sharing this orientation, is an example of sociological inquiry into the production of culture. "The production of culture perspective," as described by Peterson, "takes as its point of departure the observation that the nature and content of symbolic products are shaped by the social, legal and economic milieus in which they are produced." He specifies five factors that alone or, more typically, in concert facilitate or constrain the evolution of popular culture: changes in the law, technology, market, organizational structure, and occupational careers.[23]

Communication products, whether eventually part of mass communication or more narrowly distributed as works of art, are normally the product of a network of cooperating persons, each playing some role in the final shape, distribution, and appreciation of that product—as Howard S. Becker demonstrates in his sociological study of art worlds. Becker, in an application of the sociology of occupations to artistic work (including film), examines the complex division of labor and the interaction needed among a variety of persons comprising any "art world"—that is, "all the people whose activities are necessary to the production of the characteristic works which that world, and perhaps others as well, define as art."[24] These cooperative efforts are needed to sustain the art worlds that are responsible for the form in which any particular work occurs.

Participants in this process include not only the recognized originator of the work (painter, writer, filmmaker), but also a wide variety of people engaged (usually through their jobs) in supplying the materials and personnel necessary for the work's production, distribution, and appreciation by its public. Each participant, according to Becker's study, interacts with others within a generally ac-

---

[21] For examples, see footnote 1.

[22] John Ryan and Richard A. Peterson, "The Product Image; The Fate of Creativity in Country Music Songwriting," in Ettema and Whitney, *Individuals in Mass Media Organizations*, pp. 11–32; quote, p. 13.

[23] See Richard A. Peterson, "Five Constraints on the Production of Culture: Law, Technology, Market, Organizational Structure and Occupational Careers," *Journal of Popular Culture*, 16, 2 (1982), pp. 143–153; Clinton R. Sanders, "Structural and Interactional Features of Popular Culture Production," *Journal of Popular Culture*, 16, 2 (1982), pp. 66–74.

[24] Howard S. Becker, *Art Worlds* (Berkeley and Los Angeles: University of California Press, 1982); quote, p. 34.

cepted set of conventions (expectations, norms) about his or her proper role in this enterprise, what constitutes legitimate or illegitimate demands, what is technically and professionally possible or impossible, good or bad work, and the like. These conventions (never completely fixed but subject to some change over time), together with technical considerations, and economic, political, and other constraints, influence the final communication or art product. Together, the participants in each art world determine what is art and thereby affect the rewards and recognition given to particular artists and performers.

This study illustrates the need to look beyond the "stars," famous artists, creators, and other individuals playing glamorous, seemingly independent roles in the production of culture and to look for the patterned interactions among the range of participants in that production and in the social process through which the product is accepted by some audience.

Our understanding of mass communication as a social production will be broadened as future case studies examine the processes of distribution and exhibition as well as production, and as they extend our knowledge about key and supportive occupational roles in these processes. We look forward also to systematic comparisons with social processes at work in institutions and organizations other than the mass media, such as factories and hospitals.[25]

COMMUNICATION AS WORK

We have considered two approaches to the sociology of the mass communicator: (1) sociological studies of mass communicators' backgrounds and career patterns, factors that are presumed to affect their role performance and, ultimately, the communications content that they produce; and (2) studies of specific occupational roles within complex communication organizations that influence the communicator's creativity. We turn now to a third line of research on occupations that has been productive, one that stresses the day-to-day demands of the job that directly affect the form, quantity, and quality of mass communication content.

Many of the initial studies of communication as work were done by former journalists and other communicators or performers who are now sociologists or mass communication researchers. These studies depict the occupational world of the communicator in terms and details not readily known to social scientists or others who have not worked in a mass communication organization. The accounts help to shatter our preconceptions about what happens on the job and disclose some of the pressures affecting the communications output.

Warren Breed provides an insightful analysis of social control in the newsroom.[26] His study shows how reporters, whether under direct order or not (usually not), are influenced by the policy of their newspaper and by the sometimes explicit, although often implicit, norms about the content of their stories

[25] Holz and Wright, "Sociology of Mass Communications."

[26] Warren Breed, "Social Control in the News Room," *Social Forces*, 33 (1955), pp. 326–335. Also see Peter Clarke and Susan H. Evans; "All in a Day's Work," *Journal of Communication*, 30; 1 (Autumn 1980);pp.112–121.

that are conveyed through other reporters and supervisors in the newsroom. Breed interviewed 120 newsmen working for middle-sized newspapers. He discovered that new reporters were never formally informed as to the paper's policy. Rather, they learned this through a subtle process of socialization on the job.

Among the ways by which policy became apparent to staffers were: reading their own paper and thereby discovering its characteristics in news coverage; being the recipient of editorial actions and sanctions, such as criticism and blue-penciling of stories (usually without any direct statement about the policy violated); hearing gossip; attending staff conferences; reading house organs; and observing the publisher or other executives and hearing their opinions expressed. Staffers conform to a newspaper's policy for a variety of reasons, among them: responsiveness to the institutional authority of the publisher; potential sanctions for violation of policy; feelings of obligation and esteem for superiors on the paper; aspirations for upward job mobility; lack of conflicting group allegiances; the pleasant nature of the work; and the displacement of goals, whereby such goals as enlightening and informing readers are displaced by the common goal of getting or producing "the news" every day.

In *The Media Monopoly,* journalist and media analyst Ben Bagdikian suggests that such informal "learning" of the implicit policies of corporate chiefs is common in the mass media today. "Most bosses," he comments, "do not have to tell their subordinates what they like and dislike." Sometimes the firing or demotion of one reporter, editor, newscaster or the "killing" of a news story, television program, or book, for example, implies (correctly or not) policy to other workers, who then "behave as though under orders from above, although no explicit orders have been given."[27]

The economic or political power to hire and fire, reward or punish, is obviously an important one to all concerned. Research by Lee Sigelman makes the point that news reporters may be well aware of a newspaper's major policy and ideological stance prior to joining its staff and, given the chance, work for the organization where they are most likely to feel comfortable.[28] Reporters may change employers, too, provided there are job opportunities, and thereby leave a newspaper whose policies are unacceptable to them.

Conformity is rarely complete, of course, and conflicts arise. Breed reports on a variety of ways by which reporters bypass policy without violating their occupational role. Failing that, staffers may adopt a rationalized view of news work—"It's only a job; take your pay and forget it."

Work routines and time pressure influence communicators' selection of news, as several studies demonstrate. Studies of so-called news gatekeepers, such as news editors, often conclude that the selection of content is influenced less by the editor's personal desires, ideology, and taste than by the practical need to select from among competing stories in a hurry. Selection is guided by the communicator's awareness of what kinds of stories are likely to fit the news organization's views about proper coverage.

[27] Ben H. Bagdikian, *The Media Monopoly* (Boston: Beacon Press, 1983).

[28] Lee Sigelman, "Reporting the News: An Organizational Analysis," *American Journal of Sociology* 79 (1973), pp. 132–151.

Thus, Ben Bagdikian reports that gatekeepers scan five to seven times more potential stories than can be used daily. A metropolitan newspaper may have an intake of 2,500 stories a day, but print about 300 items. Gatekeepers must sort potential stories quickly. Bagdikian reports that observation of 45 gatekeepers (managing editors, news editors, telegraph editors, wire editors) at work on news-papers throughout the country shows that "the typical gatekeeper of news makes his decisions with remarkable speed. . . . The average for observed gatekeepers was about six seconds per story selected for use. . . . This is a virtuoso perform-ance of decision making. Judgment is exercised almost instantly without time for reflection or reference. Whatever values the gatekeeper brings to these decisions he brings by reflex."[29]

David Manning White's original case study of one wire editor's reasons for selecting or rejecting specific stories for publication also highlights these occu-pational judgments. While some of the reasons the gatekeeper gave to explain his selection clearly reflected personal preferences (he liked human interest stories), more often he said that he chose or rejected items because of his profes-sional judgment about what stories would best inform and interest the readers.[30]

Additional information comes from Walter Gieber's study of telegraph edi-tors on sixteen Wisconsin daily newspapers that subscribed to the Associated Press wire service. These gatekeepers decided which of the wire stories became reported as news in their papers. Gieber concludes that all the editors were work-ing under the pressures of the job within the organizational structure of the newsroom—the pressure of getting the copy into the newpaper. They were pre-occupied with the work itself rather than having time, during decisions, to re-flect on the social meanings and impact of the news. Gieber concludes that the telegraph editor was primarily "task oriented"—that is, "concerned with goals of production, bureaucratic routine and interpersonal relations within the newsroom." He was, in our terms, enacting an occupational role within the con-ditions set by the organizational setting, occupational norms, and values found in our society.[31]

The fact that studies of gatekeepers focus on their selection or rejection of available "stories" does not mean, however, that the news process is a matter only of choosing from a number of self-evident news events. Rather, the process also includes the working practices by which news people, and others, transform any happening into a news event for purposes of reporting about it, and the ways in which a story gets formulated and presented. Several studies have begun to unravel and codify these practices. We select one example for discussion here.

Insights into how the routine demands of work affect the performance of news reporters are provided by Gaye Tuchman's studies of a contemporary American daily metropolitan newspaper and local independent television sta-

[29] Ben H. Bagdikian, *The Information Machines: Their Impact on Men and the Media* (New York: Harper & Row, 1971).

[30] David Manning White, "The 'Gatekeeper': A Case Study in the Selection of News," *Journalism Quarterly*, 27, 74 (1950), pp. 383–390.

[31] Walter Gieber, "News Is What Newspapermen Make It," in *People, Society, and Mass Com-munications*, ed. Lewis Dexter and David White (New York: Free Press, 1964), pp. 173–182; quo-tation from p. 175.

tion. Tuchman notes that the newspaper reporter works within a social and organizational context that every day poses many risks of failure—risks imposed by deadlines, libel suits, and reprimands or criticisms from superiors and members of the public. To be successful, he or she must write stories quickly (often being given less than a day for preparation, news gathering, and writing of the story), ably enough not to require extensive rewriting (for numerous revisions may delay publication of the newspaper, leading to a series of complications that can reduce profits), and with sufficient accuracy to protect the reputation of the newspaper and to avoid libel suits. Tuchman writes:

> [E]very story entails dangers for news personnel and for the news organization. Each story potentially affects the newsmen's ability to accomplish their daily tasks, affects their standing in the eyes of their superiors, and affects the ability of the news organization to make a profit. Inasmuch as the newspaper is made of many stories, these dangers are multiplied and omnipresent.[32]

Confronted by such high risks in their daily occupations, journalists invoke claims of objective reporting as their defense against potential criticism. But objectivity is a concept, not a phenomenon. Not every fact or statement in a news story can be independently verified for its truth. Under these circumstances, journalists follow any of a number of work strategies and practices to strengthen their claim of objectivity. Tuchman analyzes three major factors that strengthen the reporter's sense of objectivity. These involve the form in which the news is presented, its content, and the reporter's judgment, which is derived in part from interorganizational relationships.

News stories are cast into particular forms that exemplify "objective" news procedures, such as presentation of conflicting possibilities, presentation of supporting evidence, use of quotation marks, and structuring information in a sequence of decreasing importance. Content may be classified to separate news analysis and features from straight, "objective" stories. The news reporters' judgment as to what constitutes straight and important news may be influenced by their knowledge about how potential news sources, especially representatives of social institutions and organizations, work. This preconception of social reality, plus their "common sense," contributes to journalists' news judgment, which in turn affects their decisions as to whether or not an event, "fact," claim, or other item should be accepted and reported as news.

Tuchman characterizes these common news procedures as "strategic rituals," developed to protect working communicators (and their organizations) from blame. Hence objectivity is transformed from a subjective concept into a set of normative work practices. In televised news films, according to Tuchman's research, a number of conventions about visual presentation also have come to be regarded by news people as exemplifying cinematic objectivity.

[32] Gaye Tuchman, "Objectivity as Strategic Ritual: An Examination of Newsmen's Notions of Objectivity," *American Journal of Sociology*, 77 (January 1972), pp. 663–664. See also Gaye Tuchman, "Making News by Doing Work: Routinizing the Unexpected," *American Journal of Sociology*, 79 (July 1973), pp. 110–131; "The Technology of Objectivity: Doing 'Objective' TV News Films," *Urban Life and Culture*, 2 (April 1973), pp. 3–26; and *Making News: A Study in the Construction of Reality* (New York: Free Press, 1978).

THE SOCIAL PRODUCTION OF NEWS: OCCUPATIONAL ROLE ANALYSIS

In our day-to-day lives, most of us give little thought to how news is produced. We take it for granted that there is something called news. And we tend to accept what we see or hear daily in the news media as relatively objective accounts of real events that occur somewhere "out there," even though we are more or less aware that some selection and editing must take place before the accounts reach us. We see the journalist's job as mainly finding, selecting, and describing important, or at least interesting, news events. We have a romantic image of the courageous, independent, and persistent reporter who "gets the story" for us.

While there may be some truth in this popular view of the journalistic process, a sizable body of current research, as we have seen, suggests otherwise. News items, from the research perspective, seem to be less the product of enterprising individual reporting than they are institutionally manufactured—the products of social processes operating through complex media organizations and embedded in the larger social system. These studies of the production of news and documentary materials by the mass media demonstrate the complexity of the construction of news (as well as other mass media content) that involves interplay among occupational roles, social norms, organizational requirements, and practical constraints—to mention but a few of the factors that need to be taken into account. In this section I will discuss two of these studies (making no attempt to summarize their full and detailed accounts) in terms of our special interest in occupational roles.[33]

CASE 3: Washington Reporting

Leon Sigal's study of the *Washington Post* and the *New York Times* is a good case with which to begin. Sigal, a political scientist, did not present his study in the explicit sociological terms we use here. Nevertheless, much that he reports is sociological in character and can be reconceptualized in terms of occupational role analysis, as we will do here.

[33] I have chosen to limit our discussion to two cases involving the production of national news in the United States. For some other examples of sociological studies of news and documentary production, see David L. Altheide's *Creating Reality: How TV News Distorts Events*, Vol. 33 of Sage Library of Social Research (Beverly Hills, CA: Sage Publications, 1976); Mark Fishman, *Manufacturing the News* (Austin: University of Texas Press, 1980); Linda R. Lannus, "The News Organization and News Operations of the Urban Press: A Sociological Analysis Based on Two Case Studies" (Ph.D. dissertation, University of Pennsylvania, 1977); Harvey Molotch and Marilyn Lester, "Accidental News: The Great Oil Spill as a Local Occurrence and National Event," *American Journal of Sociology*, 81 (1975), pp. 235–260; E. Barbara Phillips, "Approaches to Objectivity: Journalistic Versus Social Science Perspective," in Hirsch et al., *Strategies for Communication Research*, pp. 63–77; Bernard Roshco, *Newsmaking* (Chicago: University of Chicago Press, 1975); and Gaye Tuchman's *Making News*. For two British studies, see Phillip Elliott, *The Making of a Television Series: A Case Study in the Sociology of Culture* (London: Constable, 1972). Philip Schlesinger, *Putting 'Reality' Together: BBC News* (London: Constable and Company, 1978).

The study reports on the occupational role behavior of journalists working within the bureaucratic organization of these two newspapers. It also examines the role relationships between journalists and government officials who serve as sources (and sometimes as the subjects) of news. Sigal's analysis suggests that the institutionalized role relationships among newsroom personnel, and between reporters and their governmental news sources, lead to a consensus about the nature of mass-communicated news—mainly news about government activities, in this case.

Sigal sees much of the work of these news people as relatively routine and following regular patterns. Nevertheless, on-the-job role interactions sometimes involve conflicts (which he labels as bureaucratic or office politics) that seem to be built into the organizational nature of things, reflecting jurisdictional disputes over who covers certain news events and in what ways—conflicts that can seriously affect the final news content in the paper. He also sees governmental officials (as news sources) as persons playing occupational roles whose activities are regulated by organizational routines and by division of labor within their respective government agencies. The assumption underlying his analysis is that "organizational processes and bureaucratic politics account for more of news content than, say, the political proclivities of individual newsmen. In short, what newsmen report may depend less on who they are than how they work."[34]

"Bargaining" is a key process in these role interactions, according to this analysis. Bargaining occurs among news people working for the same newspaper, among reporters from different newspapers covering the same news beat, between reporters and news sources, and between news sources themselves. For example, desk editors (editors in charge of all reporters and others working on a specified area of news, such as national, foreign, metropolitan, or sports) compete with one another and bargain with management for such resources as more, and more prominent, space for their news stories in the newspaper, more staff for their news desk, and more time to prepare copy. To the extent that an editor is successful in this competition, that area of news will get fuller coverage and more desirable publication space and thus will appear more prominently in what the public receives as the news of the day.

Participants in these bargaining interactions, although often unequal in ultimate power, usually have something the other party wants or needs, or some arsenal of sanctions available to them, so that a system of reciprocal social control prevails among them. Editors, for example, have occupational power over reporters—through their legitimate rights, for example, to assign reporters to cover certain stories, editing of these stories, and placing or "killing" the stories submitted. But the reporter's role, in turn, is not without some power over the editor. The editor is dependent upon the reporter in the field for stories, contacts with sources, and other activities vital to the news production process. Sigal's study presents many examples of this interdependence among occupational roles and the kinds of sanctions available to editors, reporters, and others (including news sources) during occupational interactions.

[34] Leon V. Sigal, *Reporters and Officials: The Organization and Politics of Newsmaking* (Lexington, MA: Heath, 1973), p. 5.

Role Sets and Role Interaction

It is useful at this point in our discussion to reintroduce the sociological concept of _role set_ and to suggest its value for the study of interactions during mass communication news production. (We have already mentioned role sets in our discussion of Cantor's study of the Hollywood television producer.) The term refers to the role partners with whom people interact while playing some role of their own, in this instance occupational roles. Reporters, for example, interact at times with editors, other reporters, news sources, and others during the course of putting together a story. It is possible to generate a list of the members of a communicator's role set from common knowledge or from descriptive accounts of on-the-job behavior. A relatively small number of key role partners may be especially interesting for theoretical or practical reasons—for instance, those role partners whose own performance significantly influences what the reporter does in producing news. Of course, that is not easy to specify in advance of some data.

We might begin by arbitrarily limiting attention to a few role partners. These initially specified members of a reporter's role set might include, for example, publisher, managing editor, desk editor, copyeditors, other reporters, and news sources. (Clearly this approach greatly oversimplifies matters. It also ignores the fact that each of these occupational titles subsumes a variety of jobs within it.) Even such a delimited framework, however, is complex and can become cumbersome.

These six roles would yield an interaction matrix of twenty-one possible kinds of role interactions, such as between publisher and editor, editor and reporter. It is important, therefore, to remind ourselves that from a sociological perspective, we are more concerned with looking for patterns of meaningful social interaction than with describing all possible episodes of interaction between persons engaged in news gathering and production, useful as such descriptions are as data for the detection of patterns. We need guidance here.

The first thing we can ask is this: How likely is a type of role interaction to occur on a regular basis? Some seem unlikely to occur regularly on a large newspaper, such as interaction between the owner or publisher and most reporters. One might choose temporarily to ignore such infrequent occurrences or, instead, to make their infrequency a topic for analysis. (What might contribute to a pattern of relatively rare interactions between publishers and reporters? What is its significance for news production? Better still, are there conditions under which the pattern changes? Such interaction might be more common and regular on smaller or community newspapers; and it might occur on larger newspapers under unusual circumstances. These exceptional circumstances, however, might prove to be critical instances that illuminate the power structure and therefore are well worth study.) It is difficult to specify in advance which role relations might be common or uncommon, or how to go about discerning some patterns.

Analysis of occupational role interaction can be elevated to another theoretical plane, and perhaps another level of understanding, by looking beyond the immediate specific role interactions per se (what happens between an editor and reporter) and considering certain of their qualities, such as secrecy, visibility, symmetry in power arrangements, durability. Robert Merton has suggested, for example, that the relative observability of one's interaction with one role partner by others in the role set is an important consideration. It affects the ability to manage role strains built into the social system (as when various members of a role set make conflicting, even contradictory, demands upon us).[35] We could ask, as an example, how visible is a reporter's interaction with each member of the occupational role set?

A reporter's interactions with news sources, for example, are not usually observable by the editor, and hence the reporter enjoys a certain amount of autonomy in this part of the job. The autonomy may be increased, as Sigal's study notes, if the reporter is away from the home office working on a beat, in the field, or stationed at some remote bureau. This greater freedom, however, is not without its costs. Sigal reports that the more distant the reporter is from the home office, the less opportunity he or she has for complaining about or trying to control what happens to the stories submitted through face-to-face interaction with copyeditors. Reporters in truly remote sites may not even see what has happened to their story until days after it has been submitted—a bit too late to change things!

Another important quality of role interactions, Merton suggests, is their continuity (including perhaps duration and repetitiveness), especially among the same persons.[36] Continuity allows for personal sanctions if things go wrong in the role relationship. And even occasional minor dissatisfactions can cumulate into stressful and unpleasant encounters. When things go well, frequent and continued contacts can complicate or facilitate future role interactions as each person comes to know more about the other. Consider, as an example, the relations between reporters and news sources.

Sigal notes that reporters covering a specific government agency in Washington have to deal with the same people as news sources time and time again. These individuals, in turn, are quick to read the reporter's published stories. If a story offends a source, or that person's agency, then the reporter risks important sanctions, such as being denied future press privileges necessary to do the job. At the least, the reporter faces an unhappy person when next they meet. Further, as time goes by the reporter may genuinely come to see events from the perspective of the news source and thereby risk being co-opted.

These examples illustrate only a few of the ways in which theoretical considerations about role sets and role interactions can be applied to the study of newsmaking.

[35] Merton, *Social Theory and Social Structure*, pp. 281–386, esp. 374–376.

[36] Robert K. Merton and Elinor Barber, "Sociological Ambivalence," in *Sociological Theory, Values, and Sociocultural Change*, ed. Edward A. Tiryakian (New York: Free Press, 1963), pp. 91–120, esp. pp. 110–111.

CASE 4: The News Source as a Communication Role

Sigal's study of national newsmaking illustrates how reporters' constant need for news and how government officials' need for publicity and favorable coverage for their agencies combine into a symbiotic relationship between Washington reporters and officials. National news, he argues, is an outcome of the bargaining interplay of newsmen and their sources. But to say this is not to imply that all, or even most, news is gathered through a kind of higgling between reporter and interviewee. Much of the news is obtained through routine, well-organized channels and procedures in which the norms governing both journalists and sources are fairly well established, even if unwritten or implicit. Sigal reports, for example, that better than half of the foreign and national news stories on the front pages of the *New York Times* and the *Washington Post* between 1949 and 1969 appeared to come from such routine news channels as press conferences, press releases, and official proceedings.

We turn now to another study of national newsmaking in the United States, Herbert Gans's research on CBS Evening News, NBC Nightly News, *Newsweek*, and *Time* magazines.[37] While Sigal sees the prime dynamic of newsmaking as a form of bargaining, Gans likens it to a tug of war between news source, journalist, and audience. He conceives of news as information that journalists transmit from sources to audiences—summarizing, refining, and fashioning it into stories for the public. The role relationships between news sources and journalists help to determine what kinds of information become available to journalists and hence, perhaps, to the public.

National news sources who provide information for reporters (working for television networks and for national news magazines, in this case study) do so mainly in their social roles as members or representatives of organized and unorganized interest groups and of other sectors of society, in Gans's view. He suggests that the role relationships between these news sources and journalists is reciprocal—sources seek access to journalists, and vice versa. But on balance, news sources are more active and aggressive in trying to bring their information and their side of the story to journalists (in the hope of thus reaching the public) than journalists are in seeking out many or new sources. Journalists are more limited than national news sources are by restraints of time, budget, and other conditions of their work. Therefore journalists are likely to seek out a relatively small number of regular news sources who have proved useful in the past.

Gans sees the source-journalist relationship as a tug of war in which sources try to put the best light on themselves (or their organization or group) by attempting to "manage" the news, while journalists, in turn, seek to "manage" the sources to get the information they need and want for their stories. In this tug of war, the success that sources have in gaining access to journalists (and hence improving their chances of getting their side of a story to the public) is affected by at least four factors: (1) incentive (eager sources tend to become regular ones

[37] Herbert J. Gans, *Deciding What's News: A Study of CBS Evening News, NBC Nightly News, Newsweek & Time* (New York: Pantheon books, 1979).

for the journalist); (2) power (social, economic, and political, including the power to create news); (3) ability to supply information regarded as suitable for news; and (4) geographic and social proximity to the journalists.

Gans comments too on the apparently symbiotic relationship and the mutual obligations that develop between reporters and sources over time—especially between agency beat reporters, regularly assigned to cover some organization or field, and their regular sources. These developing relationships can both facilitate and complicate the journalist's work.

Continuity in role interactions with sources helps a reporter to judge which are likely to be productive, reliable, trustworthy, authoritative, articulate, and proved sources of useful information in the past. Frequent interaction helps assure these qualities. Those sources who talk with journalists frequently are most readily evaluated, and some soon become regularly relied upon for information.

But continual, frequent interaction with the same sources carries the risk that the journalist may, in time, be coopted. More and more, the reporter comes to see things from the point of view of his or her sources and is cut off from alternative viewpoints. This does not imply dishonesty or intentional bias. It may be the result of increased specialized knowledge acquired on the beat, pressure from sources, or some other factors. Complications may arise as journalists and sources begin to relate to one another as persons or in roles other than that of reporter and source. Reporters become friends, even confidants, of the officials with whom they are continuously dealing as sources. If this new relationship intrudes too much into their occupational performance, journalists may lose the confidence of other reporters and supervisors; eventually they may be transferred to a different news beat.

Reasearch suggests, then, that practical pressures of deadlines, budget, need for confidence in judging sources, and other considerations can lead reporters to rely often upon official or at least established news sources. These people supply information to journalists as part of their occupational or other social roles and form part of the reporter's regular, tested occupational role set. Other potential sources who fall outside this established system may occasionally be called upon for information or viewpoints if they happen to seem suitable in some way— they are conveniently reached, socially approachable, or look responsible. To put it another way, a person who is not ordinarily a news source in the reporter's occupational role set is not likely to become one unless he or she is known to the reporter through some other social roles, or is referred, even recommended, by someone trusted, or is somehow seen by the reporter as a suitable, approachable, and informed source on the immediate news story.

It should come as no surprise to the reader, then, that such social patterns in news coverage have important consequences for what gets reported in mass-communicated news. Thus Gans notes that when reporters cannot rely on regular or established sources, they are likely to turn to other persons whom they know (and presumably trust) in some nonoccupational role, persons likely to be close to the journalist and similar to him or her socially. They are persons to whom the reporter has relatively easy access (and vice versa).[38] And—what may

[38] A similar pattern of selection of information sources for mass communication is reported in a study involving quite different circumstances—a different mass medium, a different genre, a differ-

have significance for news content—they are persons likely to share the reporter's view of society. As a consequence, they are unlikely to bring new or radical viewpoints to coverage of a news event. Gans informs us that "Reporters assigned to cover a new social problem or lifestyle often begin by calling up friends, asking them for the names of friends and acquaintances who can serve as sources. In the process, reporters inevitably select sources of roughly equivalent status. . . ."[39]

Research on the news source as a social role contributes much to our understanding of the social process of producing mass-communicated news.[40] Research on role interactions between journalists and news sources (or lack of interaction with certain potential news sources) provides one source of clues about patterns of news work that help determine what becomes mass-communicated news and what does not.

CONCLUDING NOTE

Our analytical perspective is on communicators in a context—the context being the complex organizational structure of the mass media industry and the focus being their part in this structure as they play out their occupational roles.[41]

Much of our public information about mass communicators comes from depictive accounts: novels, biographies, histories, and journalistic reports about the mass media, which describe representative persons of power and influence in them and give the "inside story" of how things operate. Useful as these personalized accounts are, they are not intended to be sociological analyses. They may present valuable information and provide useful insights into sociological phenomena. We need and welcome additional narrative accounts of the world of the mass communicator. Even more instructive, however, would be further sociographic accounts of the mass communicator's roles and sociological analyses

---

ent society—in Philip Elliott's account of the production of a documentary series on prejudice for British television. Persons selected to appear on the program as guests and interviewees—to report on research, describe incidents of prejudice, discuss and analyze prejudice, and the like—were chiefly people who came to the attention of members of the television production team in some way. These ways included, as examples, persons known to someone on the team or recommended to them, spokespeople for known organizations, persons already publicized by some mass medium, mass media "stars," celebrities, and what Elliott terms "global thinkers"—ready, willing and able to talk about (but not necessarily knowledgeable about) any topic. See Elliot, *The Making of a Television Series*. For an example of the selection and grooming of television talk-show guests, see Gaye Tuchman, ed., *The TV Establishment* (Englewood Cliffs, NJ: Prentice-Hall, 1974), pp. 119–135.

[39] Gans, *Deciding What's News*, p. 125.

[40] See, for example, Bernard Roshco's *Newsmaking*, esp. pp. 60–101.

[41] Another example of this approach applied to musicians working in the mass media is provided by Robert Faulkner, *Hollywood Studio Musicians: Their Work and Careers in the Recording Industry* (Chicago: Aldine-Atherton, 1971). Faulkner's analysis proposes that "much of the behavior of creative and performing artists in mass media setting can be viewed as *work*. They write, perform, and produce in highly organized teams that demand coordination; they face routine work pressures, try to handle mistakes at work, control the activities of colleagues, and cope with the risks of personal failure" (p. 5). Faulkner documents these points through detailed interviews with seventy-three successful Hollywood studio musicians, freelance artists, many of whom had prior successful careers as musicians with symphony orchestras or jazz and big bands.

of how these roles affect the content of our mass media.[42] The studies discussed in this chapter, along with others, demonstrate the importance, feasibility, and fruitfulness of such research.

From such sociological investigations we learn much about how major roles in the complex organizations of the mass media influence the final content, the conditions under which these influences are strengthened or weakened, the processes by which they are exercised, variability in actual role performance, some of the factors accounting for the most common forms of variability in role performance, and some of the implications of this variability for the production of mass communication content.[43] This kind of research takes us far from the simple view of the mass communicator as an individual or as an autonomous creative artist and approaches mass communication as a social process.

[42] For additional clarification of the nature of depictive, sociographic, and social theoretical analyses of social roles, see Merton and Barber, "Sociological Ambivalence," especially pp. 99–105.

[43] Our focus throughout this chapter has been on the professional mass communicator. Much can be learned through comparison with studies of nonprofessionals engaged in the production of communications, although these may not always meet our criteria of mass communication. For an interesting example, see Sol Worth and John Adair, *Through Navajo Eyes: An Exploration in Film Communications and Anthropology* (Bloomington: Indiana University Press, 1972).

CHAPTER 4

Sociology of the Audience: Interpersonal Communication and the Mass Audience

We need a word for the more than 100 million television viewers of the Super Bowl games and for all the people who attend to mass-communicated news and entertainment. "Audience" is convenient so long as we remember that it means something different here than it does when applied to people attending a performance of a Broadway play or to those football fans who managed to get into the stands to see the Super Bowl game on the spot. For one thing, the audience in mass communication gives little or no direct response to the performer during the show—no applause, laughter, coughing, walking up or down the aisle, talking, or other signs of approval or disapproval, understanding, or lack of it.

IS THE AUDIENCE A MASS?

Mass communication, in our terms, involves audiences that are relatively large and heterogeneous and whose members are anonymous so far as the mass communicator is concerned—hence the apparent suitability of the term *mass audience*. But in using the term we do not mean to imply (as some usage of it has) that the audience is a "mass" in the sociological sense of that term.

What is a mass? One sociologist, Herbert Blumer, isolates four components that, taken together, identify a mass:

> First, its membership may come *from all walks of life*, and from all distinguishable social strata; it may include people of different class position, of different vocation, of different cultural attainment, and of different wealth. . . . Second, the mass is an anonymous group, or more exactly, is composed of *anonymous individuals*. Third, there exists *little interaction* or exchange of experience between the members of the mass. They are usually physically separated from one another, and being anonymous, do not have the opportunity to mill as do the members of the crowd. Fourth, the mass is *very loosely organized* and is not able to act with the concertedness or unity that marks the crowd.[1]

If this concept of the mass were applied to mass communication audiences, they would be regarded not merely as large and heterogeneous in membership,

[1] Herbert Blumer, "Collective Behavior," in *Principles of Sociology*, ed. Alfred McClung Lee (New York: Barnes and Noble, 1946), pp. 185–186.

but also as composed of individuals who are physically and socially isolated from one another, are anonymous while in the audience, and do not communicate with one another. In short, they would be regarded as separate atoms that together comprise the whole—the mass audience. This view of the audience, as we will see in this chapter, is not consistent with the approach and findings of sociological studies of people's communication behavior.

The older concept of the audience as a mass usually was accompanied by the belief that the mass media affect all audience members directly by reaching each person as a socially isolated individual, directly influencing his or her knowledge, opinions, attitudes, beliefs, and behavior. This view of the process of mass communication is called the *hypodermic needle* model. Each individual in the mass audience is regarded as directly and personally "stuck" by the medium's message.[2] Once the message has stuck someone, it may or may not have influence, depending on whether or not it is potent enough to "take."

Both the old concept of a mass audience comprised of socially isolated individuals and the hypodermic needle model of the communication process—once popular views—lack empirical support and theoretical justification in contemporary sociological research on mass communication. A newer concept of the audience takes greater notice of the *social context* of audience participation. People may be unknown to the mass communicator, but they are rarely completely anonymous to others around them while receiving mass-communicated news and entertainment, and whether or not they happen to be alone at that moment, they still have social identities as responsible members of their society. They belong to networks of primary and secondary groups—family, friendship groups, occupational circles, and so on—which influence their opinions, attitudes, and behavior. These groups affect how people are exposed to mass communication, how they interpret or react to any specific communication, and the extent to which they will or can change their behavior.

For example, in one of the earliest studies of how mass communication use may be related to peer group membership, sociologists Matilda and John Riley report that children who were well-integrated members of their peer groups had less preference for radio and television shows of action and violence than had other children. They also were more likely to use such action programs for advancing the play activity of their group than the children who were not integrated peer group members. Less well-integrated children were more likely to prefer these action stories and to dwell upon the literal interpretation of the message (for example, as creepy or scary).[3] Here is but one of many research examples of the fact that the social relations of audience members affect both selection of and response to mass communication.

Research also reminds us that the members of an audience often are, at the very moment of exposure, participating in a group experience. Group television

[2] For a discussion of these earlier models of communication, see Elihu Katz and Paul Lazarsfeld, *Personal Influence: The Part Played by People in the Flow of Mass Communications* (Glencoe, IL: Free Press, 1955), chaps. 1 and 2.

[3] Matilda Riley and John Riley, "A Sociological Approach to Communications Research," *Public Opinion Quarterly*, 15 (Fall 1951), pp. 445–460.

watching or radio listening was a common practice in the United States a few years ago, and family television viewing remains a custom. There are parallels in other societies. Going to the movies also is often a shared social experience.[4] Again, the non-anonymous, social nature of the situation may affect the audience's response.

Finally, people's social connections provide a communication network, on a personal face-to-face basis. This informal network often gives a person indirect access to mass communication material. Mass-communicated messages do not always reach all members of their ultimate audience directly, as the hypodermic needle model assumes. Sometimes mass communication is a multistep process: The message first reaches opinion leaders, or influentials, who in turn either pass the message on by word of mouth to persons who consult them, or utilize the message in the advice or information they pass on within their circle of influence.

The connection between interpersonal and mass communication has proved to be so important to an understanding of the sociology of the mass audience that it deserves an extensive treatment in this chapter. Later we will consider other sociological features of the mass audience and point to some sociological questions about audiences that have gone neglected for far too long.

INTERPERSONAL COMMUNICATION AND THE MASS AUDIENCE

The sociological studies described here bear on mass communication as social process. First, we discuss three pioneer pretelevision studies of opinion leaders and the linkage of these leaders with the mass media. We then examine selected recent research on opinion leadership. The analyses of opinion leaders and the multi-step flow of communication presented here are based primarily on studies on American audiences. There has been some research on these topics in other societies, but the most extensive work has been done in the United States. The extent to which the American pattern can be generalized to other groups is as yet unknown. Even within our own society, there is much still to be learned about the conditions under which the multi-step flow operates—how prevalent it is among various minority groups, at different age levels, and in times of historical crisis. Finally, we review research on the diffusion of innovations, news, or information within a community and again highlight the connections between personal and mass communication in the total communication process.

[4] For examples, see Leo Handel, *Hollywood Looks at Its Audience* (Urbana: University of Illinois Press, 1950), pp. 113–115.

THREE PIONEERING STUDIES

CASE 1: *Opinion Leadership and Mass Communication in a Presidential Election Campaign*

The best known, and probably the earliest, sociological study showing the importance of individuals in mediating between mass media and the general public is a pioneering study of voting behavior during an American presidential election campaign in the pretelevision days, by Paul F. Lazarsfeld and his colleagues. In many ways it set the theoretical and methodological basis for future research on opinion leadership.[5]

The researchers were mainly interested in discovering how and why people vote as they do. The study is based on personal interviews with a sample of adults in Erie County, Ohio, who were interviewed once each month from May to November—that is, just prior to and throughout the election campaign. (This practice of repeatedly interviewing the same persons over an extended period of time during which they might be going through some change, or experiencing pressures toward change, is called the *panel technique,* and it has been used in several subsequent studies of opinion leadership as well as on other research problems. Lazarsfeld's study helped its introduction into American sociological and communications research.) Respondents who changed their vote intentions between interviews, as reflected in their answers, could be identified almost at the moment of change, and the reasons for change could be studied. Voters who did not change their minds during the campaign could also be studied.

The researchers were especially interested in studying the impact of the political campaign itself, including its mass media components—mainly radio, newspapers, and magazines, at that time. To their surprise (for many political analysts as well as members of the public would have expected the opposite), there was very little sign that the campaign directly changed people's votes or stated voting intentions. This is not to say that the campaign had no effect whatsoever or that it did not convert any voters. But the basic impact of the mass campaign was to reinforce the original voting intention of some citizens and to activate latent predispositions of others.

The tendency of the campaign to reinforce existing political preferences can be partially understood from data on the patterns of exposure to communication during the campaign. People were selective, tending to pay attention to those materials that reflected their original predispositions. Republicans were more likely to expose themselves to Republican campaign messages and to media supporting their party than they were to heed the Democratic side of the campaign, and vice versa.

The reinforcement effect can be understood also in terms of the political homogeneity of social groups. The study showed repeatedly that people voted "in

[5] Paul Lazarsfeld, Bernard Berelson, and H. Gaudet, *The People's Choice* (New York: Columbia University Press, 1948). Since all the findings summarized in this section are derived from this work, specific page references will be cited only for direct quotations from the study.

groups" in the sense that persons belonging to the same church, family, social clubs, and similar institutionalized groups tended to vote alike. Of course, the tendency toward political homogeneity of social groups can be partially explained by the fact that people living under similar social and economic conditions are likely to share similar needs and interests and to interpret their experiences in similar political terms. But a fuller explanation must also take into account the political importance within these groups of personal influence through face-to-face communication. The researchers noted: "Whenever the respondents were asked to report on their recent exposure to campaign communications of all kinds, political discussions were mentioned more frequently than exposure to radio or print."[6] It was in the discovery and analysis of such effective personal contacts that the concept of the opinion leader and a new hypothesis—the multi-step flow hypothesis—developed.

The term *opinion leader* refers to someone who, through day-to-day personal contacts and communication, influences someone else's opinions and decisions on some matter and seems to do this fairly regularly or for many people, or both. Opinion leadership can thus be seen as a role involving some pattern of communication behavior. Those who act as opinion leaders (or who serve as opinion leaders perhaps without knowing that they are doing so) are not necessarily the official, formal or public leaders or officeholders in the community; nor are they necessarily members of a social or political elite. Rather, they are usually ordinary members of the society in many respects. Some people in each stratum or subgroup seem to serve as opinion leaders for others at times. In the voting study by Lazarsfeld and his colleagues, some people from all occupational levels in the sample were serving as political opinion leaders for their friends, relatives, neighbors, or others during the election campaign.

How can researchers identify people who act as opinion leaders and so classify them in order to study their communication behavior, including their uses of mass communication? One method is to ask respondents for the names of those to whom they go for advice, information, or views before making up their own minds about some topic or coming to a decision, such as voting. These so-called nominated opinion leaders might then be contacted and interviewed about their communication behavior. This method has been used in small communities or groups where the researcher can find the persons nominated without too much expense or delay. But in large cities or in a national population, the method is less practical because of the difficulties involved in contacting and interviewing the nominated opinion leaders.

Another method is for the researcher to classify the respondents in a sample survey as opinion leaders or not, for purposes of the study, on the basis of their answers to certain questions. These people are called "self-designated" opinion leaders, although they are classified by the researcher on the basis of whether or not they say that they have been asked for their opinions or advice, have given their opinions or advice to someone, or are usually likely to be asked for their views. (The term *self-designated* opinion leader does not mean that the respon-

---

[6] Ibid., p. 150. The quotations from this work are by permission of the publisher, Columbia University Press.

dent calls herself or himself an opinion leader or even thinks of herself or himself in such terms.) The researcher can study their communication behavior, use of the mass media, and other of their characteristics without having to track them down wherever they might be, since they are already members of the sample being interviewed. This is clearly a practical benefit, although it means that the researcher must infer opinion leadership without knowing whether or not the self-designated opinion leader really influenced anyone.

In the study at hand, each member of the sample population was asked the following two questions near the middle of the election campaign: (1) "Have you tried to convince anyone of your political ideas recently?" and (2) "Has anyone asked your advice on a political question recently?" Anyone who answered "yes" to either or both questions was considered a self-designated opinion leader for purposes of the study—a technique that has been followed in many later and current studies of opinion leadership and mass communication. Ancillary information and observations were obtained to help support the validity of the opinion leader/nonleader classifications based on these personal reports on behavior.[7]

This classic study produced important findings about opinion leaders, clues for further research, and set the stage for subsequent studies of personal influence and mass communication. First, as noted above, opinion leadership was found to be distributed throughout the social structure, suggesting that personal influence may be exercised horizontally, so to speak, within social classes or other status groups, and not necessarily solely or even primarily vertically, say from the top social strata downward in an elite leadership pattern. Second, the political opinion leaders were found to be especially alert, interested, and active politically. Third, and especially significant from our point of view, opinion leaders were more fully exposed to the mass media campaign that were nonleaders.

Opinion leaders were more likely than nonleaders to have read specific magazine articles about the campaign and newspaper stories and columns about the election. They were also more likely to have listened to radio speeches and to have followed the political conventions. Furthermore, they were heavy users of the mass media, regardless of their interest in the election—that is, opinion leaders were more likely to use the media than even those nonleaders who were equally interested in the election.

Fourth, and most important, there was the suggestion that the opinion leaders used the ideas and information obtained from the mass media in the advice or information they passed on to their followers:

> In the present study we found that one of the functions of opinion leaders is to mediate between the mass media and other people in their groups. It is commonly assumed that individuals obtain their information directly from newspapers, radio, and other media. Our findings, however, did not bear this out. The majority of people acquired much of their information and many of the their ideas through personal contacts with the opinion leaders in their groups. These latter individuals, in turn, exposed themselves relatively more than others to the mass media.[8]

[7] Ibid., p. 50.
[8] Ibid., p. xxiii.

This suggestion that some information flows from the mass media to the opinion leaders and from them to the mass audience is expressed in the hypothesis of a "two-step" flow of communication.

CASE 2:   *Patterns of Influence in a Small Town*

Further research on community influentials was conducted by Robert K. Merton, who studied interpersonal influence and communication behavior in a small Eastern community of about 11,000 persons.[9]

To locate the influentials, Merton asked his interviewees to name people to whom they turned for advice or help when making personal decisions (selection of furniture, educational plans, choice of a job) and to name persons who, so far as they knew, were generally asked for advice on these matters. Several hundred names were given, several dozen of which were found to have been mentioned four or more times by the respondents; these people constituted the opinion leaders or influentials for purposes of the study. The researchers hoped initially that their data would help to identify the types of people regarded as influential by their neighbors, to gain clues to the methods through which they became influential, and to determine how their patterns of communication behavior were related to their role as influentials.

In the course of interviewing the townspeople and some of the influentials, Merton and his colleagues made an important discovery that has extended our knowledge about opinion leaders in general and about the link between them and mass communication in particular. It became evident that the entire concept of "the influential" is not adequately specific, for there was no such single type who stood apart from others in the community. Rather, there seemed to be different types of influentials, at least two of which were evident among the town's opinion leaders. Merton identified these as local and cosmopolitan influentials. The chief criterion for separating the two types was their orientation toward their town, the local influential being preoccupied essentially with community affairs, the cosmopolitan influential being also concerned with the larger world, both national and international, and its problems.

Once this distinction was made, a considerable part of the research centered on detecting similarities and differences between these two types of influentials. The local influential was more likely to have been born in or near the community, whereas the cosmopolitan had been more mobile and was a relative newcomer to the town. Local influentials were also more concerned with knowing a large number of townspeople, whereas cosmopolitans were more restrictive in their associations, tending to make friends with people on the same status level. And local influentials were more likely to participate in voluntary associations designed for making contacts and friends, whereas the cosmopolitan tended to

[9] Robert K. Merton, "Patterns of Influence," in P. Lazarsfeld and F. Stanton, *Communications Research 1948–1949* (New York: Harper, 1949), pp. 180–219. The findings summarized in this section are selected from several parts of the original work.

belong to organizations that focused on special skills or interests, such as hobby groups and professional societies.

Local and cosmopolitan influentials also differed markedly in their communication behavior. Both types, to be sure, used the mass media more than the average person in the community. Nevertheless, they differed in their tastes and in the uses to which they put the communication material. Consider, for example, their patterns of magazine reading. Both types of influential read magazines more than the average citizen did. But the cosmopolitan leader was a heavier user, especially of news magazines. Merton explains this difference in terms of the functions magazines serve for each type of influential. For cosmopolites, magazines in general, and news magazines in particular, are an important link with the outside world, providing information that helps to reduce their sense of cultural isolation and enables them to maintain their leadership on nonlocal topics. For local influentials, on the other hand, news magazines are luxuries, since they do not contain much material about local affairs—the topics on which they may be called for an opinion. Similarly, local influentials read more local newspapers, whereas cosmopolites were more likely to be regular readers of the metropolitan New York papers. The locals' interest in radio news was limited primarily to straight newscasts, whereas the cosmopolites preferred news commentators and analysts who could help them to interpret events.

Merton suggests the hypothesis that local influentials are polymorphic. That is, their connections in town (on which rests their influence) cover several different fields, and they can exert influence in a variety of spheres. On the other hand, the cosmopolitans' influence is more likely to be monomorphic; that is, it is restricted to the field in which they are consulted as an expert—national or international politics, fashion, world business, or some other subject. The following study supports the hypothesis that opinion leadership in such matters tends to fall into several hands.

CASE 3: *Personal Influence in a Larger City*

Our knowledge about opinion leadership, its relation to mass communication and to the multistep flow of information and influence, advanced further with the publication of *Personal Influence*, by Elihu Katz and Paul F. Lazarsfeld. It reported results of a panel study of decision-making among a random sample of 800 women in Decatur, Illinois, a city of about 60,000 people at the time.[10]

Four problems occupied the researchers throughout this study. First, they were interested in determining the impact of personal influence, as compared with the impact of the mass media, in four areas of common decision-making: marketing, fashion, public issues, and (what was then common) choice of motion pictures. Personal contacts seemed to have had greater influence than the mass media (as measured by an index of effectiveness) in people's decisions about marketing, movie selection, and (to a lesser extent) fashions. (Data on de-

[10] Specific page references will be cited only for direct quotations from the study.

cisions about public issues were not reported in this context.) This does not mean that mass communication had no impact; on the contrary, sometimes the mass media played an important contributory role in peoples' decisions and occasionally they played the decisive role. But the data do suggest a relatively greater impact of face-to-face communication in these situations.[11]

Why should personal communications seem to be a more effective means of persuasion in these circumstances? In their earlier study of voting behavior, Lazarsfeld and his colleagues suggested five advantageous characteristics of personal relationships.[12] First, personal contacts are more casual, apparently less purposive, and more difficult to avoid than mass communication. Many people are highly selective of mass communication, avoiding materials that go against their personal opinions or in which they are not interested. But people are less likely to anticipate the content of the personal communication or to take steps to avoid it. Second, face-to-face communication permits greater flexibility in content. If the communicator meets resistance from the audience, he or she can change the line of argument to meet audience reactions. Third, the direct personal relationships involved in face-to-face communication can enhance the rewards for accepting the message or argument and the "punishment" for not accepting it. Fourth, some people are more likely to put their trust in the judgment and viewpoint of persons whom they know and respect than in those of the impersonal mass communicator. Fifth, by personal contact the communicator can sometimes achieve his or her purpose without actually persuading the audience to accept a new point of view. In voting, for example, a forceful party worker or a friend may persuade individuals to go to the polls and vote without actually altering or activating their interest in the campaign or their position on the issues.

In the Decatur study, the authors emphasize the advantage of the interpersonal aspects of face-to-face communication in affecting marketing, fashions, and movie selection. The mass media depend primarily on the content of their communications, especially on whether the content makes the object or viewpoint presented attractive to the audience. Personal communications, on the other hand, influence people not only through what is said, but also by personal control, in which the source of the directive is as important as the content itself. "People can induce each other," write Katz and Lazarsfeld, "to a variety of activities as a result of their interpersonal relations and thus their influence goes far beyond the content of their communication."[13]

---

[11] The numerical value of the index of effectiveness is the proportion of persons who assess a particular medium as being most influential in their decision-making on some subject to the total number of people making that decision who report being exposed to that medium. In a simple equation:

$$\text{index of effectiveness} = \frac{\text{effective exposure}}{\text{total exposure}}$$

For example, in marketing decisions, contacts with friends, relatives, or neighbors had an index of effectiveness of .39, in contrast with an index of .25 for radio advertising, .07 for newspaper advertising, and .07 for magazine advertising.

[12] Lazarsfeld, Berelson, and Gaudet, *The People's Choice.*

[13] Katz and Lazarsfeld, *Personal Influence*, p. 185. The quotations from this work are by permission of the publisher, Macmillan, Inc. Copyright 1955 by The Free Press.

A second aim of the Decatur study was to investigate characteristics that differentiated persons acting as opinion leaders from nonleaders in the four topics under study, especially in terms of the person's position in the life cycle (for example, young women), socioeconomic status, and patterns of gregariousness. Third, the researchers investigated the flow of influence—for example, whether it went from the older women to the younger or from the rich to the poor. Fourth, they studied the ways in which personal influence was tied to the mass media—that is, what the communication habits of opinion leaders were and how much these leaders, in turn, were influenced by the mass media.

Let us now consider a few of the findings about opinion leaders, their communication behavior, and data bearing on the hypothesis of a multistep flow of communications. Opinion leaders were identified through their answers to questions about their role in giving advice on the topic under study. For example, each woman was asked about movies in June and August: "Have you recently been asked for advice about what pictures to see?" If she said "yes," detailed data were gathered about the incidents. Also, each woman was asked in August whether she thought she was more or less likely than other women in her circle of friends to be asked her advice on such topics. From the answers to such questions, an index was constructed for classifying opinion leaders and nonleaders in each area of opinion under study.

Examination of the characteristics of these opinion leaders supports many of the hypotheses suggested by the earlier studies on personal influence by Lazarsfeld, Merton, and others. As in *The People's Choice*, where opinion leaders on politics were found in all walks of life, in the Decatur study, opinion leaders on marketing, fashion, public issues, and motion pictures are widely distributed. Each stratum of society seems to have its own group of opinion leaders. Furthermore, different people usually serve as opinion leaders for each topic, much as there were separate influentials for local and cosmopolitan issues in Merton's study. There was no evidence of a generalized leadership factor that might make an opinion leader in one area more likely to be a leader in others.

Considering three areas (fashions, marketing, and public affairs), the researchers found that only 3 percent of the women in the study were opinion leaders in all three fields at the same time; 10 percent were leaders in two fields; 27 percent were opinion leaders in a single area. Hence, at least in areas that do not restrict themselves to local issues, personal influence appears to be monomorphic, as had been suggested in Merton's research on cosmopolitan leaders.[14]

What were the communication habits of opinion leaders? Here too, several of the relationships noted in earlier studies are corroborated. The opinion leaders' generally high exposure to mass media is again evident. First, leaders in every sphere of influence tended to be more highly exposed to mass communication than were the nonleaders. They read more books and magazines than nonleaders and attended the movies more often. Second, the selective nature of this exposure to the mass media was apparent. Leaders read magazines that dealt with their specialty; fashion leaders were more likely to read fashion magazines

[14] For an alternative view, see Alan Marcus and Raymond Bauer, "Yes: There Are Generalized Opinion Leaders," *Public Opinion Quarterly*, 28 (1964), pp. 628–632.

than either nonleaders or opinion leaders in other fields. Opinion leaders in the fields of fashion and public affairs more frequently read mass media that reflect a cosmopolitan orientation (such as out-of-town newspapers and national news mgazines) than did leaders in marketing or motion pictures. This supports Merton's observation that such media are selected because they serve a specific function for the opinion leader. Third, some support for the multistep flow of communication was obtained:

> So far we have seen that the opinion leaders tend to be both more generally exposed to the mass media, and more specifically exposed to the content most closely associated with their leadership. Presumably this increased exposure then becomes a component—witting or unwitting—of the influence which such influentials transmit to others. As a result of these findings, the idea of the "two-step flow of communications" gains credence.[15]

Of course, the term "two-step flow" is more heuristic than definitive; that is, it suggests that some, but by no means all, communication content reaches a mass audience indirectly through the mediating efforts of opinion leaders.[16] But it is quite possible—as, indeed, some of the findings in the Decatur and in subsequent studies indicate—that there are more than two steps in this process. Sometimes opinion leaders look, in turn, to other people for information and advice on that subject. Some of these second-level influentials may depend on the mass media, whereas others turn to still a third circle of opinion leaders for advice, and so on.

That the communication process may be more complex than originally suggested by the term "two-step flow" does not detract from the important reconceptualization signified by the term. The concepts introduced and explored in the three pioneer studies summarized above, and in other related research, have had great impact on subsequent theoretical and empirical work on the relation between interpersonal and mass communication within the United States and in other societies. Studies have examined the parts played by interpersonal and mass communication in such diverse processes as the adoption and diffusion of innovations, the diffusion of information and news, political elections, consumer behavior, public health campaigns, modernization and other forms of social change, and birth control.[17] The scope of these studies has ranged from small communities through selected segments of the population (for example, physicians, scientists, farmers) to larger sectors of the total society.

These new studies have contributed much to our knowledge of the commu-

---

[15] Katz and Lazarsfeld, *Personal Influence*, p. 316.

[16] Evidence that messages often reach individuals directly without the mediating efforts of opinion leaders is presented, for example, in a voting study by Bernard Berelson, Paul Lazarsfeld, and William McPhee, *Voting* (Chicago: University of Chicago Press, 1954).

[17] For example, see Walter Weiss, "Effects of the Mass Media of Communications," in *The Handbook of Social Psychology*, 2nd ed., ed. Gardner Lindzey and Elliot Aronson (Reading, MA: Addison-Wesley, 1969), vol. 5, chap. 38; Everett Rogers, "Mass Media and Interpersonal Communication," in Ithiel de Sola Pool et al., eds., *Handbook of Communication* (Chicago: Rand McNally, 1973), chap. 11, and Josephine R. Holz and Charles R. Wright, "Sociology of Mass Communications," *Annual Review of Sociology*, 5 (1979), pp. 193–217.

nication process. Nevertheless, a theoretical synthesis of their findings remains premature, because the studies vary in their conceptual definitions, operational measures, and methodologies. Thus it is difficult to tell whether findings from one study genuinely corroborate or contradict those from another. Rather than attempt a comprehensive review of these findings (a task far exceeding the scope of this chapter), we will select a few recent studies or areas of research that illustrate, but by no means exhaust, our growing sociological insights into the relation between personal influence and mass communication.

NEWER RESEARCH ON OPINION LEADERSHIP AND SOCIAL INTERACTION

CASE 4:   *International Study of Opinion Makers*

Research at Columbia University's Bureau of Applied Social Research extended the tradition of opinion leadership research, which was initiated in the studies of the 1940s, into a new consideration of national elites and power structure. Comparative studies were conducted in the United States, in Yugoslavia, and in several other European nations. The researchers concentrated on individuals who, primarily because of the formal positions that they hold but not entirely limited to this base, are influential in matters of national concern.

The direct link to earlier research on opinion leaders is especially evident in the American leadership project, which follows the tradition of voting studies and research on the phenomenon of local opinion leaders. Allen Barton, a sociologist who is one of the codirectors of this project, places the research within this tradition, as follows:

> These opinion-leaders tended to read more and listen more to political communications. Therefore the journalists and editors of the mass media and the politicians and interest-group spokesmen whose statements appeared in these media could be considered as remote "opinion-makers" for local opinion-leaders who in turn influenced others. This naturally led to the question, who influenced the "opinion-makers"? Could the method of studying opinion leadership developed in studies of the general public be applied to the national figures who communicate to them through the mass media? Are these leaders of national institutions, the political parties, the economy and the mass media themselves, interconnected in networks of informal relationships which influence their opinions, norms, ideologies, political behavior, and the content which they communicate to the public?[18]

To answer these and other questions, the researchers selected six major institutional sectors of American society—mass organizations, legislators, government administration, economic administration, mass communication, and

[18] Allen H. Barton, "Determinants of Leadership Attitudes in a Socialist Society," paper of the International Study of Opinion Makers, prepared for the International Political Science Association, Munich, Germany; mimeographed (New York: Bureau of Applied Social Research, 1970). Quotations are from pp. 1–2 and 3, by permission of the author. See also Allen H. Barton, Bogdan Denitch, and Charles Kadushin, eds., *Opinion-Making Elites in Yugoslavia* (New York: Praeger, 1973).

intellectuals—and sampled from among individuals who held top formal positions in each sector. These formal leaders were interviewed to determine the extent to which they communicated with the public and one another, proposed public policy, or attempted to influence policy decisions. They also were asked sociometric questions about whom they regarded as generally influential, who their personal opinion leaders were, and who their discussion partners on policy questions were. By following the sociometric chain further, it was possible to locate the opinion leaders and discussion partners of these newly identified "leaders" of the original sample of top national institutional leaders. "By these procedures," the researchers note, "we can locate those who actually function as opinion-makers, within the set of positional leaders of major social institutions and outside that set."

These research projects have demonstrated both the feasibility and the value of the approach. Reports on the findings are wide ranging, including information about the limits of consensus on economic and foreign policy issues among American leaders, the shape of the national power structure, determinants of leadership attitudes, the informal social structure of elites, the social circles of intellectuals in the society, communication intake and output among opinion makers in the society, and other matters. Although space does not permit a summary here, one set of findings on the flow of communication among national figures warrants mention; it concerns the relations between American "elite intellectuals" and "men of power."

This particular line of research stems from the earlier work of Charles Kadushin, a sociologist interested in the study of social circles, a concept related to patterns of personal influence. For purposes of the study, elite intellectuals either are individuals who contribute fairly frequently to magazines or journals that were influential among intellectuals or are designated as influential intellectuals by these writers. Men of power were identified by their positions in various institutional sectors, as described above. Kadushin examined the extent to which intellectuals were nominated as influentials by men in positions of power and the extent to which intellectuals reported that they had direct contact with such national decision-makers. Little direct interpersonal communication occurred. Relatively few American intellectuals (as defined in this study) directly communicated with men of power on social and political matters; and men of power rarely sought the views of intellectuals, except on matters requiring technical expertise. Nevertheless, Kadushin points out, intellectuals may have an indirect influence on men of power through a "trickle down" process of communication.

Leaders in the mass media and men of power in other sectors of the elite either occasionally or frequently read the magazines and journals of opinion in which intellectuals publish—the *New York Times Magazine, Foreign Affairs, Harper's* and the *Atlantic,* to mention but a few. These magazines provide one channel through which a society's intellectuals can have an indirect effect on men of power and, through them, on social policy. In addition, it is possible that through their writings and other public activities, intellectuals help create a general climate of opinion within which social problems are defined and policies

formed. Nevertheless, Kadushin notes, by and large the writings and other public communications of intellectuals are directed more at one another than at the
power elite.[19]

CASE 5:   Opinion Seeking, Opinion Avoiding, and Opinion Leadership

Sociologically, opinion leadership is not an attribute of an individual, like a personality trait, but a social act or set of acts involving interaction between two or
more individuals. Sociological interest focuses on such questions as the conditions under which such interaction is likely to occur, the nature of the interaction, regularities in the social characteristics of people likely to play the role of
opinion leader on various topics under different conditions, and the communication behavior and other activities of individuals playing the role of opinion
leader or "follower" on some topic. Attention has been drawn to the active role
of some "followers" in soliciting opinions, information, or advice from others.

Elsewhere, Muriel Cantor and I found it useful to distinguish between opinion leadership, opinion seeking, and opinion avoiding in a study of opinion leadership and communication behavior among graduate students. For example,
with regard to one of the topics under study (United States foreign affairs), we
noted that certain students actively sought the opinions of others, whereas some
individuals avoided them; persons engaging in either type of activity also might
or might not play the role of opinion leader for others. We found that:

> [O]pinion seekers differ from avoiders in their level of interest in the topic and re-
> lated subjects (but not on other matters) and in exposure to mass media most likely
> to be relevant to the topic (but not in exposure to other media). . . . Opinion seekers
> are active participants in the communications system; they not only seek the views of
> their peers but also make relatively greater use of other media of communication.
> Many opinion seekers, in turn, serve as opinion leaders for others. By contrast, the
> opinion avoiders are relatively isolated from the flow of communication on a particu-
> lar topic. Not only do they avoid seeking the views of their peers, but they make rela-
> tively little use of other sources of information about the subject. They are, in turn,
> less likely than the opinion seekers to serve as opinion leaders for others.

Our findings further suggest that:

> The heavy communications exposure attributed to opinion leaders by previous stud-
> ies is correct but reflects the general characteristics of opinion seeking which many
> opinion leaders show. Other individuals who do not serve as opinion leaders also dis-
> play these characteristics if they are opinion seekers. Those opinion leaders who

[19] Charles Kadushin, Herman Kane, and Stella Manne, "The Relations between Elite American
Intellectuals and Men of Power," paper presented at the annual meeting of the American Sociological Association, 1973, mimeographed. See also Carol Weiss, "What America's Leaders Read,"
Public Opinion Quarterly, 38 (Spring 1974), pp. 1–22; and Charles Kadushin, *The American Intellectual Elite* (Boston: Little, Brown, 1974).

somehow fail to seek the views of their peers are also less likely to be "tuned in" to other sources of communication about their topic.[20]

We proposed that opinion seeking be regarded as a key role behavior in the process of personal influence and the multistep flow of communication.

Role specifications also have been suggested by others. Herbert Hyman, for example, distinguishes between "self-propelled" and "responsive" opinion leaders, depending on who initiates the exchange. For responsive opinion leadership to be exercised, it is crucial that someone activate the role of opinion seeker and thus start the communication exchange.[21]

John Robinson, in a study of communication behavior during a national election campaign, classifies people as playing the roles of opinion givers, opinion receivers, both, and inactives. About half the national sample of people interviewed were active participants in the process of personal influence about voting, many of them both giving and receiving opinions. This overlap supports the idea that personal influence often involves an opinion exchange, rather than unilateral communication from an active opinion leader to a passive follower.

About half the population studied were classified as inactives—that is, they had not tried to advise anyone about how to vote, nor had anyone tried to influence them. They did not seem to discuss the election much with others (hence engaging in what Cantor and I call opinion avoiding on this topic). A large majority of all respondents, including the inactives, said that they rely on the mass media for campaign information. Opinion givers (some of whom also were receivers) were more likely than others to get campaign information from newspapers and magazines. Thus some people (inactives) seemed to be more dependent on mass communication alone during the campaign, while others also participated in interpersonal discussions.

Robinson proposes a revised "step-flow" model that goes beyond a two-step process. It takes into account more explicitly than prior models the fact that mass communications reach some people directly and others through the mediation of opinion leaders; and it explicitly considers communication among opinion leaders themselves.[22]

It should be clear from our discussion that we conceive of opinion leadership as a social communication activity rather than as a personality trait. This orientation directs our attention to the social context of opinion leadership and to the social conditions that make it likely or unlikely for certain kinds of people to engage in opinion leadership on specific topics.

[20] These extracts from "The Opinion Seeker and Avoider: Steps Beyond the Opinion Leader Concept," by Charles R. Wright and Muriel G. Cantor, are reprinted from *Pacific Sociological Review*, 10 (Spring 1967), pp. 42–43, by permission of the publisher, Sage Publications, Inc.

[21] Personal communication, July 1983. Hyman also notes a distinction between seeking advice to solve a specific problem and seeking a "ready-made" opinion on an issue because of cultural demands that one ought to have an opinion about it.

[22] John P. Robinson, "Interpersonal Influence in Election Campaigns: Two Step Flow Hypotheses," *Public Opinion Quarterly*, 40, 3 (Fall 1976), pp. 304–319. Also see Joan S. Black, "Opinion Leaders: Is Anyone Following?" *Public Opinion Quarterly*, 46, 2 (Summer 1982), pp. 169–176. Black distinguishes between recent advisors, potential advisors, and nonadvisors on national issues.

OPINION LEADERSHIP AND SOCIAL ROLES

Opportunities for opinion leadership are related to a person's social statuses and roles, roles that affect chances for coming into contact with other people and for having or seeming to have expertise, information, or special knowledge about topics of interest and concern to them. Opinion leaders, observed Paul Lazarsfeld and his colleagues in their classic study of American voting behavior, engage in greater interaction with other people through their more *strategic social relations.*[23]

Just what social roles are likely to provide strategic social relations, however, is not easy to specify in advance. Certain occupations may do this because they involve contacts with a relatively large number and/or a wide variety of people. One's occupation also may signify some knowledge or experience that is relevant to the topic in the eyes of others. This is not to say that the occupation causes a person to be an opinion leader on the topic or that persuasion is part of the job, as with a politician, for example. (Recall that the concept of opinion leadership here is not formal leadership, but rather informal, day-to-day influence among friends, neighbors, and others, usually through conversations.) Rather, the job provides a suitable context within which such strategic interaction occurs. And occupation, alone or together with other social statuses (such as age or sex), makes certain people more likely than others to get to act as opinion leaders on specific topics.

We will explore the significance of occupation for opinion leadership through several illustrative cases. These include a survey of people interested in trees; research on communications in beauty parlors, barbershops, and pharmacies; and a study of suburban commuters.

CASE 6: *Environmental Opinion Leadership*

Early in the 1970s, when Americans were becoming increasingly concerned about the quality of the natural environment, a study was made of people who wrote to the United States Forestry Service for any of three leaflets on trees that had been announced in the mass media and other places.[24] The researcher, Rita Ramrath, mailed lengthy questionnaires to a sample of 285 persons who had requested leaflets; she obtained answers from 200 of these "environmental information seekers." All together, these respondents had requested a total of 17,000 copies of the three leaflets, an average of 85 copies per person. The leaflets were written in nontechnical terms for the public and were entitled "People, Cities and Trees," "Man's Best Friend, the Tree," and "Trees—Nature's Way to Diminish Noise."

What kinds of people seek such information about trees? To the researcher's

---

[23] Berelson, Lazarsfeld, and McPhee, *Voting*, p. 109.

[24] Rita Ramrath, "Communications Behavior of Environmental Information Seekers: Their Sources of Information and Role in Information Diffusion" (MA thesis, Annenberg School of Communications, University of Pennsylvania, 1972).

surprise, for she had expected the primary audience to be the general public, many were professionals working on environmental and conservation matters. They included, among others, foresters, nursery workers, landscape architects, lumber workers, farmers, biochemists, park administrators, public relations people, teachers and professors in such fields as forestry, wildlife, landscape architecture, botany, zoology, biology, and recreation.

At first thought it might seem that the leaflets were missing their target—the general public. Not so. For those who received them often recommended them to others, used them in giving information and advice about the environment, and sometimes redistributed them to members of the public. Sometimes they did this during the course of their work, and at other times through other social roles. Many respondents, for example, belong to voluntary associations, some of which are directly concerned with environmental matters. Some people are active in community projects to improve the environment and/or have made individual efforts of this sort, such as planting trees. Many respondents expressed great interest in environmental topics and frequently used the mass media, as well as various organizations and agencies, as sources of information about such matters. They were quite active information seekers in this field. Many also appeared to be opinion leaders.

About two-thirds of these information seekers were classified as environmental opinion leaders on the basis of their replies to questions similar to those used in the Decatur study. About a third said they had been asked recently for their advice on the specific topic in the requested leaflet, by friends, relatives, neighbors, business associates, fellow club members, and others. More than half of them had recommended a leaflet to someone, usually to two to ten other people; in total, these 200 respondents said they had recommended the leaflets to approximately 10,000 people. "Most of this recommending," Ramrath reports, "took place in the course of business dealings."[25] (Recommendations also were made, however, outside of business.) She suggests that the respondents' occupations gave them greater opportunity and occasions for recommending pamphlets than did their other social roles.

Some occupations, especially those related to environmental work, probably gave certain respondents specialized knowledge and a social identity that made them seem appropriate, legitimate, and accessible personal sources of information, opinions, and advice about environmental affairs. Furthermore, their jobs provided a suitable context for strategic interaction leading to personal influence.

Certain occupations, suggested sociologist Arnold Rose, also give people a physical place and a social role in the community that makes them potentially influential in face-to-face communication with cross-sections of people, many of whom lack direct communication among themselves.[26] Bartenders, barbers, cab drivers, truckdrivers, mail carriers, and shopkeepers come to mind as examples.

[25] Ibid.

[26] Rose suggested the term "ecological influential" for persons in such occupations, but I have not used that term here because of possible confusion with opinion leadership about ecology and environmental matters. Arnold Rose, "The Ecological Influential: A Leadership Type," *Sociology and Social Research*, II (1968), p. 186.

These occupations either require the person to move around and to interact with a large number and wide variety of people, or make it possible for such people to come to them for services. We are further informed about this possible link between occupation, opinion leadership, and the use of mass communication through our next case study.

CASE 7:   Conversations and Opinion Leadership in Semi-Public Places

In a study of urban communications, Judith Beinstein examined verbal communications between pharmicists, beauticians, and barbers and their customers in metropolitan Philadelphia.[27] She selected persons in these three occupations precisely because they seemed likely to be "ecological influentials" in Rose's terms. Many people come to these practitioners for services repeatedly, perhaps periodically; conversation with customers or clients normally is expected; and the service performed usually takes enough time to allow considerable talk. The study reports on personal interviews conducted with more than a hundred pharmacists, beauticians, and barbers working in five neighborhoods ranging from downtown to the suburbs.

Beinstein found that these persons do indeed have a lot of conversations with their clients, including and going beyond pleasantries and small talk. The topics that most respondents said they discuss frequently with their customers are vacations, social problems, and health problems. Next most cited were economic matters, food and restaurants, entertainment, fashions, and sports. From about half to three-quarters of the respondents talk frequently with customers about these topics. Slightly less than half said they frequently discuss politics and world affairs; and fewer talk about personal problems. (These were the ten topics explicitly studied.)

More pertinent to our immediate concern with interpersonal and mass communication, however, is whether the respondents act as opinion leaders and/or opinion seekers, and how these activities relate to mass communication. The study suggests that they do behave as opinion leaders on certain topics. For example, beauticians not only frequently discuss fashions with their clients, but most seem to play the part of opinion leaders on this topic. They say that customers frequently ask for their opinions about fashions. But they are not opinion leaders on all topics; for example, they say they don't talk much about sports,

[27] Certain methodological limitations of this procedure are obvious and were taken into account by the researcher. For example, information about conversations in each shop comes from the one common participant in them—the respondent, rather than from the many customers involved. The respondent knows more about the range of things discussed than any one customer; still, his or her account may be biased. The researcher gained confidence in these accounts through on-site observations of interactions between respondents and their clients during four weeks of field observations. Judith Beinstein, "Conversations in Semi-Public Places" (Ph.D. dissertation, University of Pennsylvania, 1972) and "Conversations in Public Places," *Journal of Communication*, 25, 1 (Winter 1975), pp. 85–95.

and few of them are opinion leaders on that subject. Nevertheless, *some* barbers, beauticians, and pharmacists acted as opinion leaders on each of the topics.

Respondents also said how frequently they asked customers for their own views or opinions about each of these topics. Such opinion exchanges reportedly were common, although they varied among topics and differed according to the respondent's occupation. In general, both opinion leadership and opinion exchange most often centered on topics related to the respondent's occupational specialty and to people's leisure activities, such as vacations, television programs, movies, and sports. They less frequently centered on topics of public affairs, such as world problems, politics, social problems, and economic matters.

The respondents' occupational roles, through the patterns of conversation that they permit, provide opportunities for the respondents to develop knowledge and expertise on certain topics of conversation. Further, many of the respondents sought out more information from the mass media and elsewhere (acted as opinion seekers) about topics on which they were asked for opinions during conversations with clients. Beinstein reports that the respondents

> . . . tend to talk to customers about the topics they enjoy discussing and they *tend to seek information about these topics in the mass media.* Therefore, they are likely to accumulate information and opinion about topics they prefer discussing as a result of talking with others about them and as a result of reading about them in magazines, newspapers, and books or hearing about them via television or radio. [They] bring this body of information and opinion to conversations with their customers. Thus they may become local "experts" on the topics they enjoy discussing most.[28]

And thus, through their personal use of the mass media and their pass-along conversations with clients, these respondents (sometimes acting as opinion leaders, other times perhaps just exchanging views with customers) play a role in the multistep flow of information from mass media to the public.

Expertise that makes people likely candidates for opinion leadership on specific topics also can come from social roles other than one's occupation, of course, and from a combination of occupation and other social statuses. A good example can be found in Linda Shipley's study of the communication behavior of commuters and local workers in a suburban community located between Philadelphia and New York City, the next case to which we turn.

CASE 8: Commuters and Local Workers

Shipley conducted lengthy personal interviews with sixty husbands and wives in order to study the communication behavior of persons who live in a community located between two metropolitan centers, and who are fully capable of receiving newspapers and broadcasts from both places as well as from local mass

---

[28] Beinstein, "Conversations in Semi-Public Places," pp. 225–226.

media.[29] She contrasted the behavior of those living in households where the breadwinner commuted to Philadelphia versus New York City versus the local community. Among the communication behavior studied was interpersonal communication and opinion leadership. Shipley asked respondents whether they had been recently asked about happenings in the local community, Philadelphia, or New York, and whether they were more, less, or equally likely as their friends to be asked about such events. She then constructed an index of opinion leadership (similar to that used in the Decatur study) and classified respondents as opinion leaders or not about local affairs, Philadelphia or New York affairs, or some combinations thereof.

Clearly where one works (or where one's spouse works) makes a difference. Cosmopolitan influentials among the respondents (people who were opinion leaders about events outside the local community) were more likely to be commuters. New York commuters or their spouses were more likely to serve as opinion leaders about New York affairs than were others; and Philadelphia commuters or their spouses were the likely opinion leaders about Philadelphia events. These daily contacts with New York or Philadelphia apparently made some respondents seem to be "experts," or at least good and convenient sources of information and advice about what was going on there. (It should be noted that this occurred in a community where residents could receive daily news about both New York and Philadelphia events from the mass media. Television sets were able to tune in to major stations from both cities, and daily newspapers from Philadelphia and New York were easily available.) By contrast, being a local influential was not dependent on working within the area.

The study contains some interesting qualitative material that reminds us of Lazarsfeld's observation that opinion leadership is embedded in social relations. Opinion leadership consists of social interactions and personal communication exchanges, rather than being a one-way action by a "born leader." Shipley asked respondents whether their opinions were asked for during conversations with friends, neighbors, other commuters, and co-workers; and whether they (respondents) asked others for their opinions during such conversations. "Some respondents," she observes, "report that their discussions are filled with a back and forth exchange of opinion—sometimes even a heated exchange. Others say that there is no asking for opinions, only giving of opinions. Yet others say their discussions are more conversational, less opinionated." In the words of one of her respondents, opinions are "generally not asked for, just given—freely given!" Or another: "Nobody asks. Everyone gives their own." And a final example: "We don't really ask, we just give them."[30]

This reminder that day-to-day conversations may involve social exchanges in which it is not always possible for the participants to sort out and label who is "leading" whom (if anyone!) is also nicely demonstrated in a small study by Linda Park of communications about health among suburban mothers of small

[29] Linda Shipley, "Communication Behavior of People Living in a Megalopolis: A Study of Mass Media Use and Inter-Personal Communications of Commuters and Local Workers" (Ph.D. dissertation, University of Pennsylvania, 1974), and "A Typology of Communication Behavior," *Journalism Quarterly*, 53, 3 (Autumn 1976), pp. 483–487.

[30] Shipley, "Communication Behavior," p. 224.

children.[31] When, in the course of her study, Park attempted to detect health information opinion leaders through questions about opinion seeking, she ran into a communications "stone wall." Nobody seemed to ask friends, neighbors, or family members for opinions about health matters. Why not? Further conversations with these mothers showed that the question was improperly phrased. One seeks medical opinions only from medical experts—usually physicians or other health professionals. What one does with friends and others is *exchange* information, recount experiences, and generally discuss health affairs.

There was plenty of that kind of interpersonal discussion by certain respondents (whom Park classified as high users of health information). These women sought health information from the mass media, in order to become more aware of preventive health measures, long-term health care habits, and emergency procedures. Interpersonal communications and exchanges of information with friends reinforced the mothers' continuous search for health knowledge which they considered necessary to their role as health guardians of the family. Most of these conversations were with other mothers like themselves and with women in the family.

The respondents, in turn, passed this information and "advice" to their husbands mainly when a major family decision was required (hospitalization of a child) or when the husbands' own health was involved (quit smoking!). Through the exchange of information with others, these mothers greatly increased their own knowledge and experience concerning health affairs far beyond the direct experience of any one of them and beyond what could be learned from the mass media. In this sense, participating in such an informal, interpersonal network of communication is participating in an interpersonal influence exchange, whether so labeled by the participants or not.

Park's findings highlighting the "exchange" nature of the interaction between mothers and their friends and relatives while discussing health and medical experiences remind us again—as did the patterns discerned by Beinstein and Shipley—of Lazarsfeld's earlier insight that "One might speak less of leaders than of a complex web of opinion-leader relationships."[32] Within these relationships, he observed, those people who play the role of opinion leader on some topic of discussion are likely to have interest and competence in the sphere of discussion in which they lead. Beinstein's study has demonstrated that such topical competence may come not only from occupational expertise, but also from active development of "private" but socially produced knowledge through regular extensive conversations with others and from seeking information through mass media and other channels. Shipley's study demonstrated that the daily commute to the metropolis provided "private" knowledge about the city that was seen as useful or of interest to one's neighbors; local expertise may be derived from local residence.[33] In all cases, persons engaged in opinion leader-

---

[31] Linda Park, "Health Communication Patterns Among Suburban Mothers of Young Children" (MA thesis, Annenberg School of Communications, University of Pennsylvania, 1975).

[32] Berelson, Lazarsfeld, and McPhee, *Voting*, p. 109.

[33] Relative expertise in a sphere may be as elementary and humanly understandable as being able to read and write. Such was the case, for example, in a study of migrant women in Peru. The researcher reports that women who had recently learned to read and write served as opinion leaders

ship on a topic have combined mass communication, interpersonal communication, and personal experience in building their stock of information and expertise on a topic.

Research on the connections between personal influence and mass communication among selected segments of the population reflects a persistent and theoretically important sociological interest in communication behavior as related to the study of social structure, social order, and social change. We turn now to another example of such concern, exemplified chiefly through the work of rural sociologists interested in the role of communication in the adoption of innovations and their diffusion within a community.

COMMUNICATION BEHAVIOR AND THE ADOPTION AND DIFFUSION OF INNOVATIONS

For many years, sociologists have been interested in studying the adoption of a variety of innovations in farming, health practices, consumer behavior, family-planning practices, and other areas of life. For example, as early as the 1920s, but mainly since the 1940s, rural sociologists have been studying how farmers learn about technological innovations and come to adopt them or not.

Insofar as the adoption of innovations (in farming or other areas) is voluntary rather than imposed, it may be conceived of as a process resembling how people reach "decisions" on other matters, such as voting. Studies of the adoption process have considered, among other things, the relative parts played by mass communication and by interpersonal communication in people's acceptance or rejection of innovations.

A second, but related, line of inquiry concerns the diffusion of the innovation within the community—that is, the extent and rate of acceptance of an innovation by the people concerned. These studies also consider the parts played by mass and interpersonal communication in diffusion.[34] It is not possible to summarize here more than fifty years of domestic and international research on adoption and diffusion, but fortunately, several summaries are available elsewhere. We simply note two important contributions this line of research has made in the conceptualization of the problem. Stated most simply, they are: (1) that adoption should be examined as a process, rather than as an event; and (2) that diffusion should be analyzed as a social process, rather than as simply the sum of individual adoptions.

To the observer, and perhaps to the persons involved, adoption of an innovation may seem to be an event or act: A farmer plants a new type of seed,

about adult literacy for other women who were illiterate but who, like themselves, were former country folk now working as domestic servants in the city. See Heli De Sagasti, "Social Implications of Adult Literacy: A Study Among Migrant Women in Peru" (Ph.D. dissertation, University of Pennsylvania, 1972).

[34] For an account of the communication experiences and advice given by international technical assistance experts involved in trying to diffuse innovations in twelve different developing countries throughout the world, see Herbert H. Hyman, Gene N. Levine, and Charles R. Wright, *Inducing Social Change in Developing Communities: An International Survey of Expert Advice* (Geneva: United Nations Research Institute for Social Development, 1967).

a consumer buys a color television set, a woman accepts some new device for preventing pregnancy, or each does not. In similar fashion, many other kinds of decisions by the individual may seem to be events: A citizen votes or does not, votes for one candidate or another, chooses a movie to see, buys a new automobile, or gets married. In each instance there is an apparent salient moment at which an act takes place that signifies the decision: one votes, buys, uses, or otherwise engages in some behavior different from the past.

But upon reflection it can be seen that this apparently final act is really only a part of a longer process of thought and activity that precedes it, accompanies it, and may follow it. To conceptualize the adoption of an innovation or any other kind of individual decision-making as part of a process rather than as an isolated act without a history is an important step, albeit "self-evident" once expressed. This conceptualization was one of the underlying reasons behind the use of the panel technique by Lazarsfeld and his associates in their early studies of "votes in the making." What has been emphasized by the work of students of adoption is the need systematically to specify and codify apparent steps or "stages" in the individual's decision to adopt or reject an innovation, or in any other decision for that matter.

Varying numbers of such stages have been postulated by different students of the problems. A model that has been commonly advanced for many years consists of five stages: awareness, interest, evaluation, trial, and adoption or rejection. The model suggests that in order for an individual to adopt an innovation, he or she must first become aware of its existence, become interested to know more about it, evaluate its relevance to personal needs, decide to give it a small trial, then assess the experiences with the trial and decide to adopt or reject the innovation. Other models have reduced the number of apparent stages; some have added postadoption decisions to continue or to discontinue the new activity. In some cases it is argued that the stages need not follow the order of the model; some might even be bypassed under certain circumstances. Many other modifications appear in the literature.

Research indicates that the relative importance of various kinds of communication (mass and interpersonal) differs at each stage in the adoption process.[35] Findings suggest that the mass media are especially important sources of first information about new technology, ideas or other innovations. And some studies suggest that interpersonal communication and personal experience are more important than the mass media to persons in the late stages of the adoption process, when deciding whether the innovation would be worth a trial.

A second major conceptual contribution of innovation research is its view of diffusion as a social process. The spreading of an innovation or idea within a community can be segmented into stages for purposes of analysis, such as an initial stage when relatively few people in the community try the innovation, or a later, "saturation," stage when nearly everybody is doing it. (Some researchers

[35] For examples of research on the adoption and diffusion of innovations, see Everett M. Rogers and F. Floyd Shoemaker, *Communication of Innovations* (New York: Free Press, 1971), Everett M. Rogers, *Diffusion of Innovations*, 3rd ed. (New York: Free Press, 1982), and Holz and Wright, "Sociology of Mass Communication."

hold that diffusion often follows a distribution resembling a normal curve, which can be segmented statistically.) Then it is possible to study the contributions of mass communication and interpersonal communication to diffusion through each stage.

Researchers also classify individuals according to when they adopt an innovation, relative to its diffusion throughout the community. For example, one theoretical scheme classifies individuals as innovators (among the first to try something), early adopters, early majority, late majority, and laggards. Then one can examine the roles played by mass communication and personal communication for relatively early or late adopters. Studies suggest that the mass media seem more important for early adopters, while interpersonal communications are more important for later ones. Distinctions have been made too between the role of innovators and that of opinion leaders. The first to adopt something are not necessarily the same persons who serve as opinion leaders for their friends, neighbors, or others.

There are indications that early and late deciders also may differ in their subsequent communication behavior. An example comes from a study of voters during the Carter-Ford presidential election campaign. While not strictly a study of innovation and diffusion, it does concern people's decision-making and serves to demonstrate the point. Steven Chaffee and Sun Yuel Choe report that voters who made up their minds relatively early in the year (pre-campaign) subsequently engaged in less communication activities during the campaign than prior to it. Voters who made up their minds sometime during the campaign "stepped up" their communication activities—paid more attention than they usually do to television coverage of politics and engaged in personal discussions about the campaign and the televised debates.[36]

To sum up, studies of the adoption and diffusion of innovations, like other studies of communication behavior, support the view that mass communication and interpersonal communication are related, perhaps complementary, modes of communication and influence, rather than the view that they are relatively independent means of reaching the public.

Our next topic extends knowledge about the link between personal and mass communication by considering another realm—studies of the diffusion of news. Research on how people learn about news events contributes to our knowledge about which sources of communication provide initial and supplementary information about specific events, how long it takes for news to diffuse to various segments of the population, and what parts mass communication and personal communication play in this part of the news process.

HOW NEWS GETS AROUND

One late afternoon in March 1981, a would-be assassin shot President Ronald Reagan and several other unfortunate victims on the sidewalk outside a major hotel in Washington, DC. News of the attempted assassination reached the

[36] Steven Chaffee and Sun Yuel Choe, "Time of Decision and Media Use During the Ford-Carter Campaign," *Public Opinion Quarterly*, 44, 1 (Spring 1980), pp. 53–69.

American public quickly. According to one study, half of a random sample of respondents in Indianapolis, Indiana—far from the scene of the shooting— heard about the event within 30 minutes, and fully 90 percent of them learned about it within 90 minutes of its occurrence. Forty-five percent of them first heard the news from someone else, 33 percent from television, and 23 percent heard it on the radio. Thus the mass media diffused the news directly to somewhat more than half of those people studied and indirectly (through word of mouth, or a "two-or-more step flow") to the rest.

How people first learned of the shooting was influenced by where they were when the news arrived. Those who were at home, especially those who happened to be watching television or listening to the radio at the time, were likely to have heard the news from the broadcast media. Most of the people who were at work got the story first from others, unless they happened—as in some instances—to have been using a radio or television at work.

About every other respondent said that he or she passed the news of the attempted assassination to a number of other people, for an average of three other persons apiece. Usually they told someone nearby whom they knew well—for example, a co-worker on the job, rather than a stranger who happened to be there; about a third called someone on the telephone; and some respondents said they went so far as to track down a specific person in order to give him or her the news. Thus, as communications researcher Walter Gantz observes, "those who were informed of the event via face-to-face means were more likely to be deliberately sought out rather than told simply because they happened to be nearby. These data support the position that interpersonal dissemination of news events is largely a selective, non-random process."[37] And hence, I would add, it is a process closely related to the social structure.

Almost all respondents said that they made efforts to keep up with developments in the story once they had heard about it, following accounts on television, radio, and in the newspapers that evening and the next day. Which mass media were used most for such following up of the news story differed across societal subgroups, varying, for example, by the respondent's age, education, and employment status, consistent with such groups' normal patterns of mass media use and their access to specific media.

Another example of the rapid local diffusion of news about a tragic event is provided by a study made in Dallas, Texas, shortly after the assassination of President John F. Kennedy there in November 1963.[38] Interviews were conducted with a modified area probability sample of approximately 200 Dallas residents. News that the president had been shot reached two-thirds of the sample within 15 minutes of the event, and within 2 hours 95 percent had learned of the assassination (all knew by 6 P.M., five and a half hours after the shooting). The majority of respondents first heard the news from interpersonal communications, face to face or through telephone calls; the rest were informed by televi-

---

[37] Walter Gantz, "The Diffusion of News About the Attempted Reagan Assassination," *Journal of Communication*, 33, 1 (Winter 1983), pp. 56–66. Quotation is from p. 60.

[38] Charles M. Bonjean, Richard J. Hill, and Harry W. Martin, "Reactions to the Assassination in Dallas," in Bradley Greenberg and Edwin Parker, eds., *The Kennedy Assassination and the American Public* (Stanford, CA: Stanford University Press, 1965), pp. 178–198.

sion or radio. And the news spread almost as rapidly by word of mouth as it did by the mass media, reaching most people within an hour of the first news release. It is likely, of course, that the initial source of the news for some of the individuals who then passed it along to others was a television or radio news bulletin. Therefore, the role of the mass media was magnified through diffusion by interpersonal communications, again demonstrating the importance of multiple channels of communication.

The complementary role of interpersonal and mass communication in diffusion of the tragic news of the assassination was not limited to Dallas. A nationwide survey by the National Opinion Research Center (NORC), conducted within days following the assassination, provides similar data.[39] About two-thirds of the nation's adults heard the news about the assassination within 30 minutes of the shooting; in less than 2 hours 92 percent knew about it; and by 6 P.M. 99.8 percent had heard about it. The news first reached about half the people by radio or television, and the other half by telephone calls or other personal communications. (The researchers note that a NORC survey conducted in 1945 showed that news of President Franklin D. Roosevelt's death reached about half the public through mass communication and the other half through personal communication.) After receiving the news, many people, as might be expected, turned to the mass media for further details and to other people for discussion of the tragedy.

Studies have been made of the diffusion of other items of news, some stories of less importance than the death of a president or a senator, others of similar high news value. Among the items studied were the admission of Alaska to statehood, the launching of America's first satellite, President Eisenhower's stroke, Eisenhower's decision to seek a second term as president, the result of a heavyweight boxing match, the issuing of a papal encyclical on birth control, and the shooting of Governor Wallace of Alabama.[40] It has been suggested by communication researcher Bradley Greenberg, as well as by Wilbur Schramm and others, that there is a curvilinear relation between the news value of a story and the speed and channels by which it reaches the public.[41] Stories of little news value (or that have been suppressed by the mass media) are likely to be diffused

[39] Paul B. Sheatsley and Jacob J. Feldman, "A National Survey of Public Reactions and Behavior," in Greenberg and Parker, pp. 149–177.

[40] For examples, see Greenberg and Parker, *The Kennedy Assassination*; Delbert C. Miller, "A Research Note on Mass Communications," *American Sociological Review*, 10 (1945), pp. 691–694; Otto Larsen and Richard J. Hill, "Mass Media and Interpersonal Communication in the Diffusion of a News Event," *American Sociological Review*, 19 (1954), pp. 426–443; Paul Deutschmann and Wayne Danielson, "Diffusion of Knowledge of the Major News Story," *Journalism Quarterly*, 37 (1960), pp. 345–355; Wayne Danielson, "Eisenhower's February Decision," *Journalism Quarterly*, 33 (1956), pp. 433–441; Bradley Greenberg, "Person-to-Person Communication in the Diffusion of News Events," *Journalism Quarterly*, 41 (1964), pp. 489–494; Bradley Greenberg, James Brinton, and Richard Farr, "Diffusion of News About an Anticipated News Event," *Journal of Broadcasting*, 9 (1965), pp. 129–142; John Adams, James Mullen, and Harold Wilson, "Diffusion of a 'Minor' Foreign Affairs News Event," *Journalism Quarterly*, 46 (1969), pp. 545–551; David Schwartz, "How Fast Does News Travel," *Public Opinion Quarterly*, 37 (1974), pp. 625–627; and Walter Gantz, "The Diffusion of News."

[41] Wilbur Schramm, "Communication in Crisis," in Greenberg and Parker, *The Kennedy Assassination*, pp. 1–25.

through word of mouth, as is news about major events. More routine news items, covered by the mass media, are likely to reach most people first through the mass media, although some people still will learn of these events from others. The time of day when the event occurs also affects its pattern of distribution. Other factors include where people are and what they are doing when a story breaks.

It would be misleading, however, to interpret these findings as evidence of mass media versus personal communication. Both kinds of communication play a role in the news diffusion process, especially as this process expands to include activities following first awareness of an event, when individuals often seek additional information, interpretation, and evaluation from the mass media and from discussions among themselves.

If we appear to have belabored the relationship between mass communication and personal communication, the stress is deliberate. It is all too easy to think of the audience for any of the mass media as having only this medium of exposure in common and as having it as an isolated communication experience. Our sociological perspective stresses the need to examine exposure to mass communication within the social context surrounding the individual, including his or her experiences with other mass media, and interpersonal communications with family members, friends, co-workers, and others who too make up the "mass audience."

CHAPTER 5

Sociology of the Audience: Selected Characteristics of Audiences and Communication Behavior

In this chapter we discuss briefly some of the characteristics of mass media audiences that have been studied by sociologists, social psychologists, and mass communication researchers. These include studies of the social characteristics of audiences, patterns of mass media use, special audiences for particular subjects, audience responses to attempts at persuasion and other kinds of communication, social patterns in audience preferences, the uses to which individuals put mass media, and the gratifications people derive from them. This selection of topics, while not exhaustive of the things that interest audience researchers, reflects a range of subjects studied over many years.[1] Our discussion of each topic is selective, highlighting some of the theoretical and research issues of concern.

SELECTED CHARACTERISTICS

Statistical profiles of audiences for particular mass media or their contents often provide data on the demographic characteristics of that specific audience, such as the proportion of viewers, listeners, or readers who are women, teenagers, college-educated, from various income levels, and so on. Survey research based on representative samples of the population also tell us something about the mass communication behavior of various segments of the population, such as the newspaper reading habits of men and women, or the television viewing behavior of people from various social classes. These descriptive statistics have sociological interest since, as one social theorist notes, "Such categories as sex, age, education and income happen also to correspond to some of the chief statuses in the

---

[1] For some sociological examples see Josephine R. Holz and Charles R. Wright, "Sociology of Mass Communications," *Annual Review of Sociology,* 5 (1979), pp. 193–217. On newspaper audiences, see Leo Bogart, *Press and Public: Who Reads What, When, Where, and Why in American Newspapers* (Hillsdale, NJ: Lawrence Erlbaum, 1981). On film, see Bruce A. Austin, "Film Audience Research, 1960–1980: An Annotated Bibliography," *Journal of Popular Film and Television,* 8, 2 (1980), pp. 53–60, and his "Update" in *Journal of Popular Film and Television,* 8, 4(1981), pp. 57–59. Readers might find special interest in Austin's "Film Attendance: Why College Students Chose to See Their Most Recent Film," *Journal of Popular Film and Television,* 9 (1981), pp. 43–49; and Julia Bannerman and Jerry M. Lewis, "College Students' Attitudes Towards Movies," *Journal of Popular Film,* 6 (1977), pp. 126–139. On television; see footnote 3.

social structure."[2] The findings from various audience studies are too numerous to summarize here. By and large, the audiences for specific mass media seem to differ more significantly in their social characteristics than in any recognizable personal traits. Generally sociologists have been interested in contrasting the communication behavior of people from different social backgrounds and generalizing from them.

Empirical generalizations about the social characteristics of mass audiences can be made from such independently conducted descriptive studies, including commercial communications surveys. These studies provide a useful, and major, first step. But further sociological analysis requires special effort to relate communication behavior to social structure; to measure audience changes and trends, and their social meaning; to develop social indicators of changes in mass communication behavior; and to make comparative studies across cultures—to mention but a few of the considerations.[3]

Elsewhere I have made an argument for exploring patterns of communication behavior through constructional analysis of survey data—a research design that contrasts the communication behavior of people holding strategically different places in the social structure or surrounded by theoretically significant social contexts. Examples are people who are socially mobile or stable; members of families where several generations have gone to high school or college compared to those who are the first to go (or not go); people in families where both spouses have equivalent or different amounts of formal schooling; and people who are elderly compared with those who are both elderly and have experienced another change in major status, such as widowed or retired.

Analysis of national survey data demonstrate that such *combinations* of social statuses (status sets) and interpersonal surroundings can be related to different patterns of communication behavior. For example, a person's mass communication behavior is related not only to his or her level of education, but also to the spouse's. Thus, regardless of their own level of education, respondents whose spouses were college-educated were more likely to read magazines and news magazines than people whose spouses had not gone to college. (Such patterns did not hold for all mass media behavior, however, or for all contrasted social combinations. The study was intended to be illustrative of the research strategy and was limited in data and analysis.)[4]

A pattern of multiple exposure to mass media, or overlap among audiences, and how this behavior relates to social and social psychological characterstics is

[2] Robert K. Merton, *Social Theory and Social Structure* (Glencoe, IL: Free Press, 1949), p. 212. For an original use of indicators of social position in an analysis of people's exposure to "highbrow" communication materials and to "poor quality" television programs, see Harold Wilensky, "Mass Society and Mass Culture," *American Sociological Review*, 29 (1964), pp. 173–197.

[3] A good example of the value of continuity in social research on audiences is Robert T. Bower's research on the American television audience, which replicated many questions from an earlier national survey of television viewing and thereby detected changes in American viewing behavior from 1960 to 1980. See Robert T. Bower, *Television and the Public* (New York: Holt, Rinehart and Winston, 1973) and *The Changing Television Audience in America* (New York: Columbia University Press, 1985).

[4] Charles R. Wright, "Social Structure and Mass Communication Behavior: Exploring Patterns through Constructional Analysis," in *The Idea of Social Structure: Papers in Honor of Robert K. Merton*, ed. L. Coser (New York: Harcourt Brace Jovanovich, 1975), pp. 370–413.

of some interest. Some researchers have suggested a tendency toward an "all or nothing" exposure to mass communications among American adults.[5] This term does not mean literally that people use all the mass media or none; few people in modern societies are completely isolated from the mass media. Rather, it suggests that those who are heavy users of one medium are also likely to use other mass media fairly regularly; and people who make light use of mass communication are likely to be restrictive across all the media. It would be interesting to know how common this pattern is in societies where the mass media are less widespread than they are here, and within subgroups throughout the population.

The term "all-or-nothing" also does not mean there is no competition for audiences among the mass media. Television's invasion of our leisure time, for example, has cut into the hours people formerly spent in attending to movies, the radio, and other activities. Nevertheless, certain people seem to be more media-minded than others, and they manage their leisure hours to permit some regular use of most of the mass media available to them. So the concept of "all-or-nothing" may be more useful if applied to specific subgroups than as a general pattern in modern society.

Other patterns of mass media use also have been studied and related to individuals' social characteristics. For example, people have been classified as heavy or light users of newspapers *and* as heavy or light users of television, and such combinations of communication behavior have been related to their social and demographic backgrounds and to such personal characteristics as their knowledge about political events and participation in political and social activities. Examples can be found in studies by John Robinson and others.[6] In one study of national survey data I found, among other things, that Americans who read a newspaper every day, whether or not they were heavy users of television, were more likely to know certain simple political facts (such as the names of their U.S. senators) and to talk about politics than were people who were only television-oriented or who made little use of either mass medium.[7]

[5] See Paul F. Lazarsfeld and Patricia Kendall, *Radio Listening in America* (Englewood Cliffs, NJ: Prentice-Hall, 1948), chap. 1.

[6] See John Robinson, "Mass Communication and Information Diffusion," in *Current Perspectives in Mass Communication Research*, ed. F. Gerald Kline and Philip J. Tichenor, *Sage Annual Review of Communication Research*, vol. 1, 1972, chap. 3.

[7] Wright, "Social Structure." As noted above, relatively few adult Americans fail to make some use of the mass media. In my analysis, less than one adult in ten in the study was outside the daily audience for either newspapers or television—one or the other. Even this estimate is probably too high. Secondary analyses of national survey data from the National Opinion Research Center's General Social Surveys throughout the 1970s, analyses conducted by Jeff Sobal and Marilyn Jackson-Beeck, estimate that 5 percent of noninstitutionalized American adults do not read newspapers, about 4 percent say that they never listen to the radio, and about 5 percent say that they do not watch television or look for less than a half an hour a day. J. Sobal and M. Jackson-Beeck, "Newspaper Nonreaders: A National Profile" (personal copy, undated); and "Television Viewers, Nonviewers, and Heavy Viewers," paper by M. Jackson-Beeck and J. Sobal (personal copy, undated). I wish to thank the authors for providing copies of these papers. Also see M. Jackson-Beeck, "The Nonviewers: Who Are They?" *Journal of Communication*, 27 (Summer 1977), pp. 62–72. Bogart reports data from a national survey in 1982. On any given day about half of all American adults watch television news and read one or more newspapers; about two-fifths do one or the other; and 14 percent do neither. See Leo Bogart, "The Public's Use and Perception of Newspapers," *Public Opinion Quarterly*, 48, 4 (1984), pp. 709–719.

Studies have been made of the mass communication audiences for particular subject matters. The audience for science news and information should be of interest to us, given the importance of scientific and technological developments on earth and in outer space since midcentury and their significance for our future. It provides a good example of research on special audience interests.

A unique pair of social psychological surveys was conducted by the Survey Research Center of the University of Michigan in 1957 and 1958.[8] These studies examined the nationwide American audiences for science news prior to and following the launching of the Soviet Sputnik, the first earth satellite, an event that made science a matter of national public concern at the time and an especially hot topic for mass communication. In both surveys it was clear that people who had more formal schooling were more likely to report that they usually read "all" the science news found in their newspapers. Science news reading also seemed more common among men than women. Following the launching of Sputnik, fewer women seemed to "skip over" science news, and the proportion of college-educated women who said they read "all" the science news was nearly equal to the proportion saying so among college-educated men.

The audience for mass-communicated scientific information has been studied more recently (1979), as part of a survey of our national attitudes toward science and technology, for the National Science Foundation.[9] People were classified as "attentive" to science and technology on the basis of their apparent interest in these topics, knowledge about them, and the extent to which they "regularly availed themselves" of such information. Special comparisons were made with the data from the survey in 1957. The new report states that about 8 percent of the adult public could be regarded as attentive to science and technology in 1957. This had increased to 19 percent in 1979. Attentiveness to science information continued to be positively associated with level of schooling. Men were more likely than women to be attentive to science; and younger people more so than older.

Jon Miller and Thomas Barrington employ a specific theoretical "model" and statistical analysis (a procedure called *path analysis*) to examine, among other things, the statistical contributions of gender, education, and occupational experience to "specialized science information and acquisition activities."[10] A measure of science information acquisition was constructed on the basis of the number of times a person watched television programs about science (such as "Nova"), read general science magazines, read professional journals, and visited museums. The researchers report that "persons with high levels of formal edu-

[8] See *The Public Impact of Science in the Mass Media* (1958), and *Satellites, Science and the Public* (1959), both reports of the Survey Research Center, Institute for Social Research, University of Michigan, for the National Association of Science Writers.

[9] See *Science Indicators 1980*, a report of the National Science Board of the National Science Foundation (Washington, DC: U.S. Government Printing Office, 1981), esp. chap. 6, "Public Attitudes Toward Science and Technology." This chapter cites a number of reports on the survey, the analytic report for the entire project being *The Attitudes of the U.S. Public Toward Science and Technology*, by Jon D. Miller, Kennith Prewitt, and Robert Pearson (Chicago: National Opinion Research Center, University of Chicago, July 1980).

[10] Jon D. Miller and Thomas M. Barrington, "The Acquisition and Retention of Scientific Information," *Journal of Communication*, 31, 2 (Spring 1981), pp. 178–189.

cation, exposure to post-high school science courses, and research-related employment were more likely to be regular consumers of scientific information."[11]

Their path analysis suggests that gender, in and of itself, was not directly related to tendency to follow science and technology for people who were fortunate enough to have gotten a college education. But males were more likely than females to have completed college, and thus gender indirectly relates to subsequent interest in science and in following scientific news. The statistical relation between educational level and following science news is further specified by whether or not the respondents had taken some college science courses, a fact that was correlated with current expressions of interest in science and current communication behavior.[12]

PATTERNS OF MASS COMMUNICATION BEHAVIOR

People's social and psychological characteristics also lead to different patterns of mass communication behavior, preferences, and responses. Shipley's study of mass media use by middle-class adults living in a suburb between Philadelphia and New York, for example, suggests one such typology of patterns of communication behavior that fit her group. Certain people in the study demonstrated what she labeled *saturation exposure,* frequently using all available mass media; others were *source selective,* generally following whatever content appeared in one favorite medium, such as television; still others were *topic selective,* seeking out information or details about some topic of special interest, such as sports, in several mass media; and a very few were *media avoiders,* rarely using any of the mass media on any regular basis.[13]

Another apparently general behavioral pattern is called *selective exposure.* Studies of communication behavior in natural field settings (such as during political campaigns) noted a statistical tendency for mass-communicated programs and their messages to reach individuals who are already most interested in them and who hold opinions and views generally in agreement with them. By contrast, those having less interest or holding contrary views, or both, seem less likely to be exposed to the communication. During election campaigns, for example, Democrats and Republicans are more likely to be heavily exposed to their own party's messages than to those of their opponents (although it is by no means the case that all voters are exposed only to messages from their own party). Such selective exposure may serve to facilitate the audience's reception of some mass communications and to restrict others.

A good example of selective exposure's significance in public communication campaigns comes from a study of the Cincinnati Plan, a communitywide

---

[11] Ibid., p. 184.

[12] For additional accounts of science and mass communication, see Hillier Krieghbaum's *Science and the Mass Media* (New York: New York University Press, 1967). For an interesting look into the early history of science news reporting in America, see Kreighbaum's "American Newspaper Reporting of Science News," published in the *Kansas State College Bulletin,* 25, 5 (August 15, 1941), Industrial Journalism Series 16.

[13] Linda Shipley, "A Typology of Communication Behavior," *Journalism Quarterly,* 53, 3 (Autumn 1976), pp. 483–487.

campaign intended to demonstrate how the people of a city could become informed on world issues through a mass informational campaign.[14] Shortly after the founding the United Nations, several public organizations conducted an intensive six-month mass communication campaign in Cincinnati, Ohio, presenting information about the UN and about world affairs. The effects of this six-month saturation campaign were studied by the National Opinion Research Center.

Using data from surveys of random samples of Cincinnatians before and after the campaign, the researchers found little or no evidence of changes in the population on the scale expected. They found no significant changes in the general public's knowledge, interest, opinions, or behavior concerning the UN or world affairs. What went wrong? The researchers report that the campaign had "reached" mainly those individuals who were predisposed to pay attention to it because they already were interested in world affairs and the UN (and were knowledgeable about them). The mass campaign did not reach many of the people who were initially ill-informed about the UN, apathetic, or even hostile toward it. The campaign, it appears, did not overcome the selective exposure factor.

Lately the idea of selective exposure seems to have lost favor among some communication researchers. It has more acceptance among sociologists than among psychologists. Part of the controversy stems from differences in the specific meanings that have been given to the original term, which is susceptible to several interpretations. The term *selective exposure* can mean an empirically observed regularity in patterns of exposure to mass communication by members of a society contrasted by interest, partisanship, age, sex or some other social or personal characteristic. That is how it is used sociologically. In this sense, it refers to an observed social phenomenon, rather than to a principle about individual behavior.

How these social regularities come into being—through whatever social and psychological processes—remains unspecified. They may, for example, reflect people's social positions and characteristics, such as education and social class. The term is also used to refer to a proposition about how an individual behaves—namely, that a person seeks information that supports the self and its views and actively avoids unfavorable information and viewpoints. This is how many psychologists use it. This psychological process of selective exposure has been subject to question by the results of experimental studies and is a matter of some debate.[15] The original concept of selective exposure as a social phenomenon, however, continues to be useful in mass communication research. Furthermore, at least some of this selective exposure to mass communication campaigns can be attributed to selective attention due to social circumstances, personal interests, and other considerations.

[14] Shirley Star and Helen Hughes, "Report on an Educational Campaign: The Cincinnati Plan for the United Nations," *American Journal of Sociology*, 55 (1950), pp. 389–400.

[15] For a discussion of some of the issues, see W. Phillips Davison, James Boylan, and Frederick T. C. Yu, *Mass Media: Systems and Effects,* 2nd ed. (New York: Holt, Rinehart and Winston, 1982), pp. 149–171; David Sears and Jonathan Freedman, "Selective Exposure to Information: A Critical Review," *Public Opinion Quarterly,* 31 (1967), pp. 194–213; and papers in Robert Abelson et al., eds., *Theories of Cognitive Consistency: A Sourcebook* (Chicago: Rand McNally, 1968), pp. 769–800.

Two other related concepts about audience behavior are *selective perception* and *selective interpretation*. The idea is that when people happen to be exposed to communications contrary to their interests and predispositions, the impact of the message may be weakened, even distorted, through perception and selective interpretation of the content—seeing or hearing only certain parts of the message and interpreting them to suit one's orientation.

An interesting illustration of selective perception and interpretation appears in a well-known study by Patricia Kendall and Katherine Wolf on viewers' reactions to a series of antiprejudice cartoons intended for use in a public communication campaign.[16] The cartoons satirized a highly prejudiced character, Mr. Biggott, who was depicted expressing hostility toward American minority groups in a variety of situations. The pictures were shown to a number of men, each of whom was then interviewed to determine his understanding of the cartoons and his reactions to them.

The researchers report that the antiprejudice message was misunderstood by approximately two-thirds of the viewers, many actually reversing its meaning and believing that the cartoons were designed to create racial disturbances and to intensify prejudices. Men who themselves were prejudiced initially and who did not regard prejudice as a social problem were much more likely to miss the point of the cartoons when they saw them than the others in the study. Such selective perception and interpretation may reflect not only individual predispositions, but social processes as well. People's interpretations of mass-communicated materials—in campaigns or elsewhere—often are influenced by their own position in the society and by their conversations and interpersonal communication with others.

Studies of people's response and resistance to mass communications, especially those aimed at persuasion, have a long history, much research having been done during and following World War II and continuing today. Social psychological experiments in the laboratory, classroom, and field (notably a program of studies conducted by Carl Hovland and his colleagues) have contributed to our understanding about such audience behavior.[17]

Hovland's research group, and others, studied how people's knowledge, attitudes, opinions, and behavior were changed (or not) by varieties of experimental communications. They examined how differences in the form and nature of communication content influence its effectiveness with audience members. For example, they experimentally compared responses to persuasive messages arousing fear in the viewer or listener with those that do not, and reactions to one-

[16] Patricia Kendall and Katherine Wolf, "The Analysis of Deviant Cases in Communication Research," in *Communications Research, 1948–1949*, eds. Paul F. Lazarsfeld and Frank Stanton, pp. 152–179; Eunice Cooper and Marie Jahoda, "The Evasion of Propaganda," *Journal of Psychology*, 23 (1947), pp. 15–25; and Davison et al. (1982), *ibid.*.

[17] For examples, see Carl Hovland, Arthur Lumsdaine, and Fred Sheffield, *Experiments on Mass Communication* (New Haven, CT: Yale University Press, 1957) and other books from this line of research; William McGuire, "Persuasion, Resistance, and Attitude Change," in *Handbook of Communication*, eds. Ithiel de Sola Pool et al. (Chicago: Rand McNally, 1973), pp. 216–252. For a sociological investigation of one concept from this tradition, see Warren W. DeLey, "A Sociological Investigation of General Persuasibility" (Ph.D. dissertation, University of California, Los Angeles, 1971).

sided arguments compared with those that appear more balanced. They also studied how communication persuasiveness varied with social characteristics of the audience (such as level of education), the audience's perception of the communicator (as a propagandist or an educator), and other features of the communication.

The studies show, for example, that reactions to a message are affected by people's image of the communicator's social responsibility and intentions, trustworthiness, and orientation to education or propaganda. Thus, as one example, studies show that people tend initially to resist messages coming from communicators they regard with suspicion; but later some change their opinions in the direction originally advocated by the message.[18]

This delayed persuasion is called the *sleeper effect.* One explanation suggests that people initially rejected the arguments because they were suspicious of the communicator. Later, some of these people remembered the arguments, but forgot where they had heard them. The remembered arguments and information, now no longer tainted by the memory of the original "untrustworthy" source, were accepted and led to changes in opinion.

Generalizations about communication behavior based on carefully executed controlled experiments in the laboratory and classroom often do not seem to hold up when confronted by data obtained from survey research or other studies of people in their normal social surroundings.[19] Therefore one needs to be cautious in interpreting experimental findings. The issue is not whether the experimentally derived data are correct or not, but rather what inferences apply to actual communication behavior under nonlaboratory circumstances.

The conditions under which people usually encounter mass communication, especially mass media campaigns, are far different from those of the laboratory. As we have noted, people usually are exposed to mass communication in a social context. They often have the freedom to avoid some specific program or message if they want to or to pay attention to it.[20] Perhaps most important of all, given the opportunity, people discuss the media content with friends, family, neighbors, and others. This social interaction plays an important part in what people make out of mass communications in natural settings.

Given freedom of choice, people differ too in their preference for specific communication content, and these preferences are related to their social charac-

[18] Carl Hovland and Walter Weiss, "Source Credibility and Communication Effectiveness," *Public Opinion Quarterly*, 15 (1951–52), pp. 635–650.

[19] See Carl Hovland, "Reconciling Conflicting Results Derived from Experimental and Survey Studies of Attitude Change," *American Psychologist*, 14 (1959), pp. 8–17; and Hugh M. Culbertson, "Statistical Designs for Experimental Research," in *Research Methods in Mass Communication*, eds. Guido H. Stempel III and Bruce H. Westley (Englewood Cliffs, NJ: Prentice-Hall, 1981), pp. 217–239.

[20] A combination of selective exposure, selective perception, and selective interpretation of mass-communicated news and information may help to explain that segment of the population that Hyman and Sheatsley have identified, through survey research, as a hard core of chronic "know nothings." These are individuals who say they know nothing about most topics with which public information campaigns deal and whose social and psychological characteristics make them hard to reach during such campaigns. Herbert H. Hyman and Paul Sheatsley, "Some Reasons Why Information Campaigns Fail," *Public Opinion Quarterly*, 11 (1947), pp. 412–423.

teristics. Audience members' interests and predispositions have roots in the group structure within which people live and from which they draw their expectations. Lazarsfeld's reflections on audience selectivity and its social foundations are relevant and timely here:

> In all the fields that have been touched by communications research the self-selection of audiences plays a considerable role. People with political convictions read the newspapers that correspond to their opinions. People with hobbies read the sections of the newspaper which report on these hobbies most fully. This seemingly trivial observation becomes more interesting as we add to it certain corollary findings, which can be gleaned from a variety of studies. It has been found, for instance, that people are inclined to read the same news items in newspapers which they have already heard discussed on the radio. In general, they do not look for information on new topics in magazines but for more information on topics with which they are already acquainted. . . .
>
> In general, then, people look not for new experiences in the mass media but for a repetition and an elaboration of their old experiences into which they can more easily project themselves. If we assume then that the types of experiences they have had are determined more by their social roles and context rather than by their psychological traits, it is not surprising that we find primary characteristics [age, sex, educational classification] so dominant in the correlations which communications research has unearthed.[21]

The variety of uses people make of the mass media and the gratifications they receive from them have long interested social psychological and sociological researchers. Studies of listeners to daytime radio serial programs (soap operas) are early examples. In those days, it seems, listeners to soap operas got emotional release, a chance for daydreaming or wishful thinking, and advice for handling life's problems. Today's viewers of daytime television soap operas, researchers suggest, derive entertainment gratification from them, but may not use them for advice. Whether they do or not remains a question.

Muriel Cantor and Suzanne Pingree, writing about the soap operas in 1983, concluded: "We do not yet have an answer to the question . . . Why do people watch soap operas? We do know that soaps are appealing and that they are more likely to generate active participation among viewers than other types of television; but more comparative studies need to be done to find out what soap operas mean to their viewers."[22]

The "uses and gratifications" approach to the study of audiences asks not "What do the media do to people?" but rather "What do people do with the media?" This theoretical orientation is most identified with the work of sociologist Elihu Katz and his colleagues. It has been used in studies in Great Britain by Jay Blumler and Denis McQuail.[23]

---

[21] Paul F. Lazarsfeld, "Communication Research and the Social Psychologist." Reprinted from *Current Trends in Social Psychology*, ed. Wayne Dennis, by permission of the University of Pittsburgh Press, pp. 242–244. ©1948 by the University of Pittsburgh Press.

[22] Muriel G. Cantor and Suzanne Pingree, *The Soap Opera* (Beverly Hills, CA: Sage Publications, 1983); quotation, p. 131.

[23] See Jay Blumler and Elihu Katz, eds., *The Uses of Mass Communications: Current Perspectives on Gratification Research* (Beverly Hills, CA: Sage Publications, 1974); and papers in *Communication Research*, 6, 1 (1979).

A study by Katz, Michael Gurevitch, and others provides an example. The researchers first generated a list of social and psychological needs that have been said (in the literature or by researchers) to be satisfied through mass communication. Some thirty-five needs were specified. These covered a broad range of possible uses and gratifications, as follows: (1) cognitive needs, related to strengthening one's understanding, knowledge, and information; (2) affective needs, related to strengthening emotional, pleasurable, and esthetic experiences; (3) integrative needs, related to strengthening credibility, status, confidence, and stability; (4) needs related to strengthening contact with family, friends, and the world; and (5) needs for escape and tension release.

The researchers asked a cross-section of Israeli adults to specify how each of five mass media—radio, television, newspapers, books, and movies—helps to satisfy each of the thirty-five needs specified. In addition, each person was asked what else or who else helps to satisfy each need.

In this way the researchers studied how people used different media for these purposes and whether they felt that these needs were gratified. They conclude, for example, that for the population studied, "Books cultivate the inner self; films and television give pleasure; and newspapers, more than any other medium, give self-confidence and stability." Interestingly, interpersonal communications with friends, family, and others often complemented the mass media in satisfaction of these communication needs. For example, friends were cited more often than the mass media as being helpful when one wants to be entertained, to reexperience events in one's life, and to learn how to behave among others.[24]

The uses and gratifications approach tells us a great deal about the extent to which people feel that certain needs are being fulfilled by one or another of the mass media. It leads, as does our functional orientation in this book, to the generation of research questions that go beyond the feelings of individual audience members—namely: What are the social consequences of having the needs of individuals fulfilled in this way?

A CONCLUDING NOTE

In this chapter we have presented several examples of sociological and social psychological research on audiences for mass communication. Throughout this discussion, we have followed the convention of referring to the users of mass media and interpersonal communication as audiences. In one sociological sense this terminology, while convenient, is not precise enough. A fuller sociological analysis of the audience invites newer concepts, theoretical reformulation, and research on both the normative and organizational aspects of audiences per se.

Consider, for example, the social structure of an audience. Does it resemble or reflect the social stratification of the society—with perhaps the best access to

[24] Elihu Katz and Michael Gurevich et al., *The Secularization of Leisure* (Cambridge, MA: Harvard University Press, 1976); quotation from pp. 324, 327. Also see Katz, Gurevitch, and Hadassah Haas, "On the Uses of the Mass Media for Important Things," *American Sociological Review*, 38 (1973), pp. 164–181.

communications, whether information or entertainment—going to persons of greatest wealth or other social advantage? For assembled audiences, this might mean, for example, the best seats or vantage points for them and lesser seats being distributed in a stratified fashion. For more dispersed audiences, it might mean, for example, that access to more popular television programs or most useful videotext computer information service is available according to one's ability to pay for it. Or does an audience have a stratification system of its own—for example, regular patrons (or subscribers) receiving more favored treatment than the casual or occasional stranger who happens to attend a performance or tune in to a telecast? Or is the audience structure some mixture of both? Or another shape?

How are audiences—assembled or widely dispersed—organized? What is the social organization of smaller audiences—people viewing television in public places such as a local bar, families viewing television in the home, people attending a neighborhood movie or one downtown? Do some people serve as leaders—first to laugh, for example—and set the tone for others' reactions? Are there varieties of roles played by different members of an audience? What is the larger social and cultural context within which an audience exists?

Or consider the folkways, mores, and laws that determine who should or should not be members of a particular audience and how they ought to behave while in the role of audience members. For example, can anyone be a member, or only those who pay? Anyone who pays, or only adults? How does one behave as an audience member, in the presence of others or even if one happens to be alone? If with others, should one talk or not talk? Boo, hiss, or applaud? Watch, listen, or otherwise pay attention to the communication until the very end, or interrupt the communication, even drop out of the audience?

What are individuals' rights and obligations in relation to others in the audience, to the performers, and to members of the society who are not in the audience? For example, are parents responsible for the television viewing of their children? Who determines the volume of the sound? Who decides when a copy of a magazine or newspaper is to be thrown away, and therefore no longer available to other potential readers in the household? Do audiences have some obligations to the performer or communicator? For example, do people who record a television program on a home videotape machine have any financial obligation to the original artists? Do audience members have some obligation to nonmembers—not playing a radio too loud in a public place; not reading a pornographic magazine in front of children; not revealing the plot of a movie to those about to enter the theater?

How does the social visibility of audience membership and behavior affect people's conduct?[25] Does the fact that others can see our behavior make us less likely to do something wrong or embarrassing, or does the social pressure of others in the audience make us go along with their behavior despite our private

[25] See, for example, David Karp's interesting observations of attempts to hide their social visibility by male patrons of urban "adult" bookstores, "Hiding in Pornographic Bookstores," *Urban Life and Culture*, 4 (1973), pp. 427–452.

reservations about it? What are the conditions that might lead to one or the other reaction?

As communication technology changes, we will need new information about the changing social norms surrounding eligibility for membership in mass audiences and about behavior once in. Sometimes people are not even certain about the legal norms until the issues are clarified through the courts. The courts decide, for example, whether or not it is legal to videotape television programs for subsequent viewing by oneself and others. But whether legal or illegal, how many people believe it is morally wrong to do so? Most people probably believe that it is both illegal and wrong to climb a telephone pole and tap into a subscription cable television service. But how about picking up satellite broadcasts with your own "dish" antenna? The questions are easily multiplied. We have surprising little research on past and current norms about audiences in our society, let alone those applying to users of the new communications media. Our understanding of audience norms and behavior can be enriched too through cross-cultural comparisons of mass communication audiences, their characteristics, norms, and behavior.[26]

These are but a few of the challenging research questions that arise when we reflect on audiences in this manner. They offer plenty of room and opportunity for theoretical reflection and research exploration in the future.

[26] Sociologically useful data about mass media audiences abroad are available in English. For examples of studies of television and radio audiences, see the various reports of the Australian Broadcasting Tribunal, Melbourne, Australia; Reports of the Canadian Radio-Television and Telecommunications Commission, Ottawa, Canada; *Mass Media*, a Report of the Special Committee on Mass Media, Ottawa, Canada (1970), especially vol. III; *Studies of Broadcasting: An International Annual of Broadcasting Science*, Radio and TV Cultural Research Institute, The Nippon Hoso Kyokai, Tokyo, Japan; research reports and newsletters published by Sveriges Radio ab, Audience and Programme Research Department, Stockholm, Sweden; and Daniel G. Ross, S.J., *Television in Taiwan* (Taiwan, Republic of China: Social Science Research Center, Fu Jen University, 1983).

CHAPTER 6

Cultural Content of American Mass Communication

Every American is familiar with programs, stories, features, and other materials presented by our mass media. Why, then, should such widely recognized elements of everyday life as comic strips, soap operas, and television shows require scholarly research? Isn't our common, firsthand knowledge about popular culture sufficient? Why should we *study* mass media content?

WHY STUDY MASS MEDIA CONTENT?

Several reasons for the systematic study of the content of mass-communicated news and entertainment can be given.

First, despite our frequent exposure to mass communication, our personal experience is both limited and selective. Every day the mass media put out so much material that no one can possibly see or hear it all. Most of us, to be sure, have a general impression of the range of programs, stories, news, and other content that may be available. But our exposure within that range is likely to be selective, biased by personal circumstances and tastes. Our casually acquired knowledge about our favorite daily newspaper, comic strips, television soap operas, and other media content is insufficiently broad, representative, and precise for research purposes. An accurate picture of the range, variety, and substance of what is being presented in the mass media requires a more systematic and orderly review and analysis. This requires far more work and concentration than we are likely to invest during our use of the mass media.

For example, a study of the mass media's presentations of earthquake predictions in southern California (which is described more fully in the next chapter) required a systematic record and classification of every earthquake news story or related item that appeared during a three-year period in six daily newspapers, in prime-time news on the three major television networks, in any special earthquake broadcasts on television and radio, and in any other relevant mass media content.

Second, we tend to overgeneralize from our particular personal experiences. For example, if we happen to see a dramatic television program that seems violent, we are inclined to assume that most such programs feature violence. Perhaps they do, but without a better sampling of programs we cannot be certain, nor can we say with any precision how common or rare such programs are, when they occur, and whether or not they are becoming more frequent. What we happened to see may have been unusual (although probably not, in this instance!).

Finally, in our daily use of the mass media we are not likely to try to analyze sociological aspects of their content. While watching television, for example, we are not ordinarily likely to note carefully or to analyze the social class or occupations of television heroes and heroines or villains and villainesses or to study their goals and values.

Mass-communicated content does not "speak for itself," however. Its meaning may not be self-evident. Media content can be classified and analyzed from a variety of perspectives. For example, television shows may be described and analyzed in terms of plots, themes, kinds of characters portrayed, and much more. Researchers try to classify mass communication content into categories of interest and relevance to the problem under study—earthquake predictions, television violence, or sex role portrayals. In this chapter we will discuss some research guided by sociological interests. But first it is useful to consider briefly the nature of content analysis as a research technique.

Content Analysis as a Research Procedure

Content analysis is a research technique for the systematic classification and description of communication content according to certain usually predetermined categories.[1] It may involve quantitative or qualitative analysis, or both. Technical objectivity requires that the categories of classification and analysis be clearly and operationally defined so that other researchers can follow them reliably. For example, analysis of the social class memberships of television characters requires clear specification of the criteria by which class is identified and classified, so that independent coders are likely to agree on how to classify a character. Researchers also strive for validity in the coding categories; that is, the categories should measure what they're supposed to—in this example, social class.

To illustrate, using a character's style of dress might not be a very valid criterion for judging social class membership in a television drama about American teenagers (or then again, it might). Or although some researchers may classify a verbal threat as an act of violence, others may not consider it "true" violence. While coders might agree on how many times in a show the characters were threatened, making the classification reliable, some researchers might dispute the count's validity as a measure of violence on the program.

Systematic content analysis requires that all the relevant content be consid-

[1] For a discussion of content analysis as a research technique and examples of some of its applications, see Bernard Berelson, *Content Analysis in Communication Research* (Glencoe, IL: Free Press, 1952); Ithiel de Sola Pool, ed., *Trends in Content Analysis* (Urbana: University of Illinois Press, 1959); Robert North et al., *Content Analysis* (Evanston, IL: Northwestern University Press, 1963); George Gerbner et al., eds., *The Analysis of Communication Content* (New York: Wiley, 1969); Ole Holsti, *Content Analysis for the Social Sciences and Humanities* (Reading, MA: Addison-Wesley, 1969); Klaus Krippendorff, *Content Analysis: An Introduction to Its Methodology*, vol. 5, Sage Commtext Series (Beverly Hills, CA: Sage, 1980); and Thelma McCormick, *Culture, Code, and Content*, Communications Studies, vol. II (Greenwich, CT: JAI, 1982).

ered in terms of the meaningful categories. Thus systematic analysis is distinguished from critical or analytical reading, viewing, or listening, in which reviewers may select any part of the content that supports their argument. For example, if you believe that television programs portray scientists in an unfavorable light, you probably can find some shows in which the scientists appear villanious, dishonest, or generally despicable. At the same time, someone with an opposite opinion can find examples of scientists who are portrayed heroically. Neither would be conducting a content analysis, however, for each has selected cases to illustrate his or her point. What is needed is an unbiased overview of the relative frequency of favorable and unfavorable characterizations of scientists— an overview that can come only from classifying all the scientists in a representative sample of television programming.

Researchers have used content analysis not only to study the characteristics of communication content, but also to draw inferences about the nature of the communicator, the audience, and "effects." Research on content characteristics includes studies of trends, international comparisons, propaganda techniques, style, and so on. Sometimes content is analyzed to provide insights into its producers—their intentions or political or psychological states. Occasionally, content is taken as a clue to the nature of audiences—their values, likes, and dislikes. Finally, content is sometimes interpreted in terms of its presumed effect upon the audience or society.

It is important to remember, however, that content analysis itself provides no direct data about the nature of the communicator, audience, or effects. Therefore, great caution must be exercised whenever this technique is used for any purpose other than the classification, description, and analysis of the manifest content of the communication. If, for example, we find that scientists are portrayed unfavorably on television, we cannot use this as evidence that television writers or producers *intend* to portray scientists unfavorably. Nor can we claim that these unfavorable stereotypes will deter students from choosing scientific careers.

Such interpretations of the content in terms of probable motives or possible consequences go beyond the available data. Ideally, to study what motivated the portraits, we would need research on the communicators themselves; to investigate the apparent consequences of the stereotypes, we would need direct audience research. In the absence of direct data on communicator or effects, however, researchers sometimes prefer to make inferences about them from content analysis rather than to speculate on such matters with no data at all.

A detailed survey of the many subjects that have been investigated through content analysis is beyond the scope of this book, but examples can be found in several works.[2] In the remainder of this chapter we will discuss a few illustrative content analyses bearing on some sociologically interesting topics: society's popular heroes, the world of television drama, work, minorities, cultural goals and means, and values in mass-communicated news.

[2] For examples, see Josephine R. Holz and Charles R. Wright, "Sociology of Mass Communications," *Annual Review of Sociology*, 5 (1979), pp. 193–217.

SOCIETY'S HEROES AND HEROINES

A frequently cited content analysis providing clues to our cultural heroes is Leo Lowenthal's early study of biographies in popular magazines.[3] We noted earlier that one sign of high status in a mass society is to be singled out for attention by the mass media. Perhaps an even greater sign is to be selected as the subject of a "biography" or close-up story in one of the popular media. To some extent, popular biographies are the abbreviated life histories of cultural heroes or heroines, villains or villainesses. From their experiences, the audience can glean something about success and failure as our culture depicts them. Information about the kinds of persons selected for popular biographies and what is said about them, then, is of interest here.

Lowenthal analyzed a systematic sample of all popular biographies in two magazines (*Collier's* and the *Saturday Evening Post*) for the first forty years of the twentieth century. He noted a shift in attention from "idols of production" (persons in business, politics, and the professions) to "idols of consumption" (persons primarily from the field of popular entertainment) as America approached the middle of the century.

The qualitative nature of these popular biographies also changed over time. Early biographies contained a good deal of information about the person's character development, personal history, and his or her behavior that led to success. More contemporary biographies glossed over details of character development and reported on the person's private life and leisure activities. More modern success stories gave emphasis to inherent character traits that, along with a series of hardships and "lucky breaks," led to success.

Lowenthal argues that such a formula for the road to success is hardly useful as a model for others: It defines success as largely an accidental and irrational event and reflects a degree of normlessness about the proper way to succeed in life. He also reports that the newer biographies stressed the consumer habits, tastes, likes, and dislikes of the successful person. These, he suggests, provide readers with a frame of reference about success within which they are less likely to suffer by comparison with the "great" persons of our times:

> It is some comfort for the little man who has become expelled from the Horatio Alger dream, who despairs of penetrating the thicket of grand strategy in politics and business, to see his heroes as a lot of guys who like or dislike highballs, cigarettes, tomato juice, golf and social gatherings—just like himself. He knows how to converse in the sphere of consumption and here he can make no mistakes. By narrowing his focus of attention he can experience the gratification of being confirmed in his own pleasures and discomforts by the great.[4]

A different viewpoint and interpretation of shifts in popular American heroes is provided by Theodore Greene, who studied the biographies in a sample of leading American magazines from 1787 through 1918.[5] His analysis argues

[3] Leo Lowenthal, "Biographies in Popular Magazines," in *Radio Research 1942–43*, eds. Paul Lazarsfeld and Frank Stanton (New York: Duell, Sloan and Pearce, 1943), pp. 507–548.

[4] Ibid., pp 547–548. By permission of Hawthorn Books, Inc.

[5] Theodore Greene, *America's Heroes: The Changing Models of Success in American Magazines* (New York: Oxford University Press, 1970).

that there was a demise in the value of individualism in America during that period. He sees a shift in popular heroes from important figures in the traditional basic institutions of society (for example, state, church, and military) during the early years of the Republic, to idols of power and individualism (creative artists, captains of industry, empire builders) around the turn of the century, to idols of justice (politicians) just prior to World War I, and then toward idols of organization (nonindividualistic leaders in corporate business, politics, government bureaucracy) from 1914 to 1918. Greene's study adds further historical perspective to the topic of changing cultural heroes.

Many of the qualitative tendencies noted by Lowenthal in the biographies at midcentury may persist today. Comparative studies are needed to determine contemporary tendencies in popular biographies and to address such important questions as the biographical treatment of women as compared with men.

An interesting example is a study by Shelby Hoerger in the mid-1970s comparing the models of success presented in biographies in three women's magazines—*Cosmopolitan, Ladies Home Journal,* and *Ms.*—each directed at a different type of audience. Hoerger looked to see what kinds of persons were written about, what was said about their success, and how they achieved it. She reports large and systematic differences among the three magazines in their treatment of success stories, based on a content analysis of all biographies published in them during one year.[6]

First consider the *Ladies Home Journal,* many of whose readers were married women with some college education who were currently working at home running the household. Biographies in this magazine (more than half were about women) were nearly evenly split between stories about persons with successful careers (60 percent) and about persons whose lives were outstanding for some other reason, usually relatives of prominent men. Success was often signified by wealth, or accompanied by it, which translated into financial security, a good house, and other material signs of comfort. But occupational success also at times seemed to cost one in love and marriage. Success seemed to depend on one's personal qualities and efforts, a combination of initial talents and hard work, and it took some time to occur.

Next consider *Cosmopolitan,* whose readers tended to be young women in white-collar occupations (mainly sales and clerical), most of whom were unmarried and had some college education. Its biographies (three-quarters were about women) were mainly (although not entirely) about popular entertainers, most of whom were celebrities, even "superstars." Success for them was signified by their vast and conspicuous material wealth, with its associated life style, and by their public fame and recognition. Often there was a price of personal loneliness, monotony, and loss of a normal home life. But success for these people came suddenly, sometimes "overnight," often the apparent result of knowing the right people, combined with such personal attributes as creativity, determination, talent, and a lot of luck.

Finally there is *Ms.,* whose readers tended to be young women, mostly un-

[6] Shelby Hoerger, "Models of Success in Women's Magazines: An Analysis of Biographies Directed at Different Target Audiences." (MA Thesis, Annenberg School of Communications, University of Pennsylvania, 1975).

married, working in managerial or professional occupations, mainly college graduates, some with postgraduate education. All the *Ms.* biographies were about women who were successful in their careers in business, the professions, politics, government, entertainment (mostly in the "serious" arts), and other fields. The mark of success was achievement. These women were singled out as being among the top people in their fields, or sometimes as having been the first woman to "crack" a previously male line of work. The road to success was a hard one, containing many obstacles to be overcome; the journey was long and marked by many temporary setbacks. Successful persons had prepared themselves through outstanding academic achievement in college and graduate or professional schools. They were determined in their struggle to overcome barriers to success and were supported in this determination by encouragement and help from good friends along the way.

What do we make of all this? Hoerger goes beyond the content analysis to speculate that the models of success and the success stories presented in each magazine were potentially functional for the readers. The biographies in *Ladies Home Journal* may have reinforced the values of home life, of personal qualities needed to overcome life's problems, and of success in terms of personal and family security and well-being. Thus they would reinforce the value and importance of the home life many of its readers led or hoped to achieve. Biographies in *Cosmopolitan* were hardly realistic models for the reader, but more like glamorous fantasies. Just the ticket for "escape" reading by young women who were, temporarily at least, caught up in routine white-collar jobs. Finally, readers of *Ms.*, mostly professional and career-oriented young women, were able to see biographies that might sustain and inspire them in their struggle against societal and other barriers to occupational success for women. These speculations go far beyond the data supplied by content analysis, of course. But they illustrate the kinds of theoretical concerns that link content analyses to interesting and sociologically relevant topics.

A comparative analysis of feature stories and biographies about women in *Ms.* and *Family Circle*, by E. Barbara Phillips, also shows more differences in the presentation of heroines. *Ms.* "spotlighted" 120 women in the eight issues of the magazine sampled by Phillips, while *Family Circle* contained stories about 18 women in the sixteen issues sampled. The biographies in *Ms.* were about women working in politics, government, the "serious" arts, business, the professions, and other fields. Those in *Family Circle* were about women related to rich, powerful, and famous men or about women employed in their domestic service. Phillips suggests that the heroines of *Ms.* magazine resemble the pre-World War I heroes in Lowenthal's study to the extent that they tend to be contributors to society rather than consumers of the good life. But unlike early male "idols of production" (the self-made captains of industry), women were more likely to be "exemplars of people who improved the lot of others, who struggled for social (not personal) goals."[7]

Our culture may not provide a clear, simple definition of success for women,

[7] E. Barbara Phillips, "Magazines' Heroines: Is *Ms.* Just Another Member of the *Family Circle?*" in *Hearth and Home: Images of Women in the Mass Media*, eds. Gaye Tuchman, Arlene Kaplan Daniels, and James Benet (New York: Oxford University Press, 1978), pp. 116–129.

according to a content analysis of seventeen recent career-success books for women by Barbara Bate and Lois Self. Seven of the books defined success according to external markers, such as money, power, and advancement to high status positions. Five of the books defined success in terms of one's personal feelings, suggesting, as the researchers put it, that each woman should "determine the appropriate balance between her public and private life and integrate her various roles according to her own priorities." The remaining books were judged as ambiguous about the nature of success. The researchers conclude that "writers of current success books for women are not in agreement about what constitutes success."[8]

It would be interesting to know whether career books for men also show a variety of conceptions about success, and whether success books directed at various segments of the population (as are some magazines) differ systematically in their definitions of success for the readers. We will return to the mass media's presentation of success and failure later in the chapter.

TELEVISION DRAMA: A WORLD OF ITS OWN?

American television, with its daily—even hourly—audiences of millions of men and women, young and old, from all walks of life, may be the quintessential mass medium of our times. Small wonder, then, that television programs have attracted the attention of critics and researchers concerned with American mass culture.

Some of them are mainly concerned about specific programs or about certain kinds of content, such as violence or sexual behavior, which they believe or suspect is directly harmful to individual viewers. Others are more concerned with features of television content that go beyond any single or particular program, patterns in content that may provide viewers with a common frame of reference, concepts, assumptions, beliefs, and "facts" about reality, about the world in general and their society in particular. From this perspective, life according to television may affect life as believed in by the viewers. Hence it seems important to learn what kind of world is being shown on television. Much of this research has focused on television drama—a form of entertainment that may lull viewers into a sense of reality because of the verisimilitude of its backgrounds and settings and its seemingly real-to-life characters.

The world of television drama has been dissected in many detailed and painstaking content analyses by mass communication researchers who have reported on the demographic makeup of its characters, on their actions, and on other features of shows. Such content analyses go back many years, some to the early days of American commercial broadcasting, when the National Association of Educational Broadcasters undertook a series of studies monitoring television programs in several major cities across the United States.[9] While their data are

---

[8] Barbara Bate and Lois S. Self, "The Rhetoric of Career Success Books for Women," *Journal of Communication*, 33, 2 (1981), pp. 149–165.

[9] These cities included Chicago, Los Angeles, New Haven, and New York. The researchers included, among others, Dallas Smythe, Angus Campbell, Donald Horton, Hans Mauksch, Kurt

mostly of historical interest today, these early studies provide a profile of what was being presented in those days and a benchmark against which later findings can be compared to see what, if anything, has changed over the decades. One example will suffice for our purposes here, a report on three years of television in New York City, from 1951 to 1953.[10] We select from it some data on television's fictional characters.

In part of the study, 86 televised drama programs were analyzed, first in terms of the settings and the kinds of characters in this television "world," then in terms of the apparent social and psychological characteristics of the heroes, villains, and supporting characters. Television drama during the week studied mainly portrayed contemporary but fictitious American settings. Men outnumbered women in the casts by a ratio of about 2 to 1. Very young people (under twenty) and very old people (over sixty) were "underrepresented" in the stories, which focused primarily on persons at the height of the courting and childbearing ages, employed or employable. Such white-collar positions as managers and professionals with higher statuses were heavily "overrepresented" at the expense of the routine white-collar and blue-collar jobs. Service workers and household workers were also overrepresented. Most of the characters were law-abiding, healthy, sane individuals. They were most likely to be white Americans, occasionally Europeans, and rarely blacks (only 2 percent of all characters shown during the week).

Several studies provide more recent data on characters in the world of American television drama, their activities, and related matters. One source of data is a continuing program of "studies of cultural indicators" by George Gerbner and his associates.[11] Since 1967, these researchers have conducted annual content analyses of prime-time television drama (and some weekend daytime programs) shown in the United States during sample weeks. By 1982 these studies had produced a "cumulative data bank of detailed observations based on the analysis of over 1,600 programs and 14,000 characters."[12]

Gerbner and his colleagues use content analysis as one approach in a research program that encompasses studies of mass communication production (institutional process analysis), content (message system analysis), and audiences and effects (cultivation analysis). Content analysis in this framework deals with message systems and their inferred symbolic functions of presenting the social

Lang, H. H. Remmers, and Robert Mainer. The reports, called Monitoring Studies, were published at various times during the early 1950s by The National Association of Educational Broadcasters, Urbana, Illinois.

[10] Dallas W. Smythe, *Three Years of New York Television*, Monitoring Study 6 (Urbana, IL: National Association of Educational Broadcasters, 1953).

[11] See George Gerbner, "Cultural Indicators: The Third Voice," in *Communications Technology and Social Policy*, eds. George Gerbner, Larry Gross and William Melody (New York: Wiley, 1973); George Gerbner, "Violence in Television Drama: Trends and Symbolic Functions," in *Television and Social Behavior*, vol. 1, eds. George Comstock and Eli Rubenstein (Washington, DC: U.S. Government Printing Office, 1972); Nancy Signorielli, Larry Gross, and Michael Morgan, "Violence in Television Programs: Ten Years Later," in NIMH's *Television and Behavior* (1982); and George Gerbner, Larry Gross, Michael Morgan, and Nancy Signorielli, "Charting the Mainstream: Television's Contributions to Political Orientations," *Journal of Communication*, 32, 2 (1982), pp. 100–127.

[12] Gerbner et al., "Charting the Mainstream," p. 103.

world for the audience in terms of what is, what is important, what is right, and what is related to what. It has been used to study mass media presentations of mental illness, education, film heroes, news, violence, and other subjects.

The researchers report that television drama presents a world in which men outnumber women (about 3 to 1); relatively young persons (under eighteen) and older people (over sixty-five) appear less frequently than they do in real life; there are more professionals and managers than might be expected and far fewer blue-collar and service workers (less than 10 percent of the television characters); and minorities also seem "underrepresented," especially as major characters.[13] Similar findings are reported in a series of studies by Bradley Greenberg and his associates based on their content analyses of television fiction for samples from 1975 to 1978. In each of the three years, male characters outnumbered females about 3 to 1, very young and elderly people were statistically "underrepresented," and professionals and business people were "overrepresented."[14]

Thus, while some details may have changed since the 1950s, for three decades the overall demographic composition of the world of television drama has not changed very much. It far from duplicates the demographic profile of our society (although it is not being argued here that television drama ought to do so).

What difference does this make? Content analyses provide no answer, but we can speculate. It is possible that the rare appearances, even absence, of certain kinds of people in television drama may be dysfunctional for them. It may lower their prestige in the eyes of others, threaten their own self-esteem, and deprive them of appropriate role models on the screen. Much may depend on how they are portrayed during their relatively infrequent appearances in television drama.[15] If, as is suggested by some of the research findings, they tend to be cast as minor characters, or stereotyped in socially undesirable ways, then even these rare appearances might seem negative to them.

A second and practical social consequence of infrequent roles in television drama is a relative scarcity of jobs for certain kinds of actors and actresses, such as the elderly or members of certain racial minorities. A third possibility, suggested by Gerbner and his associates, is that symbolic representation in the fictional world of television signifies social existence. They interpret demographically distorted life on television as a lesson for television viewers on who counts in society.[16]

[13] Ibid.

[14] The content analysis was one phase of a three-part project called CASTLE. The results of the content analysis were used to guide the subsequent phases. Phase 2 was a series of field surveys of young people and their mothers, examining statistical relationships between television watching and viewers' attitudes and behavior. (For an example, see Chapter 9, on socialization.) The third phase called for field experiments to test the effects of training programs designed to guide viewers along certain lines. See Bradley S. Greenberg et al., *Life on Television: Content Analyses of U.S. TV Drama* (Norwood, NJ: Ablex Publishing Corporation, 1980), esp. chap. 4.

[15] For an example of a study of young peoples' impressions of presentations of minority groups on television, and their views about this, see Hannah Kliger, "Communication and Community: Ethnic Media Images and Jewish Group Identity" (M.A. Thesis, Annenberg School of Communications, University of Pennsylvania, 1977).

[16] George Gerbner and Larry Gross, "Living with Television: The Violence Profile," *Journal of Communication*, 26, 2 (Spring 1976), pp. 173–199.

Content analyses have gone beyond recording the demographic features of television characters to consider such questions as: What kinds of persons are shown as heroic or villainous? How are various kinds of social roles portrayed? What do characters do? What is done to them? And with what apparent consequences in the story?[17]

Every-day life on television is the focus of the content analyses of television drama by Greenberg and his associates. These studies describe television drama's treatment of sex roles, antisocial and prosocial behaviors, sexual intimacy, the use of alcohol and other substances, family role structures and interactions, Hispanic-Americans, blacks, and the elderly. As an example, consider the data comparing the everyday behavior of men and women. The researchers report how often certain kinds of activities occur in television drama, and whether these are displayed disproportionately by either sex. About a score of such activities were examined. Some occurred too infrequently to warrant analysis for sex typing, but their very rarity is instructive.

Viewers were unlikely to find much drama showing office work, shopping, child care, or, unsurprisingly, yard work or sewing. The most frequent activity (among those being counted) was driving (more than five times per hour), and the next was mass media use. Men were disproportionately more likely to be shown driving, making business telephone calls, drinking and smoking, using firearms, and engaged in athletics. Women were disproportionately more likely to be shown entertaining, preparing food, and doing indoor housework. There were, however, no significant differences by gender in the frequency of being shown using the mass media, engaging in personal grooming, eating, riding, playing games, writing, extending social courtesies, and making personal telephone calls. Prior to the analysis, the researchers had specified which conduct they expected to be sex-typed on television, such as housework. They interpret the data as showing such stereotyping in eight out of the thirteen specified activities.[18]

Many people are concerned about violence in television programs—a subject of content analyses for more than thirty years. The amount of violence in American television drama recorded in these studies has been considered great and relatively unchanged over the decades. The longest continuing set of data on television violence is found in the reports of the "cultural indicators" project by George Gerbner and his associates, which began in 1967. Cultural indicators research defines *violence* as "the overt expression of physical force (with or without a weapon, against self or other) compelling action against one's will on pain of being hurt or killed, or actually hurting or killing." Violence to property, and emotional and psychological violence are not included in this category of violence.

Violence, as defined, is counted whether it appears in a serious drama or in a comedy—a view criticized by some who say it shouldn't count if it is all in fun. But the researchers reply that if it hurts, it counts. Some critics would exempt violence that seems accidental or an act of nature; but the researchers reply that

[17] For an earlier study of television's heroes and villains, see Smythe, *Three Years of New York Television*, pp. 94–103.

[18] Greenberg, *Life on Television*, pp. 89–95.

these acts are created for the story and therefore have symbolic meaning too—in television drama nothing simply "happens."[19]

Knowing what goes into the category of violence—essentially acts that harm people—we now can examine some of the findings. The researchers report that 81 percent of the dramatic programs shown during a sample week in 1967 contained violence. This has changed little over the years, except for occasional differences along the way. By 1979 it was 82 percent. The overall average for the thirteen years of content analysis was around 80 percent (about 5 violent acts per hour of dramatic programming).[20]

More than three out of every five major characters are involved in violence, according to analyses for 1969 to 1977. Victims slightly outnumber violent characters. Violence and the likelihood of being a victim varied by social characteristics. For example, men are more likely than women to be involved in violence, but when women are involved, they are more likely than men to be the victims. Elderly women and nonwhite women, although less likely to get involved in violence than some others are, were more likely to be shown as victims than as violent characters themselves.[21]

Such findings are of interest in themselves, as descriptions of television's portrayal of violence. Gerbner and his associates, however, are also interested in their symbolic meaning. They interpret the show of violence in television stories as symbolic lessons in social power, lessons that portray the social order and demonstrate "who has the power and who must acquiesce to that power."[22]

Content analyses alone cannot tell whether or not the audience is aware of such symbolic lessons about life and society, or is influenced by them whether aware of them or not. Other research methods are required to gather data for drawing inferences about mass communication's "effects," a topic to be discussed later in the book.

Nevertheless, imaginative, careful, and systematic studies of mass communication content continue to contribute to our knowledge about popular culture. They supply useful and detailed information about what is presented by the mass media—information that can be obtained in no other way. We can use that information for theoretical speculation about plausible consequences of mass communication and as leads for direct research on them.

[19] For a discussion of these and other methodological issues, along with some comparative data on violence from studies using different definitions and measures, see George Comstock et al., *Television and Human Behavior* (New York: Columbia University Press, 1978), pp. 64–84. For a discussion by members of the Cultural Indicators Project, see Nancy Signorielli et al., in *Television and Behavior*, pp. 158–173 and Gerbner and Gross, "Living With Television: The Violence Profile."

[20] Signorielli et al., *Television and Behavior*, p. 168.

[21] George Gerbner, Larry Gross, Marilyn Jackson-Beeck, Suzanne Jeffries-Fox, and Nancy Signorielli, "Cultural Indicators: Violence Profile No. 9," *Journal of Communication*, 28, 3 (1978), pp. 176–297.

[22] George Gerbner, Larry Gross, Nancy Signorielli, Michael Morgan, and Marilyn Jackson-Beeck, "The Demonstration of Power: Violence Profile No. 10," *Journal of Communication*, 29, 3 (1979), pp. 177–196; quote, p. 180.

THE WORLD OF WORK

Popular portrayals of people at work provide a potential source of imagery about an important social role. The mass media may be the only, or at least a major, source of information and impressions about particular occupations for many young people in a society, especially those who are unlikely to know someone so employed. Therefore, a number of content analyses of television and other mass media have paid particular attention to the numbers, proportions, and kinds of occupations presented; in addition, some studies have examined the personal and social characteristics associated with particular occupations.

Quantitative content analyses of American television drama (such as those cited above) have documented the general overrepresentation of middle-class occupations and the underrepresentation of working-class jobs in comparison with the proportions of individuals so employed in the national labor force.

A sociological analysis of occupational roles as portrayed on television is presented in Melvin De Fleur's analysis of a sample of six months of television programs shown in a midwestern American community in the mid-1960s.[23] De Fleur argues that children gain insight into the world of work through socialization by accidental and haphazard exposure to many learning sources, including the mass media, among which television is an especially relevant learning source. His content analysis identified each recognizable occupational portrayal lasting at least three minutes during the show. Occupational portrayals were analyzed according to the type of occupation, the background setting of the work, power over other individuals during interactions, and characteristics and traits of the workers.

The study considered the distribution of power among televised occupations, as indicated by the number of times an individual portraying a particular occupation gave orders to someone else, obeyed an order, gave permission to someone, received permission, received a title of respect, and used a title of respect toward someone else. From these actions, an index of power was calculated for each occupational category and occupations were ranked. Among the occupational groups ranked relatively high on power were foremen, ranch owners, judges, district attorneys, artists, police officials, members of the clergy, and physicians; relatively low were persons in service occupations, office workers, salesmen, semi-skilled and unskilled workers, nurses, personal servants, and enlisted military personnel. De Fleur notes that, in terms of power (a criterion regarded by children as important in an occupation, according to supplementary research), television presents least often and as least desirable the middle-level and working-class occupations in which many young viewers are most likely to have to make a living.

Of special interest here is De Fleur's observation that television seems to be preoccupied with the atypical aspects of an occupation and its performance. Physicians, for example, are rarely shown treating a routine case of measles; more often they are performing a dramatic operation. These atypical features

---

[23] Melvin De Fleur, "Occupational Roles as Portrayed on Television," *Public Opinion Quarterly*, 28 (1964), pp. 57–74.

seem to be the source of the dramatic, interesting, entertaining features of television stories. But to note this is not merely to point up the obvious. For regardless of the value of such dramatic portraits as entertainment, they also have the potential function or dysfunction of presenting distorted views of the world of work and of particular occupations to the viewers, most of whom lack day-to-day realistic experiences of what it is like to do such jobs.

De Fleur concludes that television's treatment of occupational roles is selective, unreal, stereotyped, and misleading. He cautions, however, that content analysis presents only one kind of information to be fitted into the total study of the role of television and other influences in the socialization of individuals into the world of work and other roles. Content analysis needs to be complemented by studies of the viewers' responses to the media and research on viewers' beliefs.

Even studies limited to content analysis, however, can provide sociologically interesting qualitative and quantitative data when guided by a sociological perspective. Judith Lemon presents interesting data on the apparent dominance patterns in interactions between people in television situation comedies and crime dramas, based on a content analysis of a sample of broadcasts during 1975.[24] Lemon concludes that television "maintains societal stereotypes in its portrayal of power." She indicates that occupation, which she takes as an indicator of social class, is the most important factor in dominance during interactions between two characters; next is sex (with males dominating), followed by race (whites dominating).

In general, characters in occupations having higher social status tended to be dominant during interactions with others while playing their occupational role. This held both for men and women. But since men are more likely than women to be cast in higher occupational roles in television drama, the upshot is that male dominance is a prominent feature of television drama. Thus, Lemon's study (as did De Fleur's) goes beyond the elementary (albeit important) description of the relative frequency of male and female characters on television and examines their behavior while performing occupational or other social roles.

Other cases of sociologically relevant content analyses of mass entertainment's treatment of work can be found. To cite but a few, a study of the first twenty-five years of the comic strip "Little Orphan Annie," for example, disclosed that blue-collar workers were rarely identified as people with names; rather, they were shown in group and crowd scenes, lacking in individual identity and personality.[25] By contrast, people holding middle-class and upper-class occupations were usually identified by name and played individualistic roles.

De Fleur's study notes, almost in passing, that certain occupations rarely or never appeared in television stories in the early 1960s; scientists are an example. One content analysis of daytime television serial dramas (soap operas) in the 1970s revealed that, although the actors were cast in a variety of occupations, the characters seldom if ever were shown in the process of carrying out any of their occupational tasks. The occupation was a costume for the character, who

[24] Judith Lemon, "Dominant or Dominated? Women on Prime-Time Television," in Tuchman et al., *Hearth and Home*, pp. 51–68.

[25] Donald Auster, "A Content Analysis of Little Orphan Annie," *Social Problems*, 2 (1954), pp. 26–33.

typically was engaged in personal conversations and activities. Neither characters nor plots centered on the routine tasks and problems of the world of work.[26]

Things in the world of soap operas did not change much in the following decade, it would seem. Suzanne Pingree reports, in 1983, on the results of several student content analyses of eleven different soap operas. Students recorded the number of scenes, in a sample episode, "in which characters were doing something clearly related to their occupation, such as a lawyer questioning a witness, or even 'prop' work, such as shuffling papers in the background." She reports that even this broadly defined picture of working was found in only 13 percent of the scenes studied, and concludes that "Apparently, these serial characters seldom worked. . . ."[27]

THE VISIBLE MINORITIES

Content analyses have also been directed at studying the portrayal of minority group members by the mass media. Most recently, attention has been focused on the treatment of women and minorities in television programs, as noted above. Content analyses have sometimes been undertaken because of the researcher's concern with the social problem of discrimination and prejudice against minority peoples along racial, ethnic, religious, and other lines. Symbolic underrepresentation, misrepresentation, stereotyping, and other forms of distorted portrayals of minority individuals may, it is argued, contribute to prejudicial and discriminatory treatment of individuals in real life.

In addition, these mass media portraits may be the major sources of impressions and information that certain people have about others, lacking much personal and direct contact with them. Media portrayals may also provide potential role models for audience members. The quantity and quality of minority group portrayals may have consequences for their socialization, especially for the young. These social and theoretical reasons, among others, have prompted a relatively large number of content analyses about minorities in the mass media during the past thirty to forty years.[28]

One sign of changing times is the increased visibility of members of certain minority groups in roles on television programs. The authors of a content analysis of ethnic and sex representation in television drama commented, in 1971, that: "When viewing television today, it is hard to believe that depictions of minority group members were a rarity just 10 to 15 years ago. The inclusion, for example, of a black actor or actress was almost sure to produce a controversy."[29]

[26] Mildred Downing, "The World of Daytime Television Serial Drama" (Ph.D. dissertation, University of Pennsylvania, 1974). Also "Heroine of the Daytime Serial," *Journal of Communications*, 24 (1974), pp. 130–137.

[27] Muriel Cantor and Suzanne Pingree, *The Soap Opera* (Beverly Hills, CA: Sage Publications, 1983), p. 89.

[28] For recent examples, see Holz and Wright, "Sociology of Mass Communications." For an early example, see Bernard Berelson and Patricia Salter, "Majority and Minority Americans: An Analysis of Magazine Fiction," *Public Opinion Quarterly*, 10 (1946), pp. 168–190.

[29] John Seggar and Penny Wheeler, "World of Work on TV: Ethnic and Sex Representation in TV Drama," *Journal of Broadcasting*, 17 (1973), pp. 201–214.

Smythe's content analysis of a week of television drama during the early 1950s reported that only 2 percent of the characters were blacks. Gerbner's analyses of prime-time television drama for 1969–1978 reports that about 12 percent of all characters were classified as nonwhite; about one in every ten major characters was classified as nonwhite.[30] Seggar and Wheeler, in a study of television dramas in modern settings in 1971, report that 75 percent of the characters were white Americans and about 6 percent were black Americans (the remainder were other minorities). Minorities were more likely than majority white Americans to be concentrated in personal service jobs.

Greenberg's study also provides information on the portrayal of minorities on prime-time television drama, especially blacks and Hispanic-Americans. The researchers compare the characteristics and behaviors of black characters with those of a sample of whites who appear on the same program, for a sample week in 1977. (There were 101 black characters out of a total of 585.) They report that black characters were more likely than whites to be younger, from lower socioeconomic status levels, without an identifiable job, and playing a partly or wholly comical character. There were no significant differences between black and white characters in such interaction terms as giving and seeking or receiving advice, information, or orders. The researchers observed that Hispanic-Americans are hard to find in television drama. Out of 3,549 characters during three television seasons, they identified 53 persons as Hispanics. Only ten males and one female had major roles.[31]

Content analyses have been made too of the treatment of the elderly and of other social minorities. Further examples could be added, but those cited should be sufficient to illustrate the usual form of such analyses and their typical results. Certain minorities have become somewhat more visible on American television and perhaps in other mass media content in the past decade or so. To note this is to add little more than might be obvious to the casual observer of today's mass communication. But the studies serve to document the extent of this visibility with greater precision and on a more representative set of data than can be done through casual observation. Furthermore, when extended over time through replications carried out by comparable procedures, these studies allow the detection and the measurement of trends in mass-communicated portrayals of minority groups and social roles, thereby providing a running indicator of our changing symbolic world. We caution again, however, that interpretations of such findings, either to draw inferences about causes or about effects, cannot be supported through content analyses alone.

GOALS, MEANS, AND CONSEQUENCES

Two components of culture that are of special interest to sociologists are socially valued goals and socially prescribed or disapproved means for achieving these

---

[30] George Gerbner and Nancy Signorielli, *Women and Minorities in Television Drama 1969–1978.* (Research report, Annenberg School of Communications, University of Pennsylvania, October 29, 1979.)

[31] Greenberg et al., *Life on Television*, chaps. 1 and 2.

goals. This sociological interest has carried over into a few content analyses of mass communications, in which the mass media are regarded as common sources from which people may learn about their own society and its culture, as well as about other societies. In the words of one group of sociologists:

> Such content analyses may be particularly fruitful when they work with problems and categories designed to discover underlying values repeatedly portrayed in a wide variety of settings and situations. . . ."[32]

In order to follow this interesting line of sociological investigation, content analyses must be fashioned to classify the apparent social and personal goals portrayed in mass communication, the approved and disapproved methods for achieving these goals, the degree to which these methods are shown to be successful or unsuccessful ways of achieving goals, and other consequences that follow from using such means. An example is provided by a study of television programs by sociologists Otto Larsen, Louis Gray, and J. Gerald Fortis.[33]

Observers recorded the frequency with which each of eight kinds of goals was identified in the programs under study, goals such as desires for property, self-preservation, affection, and power. Eight classes of methods for goal achievement also were identified and recorded, such as legal methods, economic methods, violence, and chance. Particular theoretical significance is given to the combination of goals and the ways shown for achieving them. These methods were grouped into three categories according to whether they are generally socially approved (for example, legal), socially disapproved (for example, violence), or either (for example, chance). An analysis was made of the extent to which characters were shown as successful or unsuccessful in achieving each of the eight types of goals when following socially approved, disapproved, or neutral methods. The researchers suggest that conduct that is not socially approved seemed to be portrayed by television as having a better chance of success than methods that are socially approved. This outcome appeared generally, regardless of the particular goal sought or the type of program on which it was portrayed.

The researchers then relate these findings to the larger phenomenon of social *anomie*, a condition characterized by Robert Merton as a cultural emphasis upon the successful achievement of goals through expedient means, with an accompanying withdrawal of emphasis upon socially approved means—a state of relative normlessness, in which "anything goes." According to the researchers, television dramatic programming appears consistently to portray a state of anomie, in which socially approved goals are often achieved by unsanctioned means. The researchers hasten to add, however, that content analysis cannot determine whether the television audience perceives this pattern and is influenced by it. Such questions can be addressed only through direct studies of the audience. The authors note that other researchers have argued an opposite view—that mass media content tends to support, rather than challenge, the society's common values and social mores, thereby contributing to the maintenance of social norms rather than to social anomie.

[32] Otto Larsen, Louis Gray, and J. Gerald Fortis, "Goals and Goal-Achievement Methods in Television Content: Models for Anomie?" *Sociological Inquiry*, 33 (1963), pp. 180–196; quotation, pp. 180–181.

[33] Ibid.

In all likelihood, some mass-communicated information and entertainment can be interpreted as supporting the traditional culture order and some not. Discernible patterns are of interest. Content analyses can examine variations over time and under different social circumstances. Further research on the media's portrayal of social goals and norms, success and failure, and people's reactions to them seems warranted in view of their importance to our understanding of how mass communication contributes to the maintenance of the social order or to pressures toward social change.

One promising approach is to study how the mass media show people coping with success and failure. Merton has suggested five types of ways, or role adaptations, by which individuals relate to specific social goals and socially approved means for achieving them.[34] These are not personality types, but role behaviors. A person may make one type of adaptation with respect to one goal, such as financial success, and a different adaptation in another area, such as love.

The five proposed types are as follows: (1) *Conformity*, believing in both the goal and society's norms about how to reach it; (2) *ritualism*, giving up on the goal but continuing to behave in the "proper" way to reach it; (3) *innovation*, wanting the goal but caring less how one gets it, trying less traditional means (even illegal ones); (4) *retreatism*, abandoning both the goal and the behavior leading to it; and (5) *rebellion*, rejecting the goal and norms for achieving it and substituting alternative goals and means not only for oneself, but for others. As examples: conformity, save some money each week toward a down payment on a house; ritualism, continue to save after you realize that inflation has driven real estate prices far out of your reach; innovation, stop saving and try to win the house through a lottery number or sweepstake ticket; retreatism, quit work and saving, sleep in the park; rebellion, start a utopian commune and win converts.

Returning to the study of mass communication content, one can question how often the media portray each of these five types of role adaptation, under what circumstances, and with what apparent consequences to the characters in the story. Frequent portrayal of social conformity as the predominant role model could indicate the conservative character of the mass media and its potential function of preserving cultural patterns. Frequent emphasis on deviant role adaptations, unless showing them as unsuccessful and leading to unpleasant consequences, could lead to uncertainty about social norms and contribute to social instability. (This is a theoretical conjecture, of course.)

A critical question is how the mass media treat failure. How do they cope with the social fact that conformity to social norms does not always lead to the valued goal, that entire segments of a population may never achieve certain of these goals? What kinds of role behavior are shown as adaptations to failure? What mechanisms are used to manage the problem? Answers to such questions await future content analyses. But we can speculate about them here on the basis of prior research.

The bulk of mass-communicated content probably supports conformity to social goals and norms as the dominant role behavior. What system could have

---

[34] Robert K. Merton, *Social Theory and Social Structure* (Glencoe, IL: Free Press, 1957), chaps. 4 and 5.

it otherwise? As examples, most characters in stories conduct their lives in an apparently "normal" way. Men and women try to be attractive and respectable in dress. The need to work and to earn one's keep in some way is almost the universal lot of adult characters, not only for law-abiding citizens, but even for those engaged in questionable or illegal activities ("This gun for hire!").

Ritualism, which continues to support conventional modes of behavior, can be found as a product of any of several symbolic mechanisms. These mechanisms I call: (1) goal reduction; (2) goal substitution; (3) goal diversion; and (4) the hand of fate. I will illustrate each by examples from available content analyses, although the original studies did not use these terms. (The number of stories or other materials examined in each study sometimes is small; I present these cases here only as illustrations of the mechanisms, not as evidence about the frequency of their occurrence or their consequences.)

Goal reduction is evident in Donald Auster's content analysis of the newspaper comic strip "Little Orphan Annie."[35] Auster analyzed the portrayal of business success and prescriptions given for achieving it. At one point, Annie compares the wealthy Daddy Warbucks with a character named Spike, who apparently had not done so well financially. She provides a rationalization for this. Daddy, she explains, was willing to take long chances, to play for high stakes, and he won. Spike, on the other hand, liked security, small towns, and a quiet life. But he too worked hard. He never achieved wealth, but by the age of forty this relative "failure" owned his own business, his own home, and some ground. Annie concludes that people "with not too much" are happy to think how much better off they are, with a little, than the very rich are. She does not point out that the goals of both men are qualitatively the same—material and financial success—although the threshold of success has been scaled down, the goal reduced, for the man whose labors never produced a fortune.

Goal substitution can be seen in a content analysis of magazine fiction by P. Johns-Heine and Hans Gerth.[36] The study compared the portrayal of success in magazine stories prior to and during America's Great Depression of the 1930s. The authors report that in success stories prior to the Depression, men of proved ambition and achievement commonly were rewarded by social ascent. Heroes in the stories during the Depression also were good men, virtuous and hard-working. But these good qualities and behavior no longer were shown as paths to social ascent. Rather, they more commonly led to other rewards: love and esteem from one's friends, family, neighbors—certainly socially desirable goals in themselves, but nonetheless substitutes for the earlier ones. Virtuous conduct brings its own reward.

Goal diversion appears in Lowenthal's analysis of biographies in popular magazines. In these stories about successful people, the very definition and meaning of success seems to be shifting over time. The framework within which success is presented and its consequences specified shifts from stories about social contribution and achievement to those that focus on the consumer behavior

[35] Auster, "A Content Analysis of Little Orphan Annie."

[36] Patrick Johns-Heine and Hans Gerth, "Values in Mass Periodical Fiction, 1921–1940," *Public Opinion Quarterly*, 13 (1949), pp. 105–113.

and private life styles of celebrities and popular heroes. The audience, he suggests, can compare itself favorably with these successful heroes if success means being able to smoke a particular brand of cigarettes, choose the right beer, wine, or liquor, wear a designer logo sports shirt, enjoy sports and other leisure activities, and so on. These symbols of a successful life style can be scaled up or down to fit the person's financial resources. Acquiring them means success; hence the diversion.

Another example comes from a study of the narrative strategy of the popular musical films during the Great Depression. The analyst, J. P. Telotte, argues that these films (starring Fred Astaire and Ginger Rogers) addressed mass audiences during the troublesome times of economic depression and high unemployment by demonstrating "a power within everyone's grasp, that of our personal expressive energies." This personal power allows the character to cope with problems and to "survive and effectively transform" the situation by using his or her natural abilities. This is exemplified in the films time and again by dancing in the face of troubles. "In their recurring invitations to dance," Telotte concludes, these movies suggested to audiences facing desperate economic problems "that we could effectively channel our expressive energies into asserting a kind of interpersonal harmony which might, in turn, enhance the world in which we live." Success becomes inner harmony.[37]

The fourth mechanism, the *hand of fate*, makes compliance with the social norms for success appear to be a necessary but not sufficient condition for success. It introduces such uncontrollable catalytic conditions as luck, "the break," intuition, and the helping hand. Auster's content analysis also illustrates this, for good fortune and mysterious forces seem to favor Daddy Warbuck's enterprises.

Returning now to the types of role adaptation, occasionally the media seem to reward innovative behavior. But this may be reserved for persons identified as extraordinary characters, usually working for good causes, such as television's A-team. One content analyses of stories in early American women's magazines, for example, showed material and financial success as one goal for women. But the socially approved way of achieving this goal, at that time, was through a successful, "sensible" marriage, rewarded by love, in which the woman's role was to bring out her husband's latent good qualities, inspiring him to achieve financial success for the family. It was less acceptable for a woman to try to make her own way by following a career. Stories about "career women" were limited to tales about outstanding success, usually achieved at the price of suffering and missing out on love and affection. For a woman to seek success through a career was innovative for the times, within the law but at the edge of violating the folkways if not the mores, and she paid the price.[38]

More recently, Helen Franzwa analyzed women's magazine stories from 1940 to 1970. Two out of every five major female characters were shown working outside the home. About nine out of every ten working women held middle-status or lower-status jobs, seen as temporary roles to be left upon marriage, an

[37] J. P. Telotte, "Dancing the Depression: Narrative Strategy in the Astaire-Rogers Films," *Journal of Popular Film and Television*, 8, 3 (1980), pp. 15–24.

[38] Johns-Heine and Gerth, "Values in Mass Periodical Fiction."

actively sought life goal. Those few women for whom work careers seemed important were shown paying a price in the concomitant disintegration of their home lives by never marrying and starting a family, or by divorce.[39]

Retreatism as a role adaptation, when shown at all, seems likely to be presented as either a comic or tragic response that spills over into several (perhaps nearly all) of the character's roles in life. When comic, the character may have certain redeeming virtues, as does Charlie Chaplin's little tramp. When tragic, retreatism is shown as causing problems, for example escaping responsibilities through alcohol, drugs, dropping out, drifting.

Rebellion is potentially the most threatening form of role adaptation, seeking as it does to change the existing culture (or some portion of it). It may be presented in popular culture as the stuff of heroes. But I suspect they are mainly historically legitimized heroes (such as any nation's revolutionary heroes). If contemporary characters display rebellion in this sense, it may be to call upon us to return to some previously cherished social and spiritual values and virtuous conduct and to abandon cultural ways seen as amoral, anomic, or evil.

Our discussion of the study of the mass media's presentation of goals and means, success and failure, and role adaptations to them admittedly raises more questions than can be answered today. My purpose in introducing it here is to illustrate one way in which a sociologically informed approach to content analysis can enrich our understanding of popular culture and the possible role of mass communication in contributing to cultural stability and social change.

SOME COMMENTS ON CULTURAL CONTENT IN MASS-COMMUNICATED NEWS

In this chapter I have focused mainly on content analyses of mass-communicated entertainment, often television programs, an area that has received a lot of attention from researchers, media critics, and the public. But there are many studies of mass-communicated news and other subjects, far too many for even a selective review here. Their research purposes are varied. As examples, some studies deal with the mass media's coverage of particular events (the Watergate affair), types of news coverage (international, national, and local news), or special subjects (science news). Sometimes the purpose is descriptive or comparative (what proportion of the news is local); sometimes there is an attempt to study distortion or bias in the news (in coverage of presidential candidates).

One sociologically interesting, but methodologically difficult, ambition of some content analyses is to make inferences about social values behind what is produced and distributed as news, cultural "lessons" for the public, and the social consequences of all this. Judging from such analyses it seems that mass-communicated news usually reflects social values that are supportive of the so-

---

[39] Helen H. Franzwa, "Working Women in Fact and Fiction," *Journal of Communication*, 24 (1974), pp. 104–109. See this issue also for other reports on women in the media, including content analyses of women in television commercials, prime-time television drama, television cartoons, and daytime serials.

cial order and of the dominant social structure of that society. This makes sense. Why would any society (totalitarian, democratic, or otherwise) retain a system of mass communication surveillance that "spits in its eye" or otherwise threatens the social order? "Underground" newspapers (or alternative news media) may be tolerated, but they are, after all, deviant and do not represent the mainstream of mass-communicated news. They come and go.[40]

All this may be clearly evident to someone who lives in the society. What is not so easy to discern are the social values that may lie behind the news in each society. This requires special attention, study, and insight. Content analyses addressed to questions about underlying social values involve more "reading between the lines" and self-reflective interpretations than seem apparent in quantitative "counts" of news "items" (although it is important to recognize the contributory role of the researcher in quantitative content analyses too, for example in establishing and defining categories and in interpreting the data produced by the research). I have chosen one study here to illustrate a search for enduring values behind the news in America. It is part of Herbert Gans's sociological study, *Deciding What's News.*[41]

Gans's content analysis concentrated on CBS television news and *Newsweek* magazine for sample periods in the late 1960s through the mid-1970s. He presents eight clusters of what he sees as enduring values in American mass-communicated news, as follows: (1) Ethnocentrism: "Like the news of other countries," Gans says, "American news values its own nation above all. . . ." (2) Altruistic democracy: The news upholds an unstated ideal of how democracy should work. The news publicizes deviations from the ideal, such as political corruption. It implies that politics should serve the public and public interest. (3) Responsible capitalism: There is "an optimistic faith that in the good society, businessmen and women will compete with each other to create increased prosperity for all," without involving unreasonable profits and gross exploitation. (4) Small-town pastoralism: The news favors small towns. It reflects rural and anti-industrial values, the desirability of nature and smallness. Cities usually are presented as the scenes of problems, crime, racial conflict, and financial trouble. (5) Individualism: The news features stories of "rugged individualists," preserving the freedom of the individual against the forces of nature and society. (6) Moderatism: Excess or extremism by individuals and especially by groups is discouraged. "Individualism which violates the law, the dominant mores, and enduring values is suspect," Gans asserts. Thus the value of "rugged individualism" does not mean praise for the deviant or the rebel. (7) The desirability of social order: News warns about threats coming from natural, technological, social, and moral "disorders," with the implicit (or explicit)

[40] For one historical account of the underground press during the 1960s, see Robert J. Glessing's *The Underground Press in America* (Bloomington: Indiana University Press, 1970). The *Berkeley Barb*, once one of the major underground papers, was reputed to have a circulation of 90,000 around 1970. This dropped to about 2,000 during the 1970s before it went out of business in July 1980, according to a newspaper story by Michael Dorgan in the *Philadelphia Inquirer*, July 27, 1980.

[41] Herbert J. Gans, *Deciding What's News: A Study of CBS Evening News, NBC Nightly News, Newsweek & Time* (New York: Pantheon Books, 1979), pp. 39–69.

understanding that order should be restored. (8) National leadership: The news accepts "the need for national leadership in maintaining that order."

Gans points out that such values are rarely explicitly stated in mass-communicated news, but must be "found between the lines." He warns that his own interpretation of patterns in the news is impressionistic, built upon his own training and values, that other analysts might draw a different picture from the news, that the audience might see yet other pictures or might not see any overall pattern of values at all. Thus he too reminds us of some of the inherent limitations of content analysis as a research technique, while nonetheless providing us with an informed, scholarly, and sociological account of some possible cultural values in our news. It seems a good example with which to close the chapter and move on to our next topic.

CHAPTER 7

Social Consequences of Mass Communication: Studies of News and Mass Persuasion

We were out doing "trick-or-treat" for Halloween and that's how I missed the great Martian invasion of 1938. We had no pocket radios in those days, so we weren't warned about the horrible events taking place around Grovers Mill, New Jersey, and the dangers threatening us as we proceeded down country lanes, through the mystery woods, and even (courage!) to the house by the cemetery. Lucky for us that we didn't meet the gray-tentacled monster that wriggled out of its metal cylinder on the Wilmuth farm—a creature with skin like wet leather, black eyes, and "saliva dripping from its rimless lips." We sure heard about it when we got home, though! By that time the rest of the family knew that it was only a radio play by Orson Welles and the Mercury Theater. But it seemed real enough at first, with emergency news bulletins and on-the-spot news reports.

More than one person in our family smelled the Martian gas drifting down from Princeton. Another, however, "knew" that no alien creature could survive the heat upon entering earth's atmosphere and therefore was skeptical of the "new bulletins" as they unfolded during the broadcast. Someone else checked a different radio station's broadcast for further news of the invasion—heard only regularly scheduled entertainment programs—and skepticism became firmer. Other members of the family who lived nearby were called on the telephone, or someone was sent to see them. These personal contacts soon properly identified the "invasion" as a work of broadcast fiction, a Halloween lark, as Welles and his cast put it in the program's conclusion. There had been excitement but no panic in our family. In this we were undoubtedly fortunate; it is said that many listeners were frightened, and that there was some panic. Our family's behavior, however, was probably typical—attempting to verify the first "news" accounts in several ways, and socially constructing the meaning of the situation through interpersonal communication with family members and with others.[1]

The fortunate fact that we did not panic also seems more typical of most people's behavior, despite the popular belief that panic is common. Recent research has caused some social psychologists to question the idea that large num-

[1] For a psychological analysis of people's reactions to the broadcast, see *The Invasion from Mars: A Study in the Psychology of Panic*, by Hadley Cantril, Hazel Gaudet, and Herta Herzog (Princeton, NJ: Princeton University Press, 1940), which contains the complete script of the broadcast. Our description of the monster is taken from the account on p. 16. The reader might be amused to learn that only a few years ago (1981), it was proposed to sell samples of dirt from Grovers Mill (site of the fictitious Martian invasion) at a dollar an ounce as a donation to the American Heart Association, according to a story by Gail Ciociola in the *Philadephia Inquirer*, July 29, 1981, pp. B1,B2.

bers of people panic in response to threatening news about dangers in the environment, such as impending hurricanes, floods, nuclear accidents (or invasions from Mars!).[2] As an example, consider a study of a modern-day radio program which, according to mass-communicated news reports, allegedly led to widespread panic. A Swedish station had broadcast a fictitious drama, in news format, about an imaginary future nuclear accident at a real nuclear power plant currently under construction. Some listeners apparently mistook the story for a genuine news bulletin. Shortly thereafter, the Swedish news media (first the broadcast media and later newspapers) reported that there was widespread panic in southern Sweden. But subsequent research by Karl Rosengren and his associates convinced the investigators that there was no mass panic by the people there or elsewhere. The researchers then examined how the mass media came to report the "panic" as a news story.[3]

One possible explanation for the popular belief that panic is common is that the news media coverage of an event tends to give high visibility and importance to those relatively few people who do react in an unusual, sometimes dramatic, way. This creates an exaggerated impression that panic is widespread. Also the fact that many people try to telephone the police, newspaper offices, broadcast studios, or other public sources of information to find out what is going on during an emergency soon swamps these telephone lines and adds to the impression that people are in a panic. Reporters and officials alike may be misled by these impressions. The mass-communicated account of events, in turn, is taken by the public (including other mass communicators and public officials) as an accurate picture of public reactions. Hence the common belief in mass panic.[4]

Returning now to the "Invasion from Mars," it is easy to understand how some radio listeners, especially people who tuned in late and missed the opening credits, mistook the fictitious "news bulletin" about an invasion from outer space for the real thing. We expect that regular entertainment programs will be interrupted to issue warnings and news about impending danger. This is as true for television today as it was for radio then. It seems fitting, then, that we open our discussion of the possible social effects of mass communication by considering the warning function of mass-communicated news. We will illustrate this discussion primarily with some recent research on public responses to earthquake predictions in southern California.

Most of us who don't live in California probably don't give much thought to the possibility of an earthquake, but it is a very real threat to the millions of people living there. And while the chances of an earthquake may seem remote to many of us, risks do exist outside California and may be the subjects of mass communication reports locally. (Indeed, this is true in my own region.) So these

[2] For a discussion, see John Lofland, "Collective Behavior: The Elementary Forms," in *Social Psychology: Sociological Perspectives*, eds. M. Rosenberg and R. H. Turner (New York: Basic Books, 1981), pp. 411–446; and Joseph B. Perry, Jr., and Meredith D. Pugh, *Collective Behavior: Response to Social Stress* (St. Paul, MN: West Publishing Company, 1978), esp. pp. 108–116.

[3] See Karl Erik Rosengren, Peter Arvidsson, and Dahn Sturesson, "The Barseback 'Panic,' a Case of Media Deviance," in *Deviance and Mass Media*, ed. Charles Winick (Beverly Hills, CA: Sage Publications, 1978), pp. 131–149.

[4] See Lofland, "Collective Behavior."

research findings have some intrinsic interest. More to the point here, however, is that southern Californians' responses to earthquake-related news can provide clues to people's reactions to the mass-communicated news about other potential threats and hazards in our environment.

SURVEILLANCE AND THE WARNING FUNCTION

On the face of it, one of the clearest social benefits from mass communication is the timely warning of impending danger that can be sounded democratically by the mass media. Thus forewarned, individuals can take steps to protect themselves and their loved ones (and in some instances their homes and possessions), and community organizations can be activated to respond to the threat. Sounds simple. Life, however, is never so obligingly simple as we think. Social research on people's reactions to disaster and to warnings about impending disaster has disabused us in this instance. As sociologist Ralph H. Turner and his colleagues comment, in a recent report on community response to earthquake threat:

> The literature on disasters and disaster warnings is replete with evidence that the nature of the danger confronting the community and the available courses of action are poorly understood by large segments of the community. In part this stems from deficient communication by scientists, public officials, and the mass media. In part it stems from the inaccessibility of some population segments to the customary communication media. In part it stems from the pattern of information diffusion and confirmation through informal networks after the messages have been presented by the media.[5]

Lack of appreciation of the seriousness of the impending danger, deficient and insufficient communication about it, interpersonal interactions—these are but a few of the many factors to confound us. Another is the nature of the warning. As Turner notes, researchers have distinguished between warnings about a general, chronic state of risk (indefinite forecasts that serious earthquakes seem likely to occur in southern California sometime within the next few decades), and increasingly more specific predictions of imminent danger. Understandably, people tend to react differently to prospects of disaster depending on how imminent and precise they seem.

Of special interest here is people's tendency to verify (or disconfirm) and interpret warnings received through the mass media by talking with friends, rela-

[5] Ralph H. Turner, Joanne M. Nigg, Denise Heller Paz, and Barbara Shaw Young, *Community Response to Earthquake Threat in Southern California* (Los Angeles: Institute for Social Science Research, University of California, Los Angeles, 1980), part one, p. 26. Also see, by the same authors, *Earthquake Threat: The Human Response in Southern California*, 1979; Joanne M. Nigg, "Communication Under Conditions of Uncertainty: Understanding Earthquake Forecasting," *Journal of Communication*, 32, 1 (1982), pp. 27–36; Ralph H. Turner, "The Mass Media and Preparation for Natural Disaster," in *Disasters and the Mass Media* (Washington, DC: National Academy of Sciences, 1980), and "Media in Crisis: Blowing Hot and Cold," *Bulletin of the Seismological Society of America*, 72, 6 (1982), pp. 519–528. I wish to express my thanks to Professor Turner and his colleagues for their generosity in making these materials and some unpublished reports available to me.

tives, officials, and other people (thus illustrating the importance of both mass communication and interpersonal communication to this communication activity). These persons play an important part in influencing our beliefs about the warning messages, our interpretations of them, and our responses to them. As Turner and his colleagues put it:

> Communication between scientists and the public and between officials and the public is not simple and direct, but is a complicated social process. Initially the communication media introduce their own slants and emphases by the way stories are written and the kinds of questions posed during interviews. . . . After the accounts are released by the media they still pass through a complex social process. . . . [which includes interpersonal communication networks. And thus] public opinion about the earthquake prediction and the appropriate individual and community response is formed through extended and criscrossing interaction chains. . . . Whether the relationships are those of colleagues, friends, or both, the pathways to public opinion consist of preexisting interpersonal relationships."[6]

CASE 1:   The California Earthquake Prediction Study

The California earthquake threat project exemplifies a comprehensive, sociologically oriented study of mass-communicated warnings and people's responses to them. A brief look at its study design will help us to appreciate the complex research design needed to tackle this topic. But first a little background information is called for. On February 13, 1976, the *Los Angeles Times* ran a front-page story saying that a bulge in the earth's surface had been discovered near Palmdale, California. The meaning of this uplift in the earth's surface was unknown, but there was serious concern that it might be a precursor to a major earthquake, costing thousands of lives. On April 8, the California Seismic Safety Commission "officially declared that 'the uplift should be considered a threat to public safety and welfare in the Los Angeles metropolitan area.'"[7] By the end of May, further developments led the *Los Angeles Times* to report "a growing conviction at the US Geological Survey that the uplift indeed presaged an earthquake."[8]

The mass media presented lots of earthquake-related news during the year following the announcement of the Palmdale bulge, including earthquake "predictions" (unrelated to the uplift) by persons given considerable attention by the press and broadcast media. It is against this background of events that Ralph Turner and his co-investigators, Joanne M. Nigg, Denise H. Paz, and Barbara S. Young, carried out their study.

In order to know what earthquake-related stories were being presented by the mass media, the researchers analyzed the relevant content from the area's press

[6] Turner et al., *Community Response to Earthquake Threat in Southern California*, pp. 66, 69.

[7] Ibid., p. 4.

[8] Ibid., p. 5.

and broadcast media during the three years of the study, 1976 through early 1979. This detailed narrative of media coverage and its analysis supplied one component of the investigation. Second, the study examined, through observation and other field techniques, the responses of governmental and other organizations to these earthquake threats. A special study was made of earthquake-related activities in the schools.

The main and basic field survey consisted of personal interviews with 1,450 adult residents of Los Angeles County in the early part of 1977. This cross-section of the population was supplemented by special samples of black and Mexican-American minorities, persons living in an area that had experienced an earthquake, and persons living in sections of Los Angeles County especially vulnerable to earthquake damage. In order to study developments over several years, a combination of panel and repeated surveys was used. Some members of the original sample plus 500 new respondents were interviewed every six months, for a total of four new sets of data.

Preparations also were made for up to five special surveys in the event that something dramatic occurred while the study was in progress. (It did. A moderate earthquake occurred on New Year's Day, 1979, during the nationally televised Rose Bowl football game. Fortunately there seems to have been only minor damage and no injuries.) Finally, a field study was made of several cases of collaborative group response to the earthquake threats, including resistance to certain proposed safety measures.

The first survey in the project was conducted about one year after the announcement of the Palmdale bulge—a year marked by mass media coverage and discussions about the meaning of the uplift, earthquake predictions and near predictions, serious earthquakes throughout the world, and questions about the safety of nuclear power plants, local dams and buildings, according to the researchers' narrative record of media content. As they report: "Forebodings of earthquake disaster are in the air in southern California." The vast majority (87 percent) of residents surveyed said that they had heard some prediction or announcement about a coming earthquake. Most people recalled only one specific instance, but three out of every ten remembered more.

The greater the range of mass media that people used and the more discussions about earthquake predictions that they held with other people, the greater the number of mass-communicated predictions or announcements they recalled. Both the variety of media used and the amount of interpersonal discussion increased for persons having more years of formal schooling. Education, then, turns out to be an important consideration in public awareness about earthquakes. The researchers report:

> Education has both direct and indirect effects on awareness of earthquake near predictions. . . . more highly educated respondents [tend] to learn about earthquakes from a wider range of media sources. The more highly educated are also more likely to have engaged in discussion. And over and beyond the effects of their greater involvement in communication about earthquakes, they are likely to have heard or remembered more near prediction announcements.[9]

[9] Ibid., p. 253.

While most respondents remembered hearing some kind of earthquake prediction, far fewer specifically recalled the Palmdale bulge or uplift. In all, one person in every four remembered hearing about the uplift, knew that it might signify a coming earthquake, and saw this as personally relevant—that is, expected some damage where he or she lived. People appeared receptive to earthquake-related topics in the mass media, two-thirds of the respondents saying that they wanted more, not less, coverage of such topics.

What about behavior? How had people reacted to the mass-communicated news and warnings about earthquake threats? What *can* a person do, when faced with conditions of ongoing high risk but relatively little specificity about the particular time or exact spot of greatest danger? Move away, perhaps—but it seems unlikely that many people would abandon their homes and jobs out of fear of general uncertain vulnerability to such disasters as earthquakes, floods, hurricanes, tornadoes, or fires. Some people expressed a certain amount of fatalism: What will be will be. Still, something can be done to improve one's chances of surviving in an emergency and its aftermath. The researchers asked people whether or not they had taken any of sixteen actions usually recommended as household preparations for earthquake-related emergencies. Most people said they had a working flashlight, a battery-operated radio, and a first aid kit. But relatively few people had taken other precautions, such as installing secure latches on cabinets to prevent items from falling out and onto someone's head, or joining in neighborhood activities about earthquake-related matters, such as neighborhood plans for the elderly or the children.

People who used a wide range of mass media sources and, even more so, people who discussed family preparedness with others were more likely to have taken a number of preparatory steps. "Decision-making about earthquake preparedness," Turner and his colleagues suggest, "is apparently similar to decision-making under other uncertain conditions. Before people take action on what they have heard, they seek information and confirmation through direct face-to-face interaction with their peers."[10]

The California project yielded many more findings than are summarized here; we have selected only a few to illustrate the richness of the research. These findings demonstrate the need to consider both mass communication and interpersonal communication as contributors to the public's awareness of danger and response to it.

The California experience also reminds us that in this day and age communicating warnings may be far from a simple matter of alerting people to a sure and imminent danger. Earthquake threats are not new to our time. But the increasing prospects of scientific prediction of them is new and, understandably, not easy to communicate to the public. The meaning of such a strange phenomenon as the Palmdale bulge, for example, is seldom a clear-cut and simple story to report, and it is not easy for people to assess its personal relevance. In this regard, communications about earthquake threats have some things in common with warnings about other modern dangers such as nuclear accidents, environmental pollution, and toxic wastes.

[10] Ibid., part five, p. 146.

Warnings are made more difficult because of the technical complexity of the problem, the probabilistic nature of the risks involved, and social, economic, political (and sometimes military) sensitivity to the issues raised. Additional examples can be found, among others, in accounts of communication before, during, and following the accident at the nuclear power plant at Three Mile Island, Pennsylvania, in 1979, and in accounts of the mass media coverage of the story about Love Canal, a residential section built over an old chemical dump site in Niagara Falls, New York.[11] (For more recent examples, unfortunately, consult the daily news!)

OTHER FUNCTIONS OF MASS COMMUNICATION SURVEILLANCE: STATUS CONFERRAL, AGENDA-SETTING, AND CONSTRUCTING PUBLIC REALITY

The threat of disaster is only one form of social crisis in which the mass media play an important role. Other kinds of crises have also been studied. Several studies have examined the apparent functions of mass media reports, especially television coverage, during periods of national shock, such as that which followed the tragic assassination of President Kennedy in 1963. These studies suggest that mass communication aids the national "healing" process by allowing the entire nation to participate symbolically and physically in the social act of mourning. Further, it provides reassurance that there is continuity in government despite the crisis.[12] Likewise, research on the mass media's coverage of the U.S. Senate's investigation of Watergate, in 1973, and the possible impeachment of the president suggests that such surveillance served to reassure people that our system of government—with its checks and balances—was sound and working properly.[13]

Some other social functions of surveillance through mass communication have been mentioned in Chapter 1, a number of which were suggested in

---

[11] For an account of journalism on the scene near the nuclear accident, see Peter M. Sandman and Mary Paden, "At Three Mile Island," *Columbia Journalism Review*, July–August 1979, pp. 43–58. For an account of viewpoints and conclusions offered by participants in a conference about the event (including views about the role of the mass media), see *The Three Mile Island Nuclear Accident: Lessons and Implications*, eds. Thomas H. Moss and David L. Sills as volume 365 of the *Annals of the New York Academy of Sciences* (1981). Also see Sharon M. Friedman, "Blueprint for Breakdown: Three Mile Island and the Media Before the Accident," *Journal of Communication*, 31, 2 (Spring 1981), pp. 116–128. For an account of the mass media's initial coverage of the Love Canal story, see Jon Swan, "Uncovering Love Canal," *Columbia Journalism Review*, 17 (January–February 1979), pp. 46–51.

[12] For examples, see Wilbur Schramm, "Communication in Crisis," in *The Kennedy Assassination and the American Public*, eds. Bradley S. Greenberg and Edwin B. Parker (Palo Alto, CA: Stanford University Press, 1965), pp. 1–25, and various studies published in that volume.

[13] As one example, see Josephine R. Holz, "Watergate and Mass Communication: A Case Study in Public Agenda Setting" (MA thesis, Annenberg School of Communications, University of Pennsylvania, 1976). For a more recent study and analysis, see *The Battle for Public Opinion: The President, the Press, and the Polls During Watergate*, by Gladys Engel Lang and Kurt Lang (New York: Columbia University Press, 1983).

the enduring essay by Lazarsfeld and Merton cited there.[14] Status conferral is one.

Status Conferral

This concept seems straightforward enough: persons, organizations, and issues that get reported by the mass media are seen as important by the public, at least for the moment. Frequent attention by the mass media, presumably, further verifies one's importance. Publicists understand this, candidates for public office believe it, and so do successful leaders of organizations and social movements (among others), all of whom seek media attention, preferably favorable. (It is important to remind ourselves, however, that not everyone seeks or welcomes the public spotlight. Some people work hard at minimizing the attention given to themselves, their organizations, and activities—an interesting phenomenon for study.) More problematic is the question of just how useful or even harmful such media-conferred status might be for the persons, organizations, or social issues touched.

Todd Gitlin, for example, argues that the media's regular and repeated need for individuals to play the role of spokespersons during the student protests of the 1960s led reporters and television interviewers to focus attention on a few students they identified as the "leaders" of the groups and students involved in various events.[15] Those singled out for continuous attention by the mass media became celebrities. In time, this celebrity status—with its attendant demands upon the students so selected—seemed dysfunctional. Celebrities risked alienation from the very organizations and students that the mass media said they "represented." In the long run, this may have been dysfunctional for the student groups and their causes if it robbed them of effective organizational leadership.

The example suggests to us a broader concern about the possible functions and dysfunctions of repeated, regular, and patterned mass communication about social movements, protest organizations, citizen action groups, and other social developments. The functional perspective is less concerned with the impact of a single instance of mass communication than with the implications of the broader class of communication activities—regular and repetitive—that the single instance illustrates. We would like to know, for example, the extent to which the routines of news coverage usually confer status upon a few media-certified "spokespersons" for social movements, organizations, and other developments, and the extent to which such status conferral, in turn, seems to benefit or harm the organizations or causes at stake. Also, what are the implications for the larger society and its maintenance and change? Answers are not easy to come by, but our functional framework at least alerts us to the possibilities that any such communication activity is likely to have both functional and dysfunctional aspects for the individuals, organizations, and society concerned.

[14] Paul F. Lazarsfeld and Robert K. Merton, "Mass Communication, Popular Taste and Organized Social Action," in *The Communication of Ideas,* ed. Lyman Bryson (New York: Harper and Bros., 1948), pp. 95–118.

[15] Todd Gitlin, *The Whole World Is Watching: Mass Media in the Making* and *Unmaking of the New Left* (Berkeley: University of California Press, 1980), chap. 5, "Certifying Leaders and Converting Leadership to Celebrity," pp. 146–179.

As another example, consider the mass media coverage of the "march" that a group of neo-Nazis planned to hold in Skokie, Illinois (a suburb of Chicago in which a relatively large number of Jewish families lived and where many had themselves been captives in Nazi concentration camps or had family and friends who were) in 1978. Research has shown that some members of the public were concerned that the publicity given to the neo-Nazi group and its leader would make them seem important and perhaps enhance their status in the eyes of some people. Publicity might serve to certify or legitimize them in some way on a national scale (apparently they were a tiny group in the Chicago area), and might increase their membership. Such status conferral, presumably functional for the neo-Nazi group, was viewed with alarm by people who regarded the prospects as threatening and harmful to society. Others, however, believed that the media should focus attention on this neo-Nazi group and its activities so that the public could be informed and warned about them. Publicity would bring the force of public opinion against them and therefore would be functional for society, according to this point of view. (We return to this case study later in the chapter.)[16]

Agenda-Setting

One major area of contemporary research on the role of mass communication in the development of public opinion and beliefs is the study of *agenda-setting,* a concept that could be seen as an extension of the status conferral function. Lazarsfeld and Merton suggest that the mass media may confer status not only on individuals and groups, but also on public issues and social movements, through frequent and favorable recognition. People's opinions about the issues may or may not be changed by media arguments, but the mere fact that some public issue or policy becomes a topic for mass media attention gives it the appearance of importance and makes it salient to the public.

In the 1970s, communications researchers Maxwell McCombs and Donald Shaw proposed the hypothesis of agenda-setting during their studies of mass media coverage of national presidential election campaigns.[17] They hypothesized that the mass media influence the public's beliefs about what topics are the key issues in a campaign through the amount of attention given to each issue. Since that time, the agenda-setting hypothesis has been extended by various authors to refer more generally, as one recent review put it, "to the ability of the mass media to influence the level of the public's awareness of issues as opposed to their specific knowledge about those issues. . . ."[18] The other side of the coin, of course, is that matters not given much attention by the mass media are regarded by people as unimportant, if they are aware of them at all. Hence access

[16] See Josephine R. Holz, "Communication About the Skokie 'March': A Case Study in the Social Construction of Reality" (Ph.D. dissertation, University of Pennsylvania, 1981).

[17] Maxwell E. McCombs and Donald L. Shaw, "The Agenda-setting Function of Mass Media," *Public Opinion Quarterly,* 36 (1972), pp. 176–184.

[18] Donald F. Roberts and Christine M. Bachen, "Mass Communication Effects," in *Annual Review of Psychology, 1981* (Palo Alto, CA: Annual Reviews Inc., 1981), pp. 307–356; quotation, p. 323.

to the mass media news process is regarded as essential to getting one's story across to the public.

The amount of attention the mass media give to social issues leads people to believe that these are important, whether or not the media influence people's opinions on them. Thus mass communication plays an important role in defining the public agenda by influencing what it is that people think about. In order to support this hypothesis, communications researchers have examined statistical correlations between the amount of attention given to various social issues by the mass media, usually in news reporting, and the apparent saliency or perceived importance of these issues for individuals or for the public, as determined by sample surveys, public opinion polls, or other means.

Agenda-setting is not an automatic or certain consequence of mass media attention under all circumstances, of course. And several researchers have noted conditions under which it seems more or less likely to occur. In an intensive study of how people obtain and process political news and information, for example, political scientist Doris A. Graber reports in 1984 on a year-long in-depth study of a small panel of people in Evanston, Illinois, contrasted according to their interest in politics and degree of ready access to mass media information. While most of the study deals with how these respondents process the news, the study touches on the agenda-setting hypothesis.

Graber reports that respondents "definitely were influenced by the many cues to the importance of stories that the media supplied." Nevertheless, she observes, "Media cues about the importance of stories lose their potency as guides to what people will read or watch or think about when conflicting pressures arise from other facets of the individual's life."[19]

Social processes other than mass communication also affect the public's judgment of an issue or person as important. For one thing, people talk to one another about social issues, and these conversations may play an important part in their judgments. This process may be highlighted when the social issue involves a point of conflict among different segments of the society. As an example, one study of public opinion formation over a controversial routing of high-voltage power lines across Minnesota farmland reports that personal discussions about the issue increased over time. (The mass media, meantime, continued to be major sources of information about the issue, however.)

The researchers, sociologists George Donohue, Clarice Olien, and Phillip Tichenor, observe: "This is a frequent pattern in the development of social issues. People often get their first information from the media, in this case newspapers. As the conflict develops and intensifies, it becomes more of a topic of conversation which supplements—but does not necessarily replace—the information from the media."[20] How much these conversations, in turn, may influ-

---

[19] Doris A. Graber, *Processing the News: How People Tame the Information Tide* (New York: Longman, 1984), pp. 111–113.

[20] George A. Donohue, Clarice N. Olien, and Phillip J. Tichenor, "Electric Power and Social Power: Analysis of Organization, Conflict and Newspapers on Public Decision-Making," *Sociology of Rural Life*, 1, 1 (March 1978), pp. 1, 2, 4. I am indebted to Professor Tichenor for his kindness in bringing this study (and others by the rural sociologists at Minnesota) to my attention and for

ence notions about the relative importance of various social issues is not known. As one recent review has noted, "The role of interpersonal communication in agenda setting demands further investigation."[21]

Agenda-setting needs to be considered in terms of the larger social and political context. Several studies have examined how it relates to social action, public opinion, and political events. For example, Donohue, Olien, and Tichenor's study of the electric power line controversy reports that the political outcome of that issue was determined more by bureaucratic governmental forces than by any possible effect of mass communication on general public opinion. "In spite of the pattern of views and opinions identified in these studies, and the views reported in other polls," they report, "public decisions being made are all in favor of the power line project and the general eminent domain principle. It is not the public exchange of information and public opinions about the issue that is decisive. A bureaucratic process is in control, and decisions on such projects are made and justified according to the general welfare which, in this case, means the general need for more electrical energy."[22]

To take another example, in 1981 researchers at Northwestern University conducted a case study of the apparent agenda-setting impact of a televised investigative report on alleged fraud and abuses in federally funded home health care programs (those that provide health care and related services in the person's own home). This television program was the culmination of a lengthy journalistic investigation that not only followed the usual methods of journalism, but also involved close collaboration with U.S. Senate staff members, particularly officials of the U.S. Permanent Subcommittee on Investigations, which was planning a series of hearings on home health care fraud. The report appeared as an 18-minute segment on "The NBC News Magazine with David Brinkley," on May 7, 1981.

The Northwestern researchers studied the apparent impact of this news event on the views of the general public, government policy-makers, interest group leaders, and public policy decisions. They conclude that viewers of the televised news report raised their sense of the importance of the issues involved, while persons in the study who did not see the program did not change their views significantly. Likewise, governmental "policy-makers" who saw the show appeared to change their stated assessments of the importance of the issue, belief that public action was necessary, and views about the public's sense of the topic's importance. (But the views of leaders of special interest groups, such as officers of the Gray Panthers, seemed to be less influenced by the show.)

"Despite these changes among the public and among certain policy makers," the researchers report, "there appears to be no relationship between impact at these levels and impacts at the actual policy-making level. What seems to have influenced the policy recommendations which came out of this case were not so much aroused members of the public but rather the active collabora-

sending me copies of the publications. For a fuller account, see P. Tichenor, G. Donohue, and C. Olien, *Community Conflict and the Press* (Beverly Hills, CA: Sage Publications, 1980).

[21] Roberts and Bachen, "Mass Communication Effects," p. 326.

[22] Donohue et al., "Electric Power and Social Power," p. 7.

tion between the investigative journalists and officials of the U.S. Senate Permanent Subcommittee on Investigations."[23]

Not every topic given publicity by the mass media gets on the agenda for public concern and becomes a matter of social and political consequence. Lang and Lang, in a major analysis of mass media and public opinion during the Watergate episodes (the series of events that led to the resignation of President Richard Nixon in 1974), strongly argue that the mass media do not dictate a public agenda independent of society's political process. Rather, they propose, mass communication interacts with political processes and public opinion in a more complex way, through public agenda-building. *Agenda-building*, which they propose as a more apt term than agenda-setting, "is a collective process in which media, government, and the citizenry reciprocally influence one another in at least some respects."[24]

The Langs relate mass communication to public opinion through a working model of ways "in which mass communication affects how political coalitions are built and how public opinion functions as a form of social control."[25] The news media, by giving visibility to certain issues and persons, create an audience of "bystanders" to political events, persons whose presence is important insofar as politicians or other participants in the political arena are aware of them and take their views (public opinion, in one sense of that term) into account. This "bystander public functions as a significant reference group for political actors who seek their consent or at least acquiescence."[26] Politicians also are dependent on the mass media for clues to public opinion and responses to issues and for clues to their own public image.

Some issues, those with a high threshold before reaching public concern and issues remote from most people's firsthand experience, require a great deal of intensive and prolonged mass media coverage before they enter the public consciousness as serious political and social issues and become matters for political action by government officials or others under pressure of the public opinion (or free to act because of changes in public opinion). Watergate was such a topic. It took months of news developments before getting onto the public agenda. The Langs suggest several ways through which mass-communicated news goes beyond agenda-setting to enter into the agenda-building process:

1. The mass media highlight some events or activities.
2. Saturation news coverage, by both cosmopolitan and local mass media, gains essential audience attention for the issue, even high-threshold ones.
3. The mass media provide a context—a field of meanings—for the public's interpretation and understanding of these events and activities.
4. The importance and meaning of events is further developed, enhanced, or reduced

---

[23] Fay Lomax Cook, Tom R. Tyler, Edward G. Goetz, Margaret T. Gordon, David Protess, Donna R. Leff, and Harvey L. Molotch, "Media and Agenda Setting: Effects on the Public, Interest Group Leaders, Policy Makers, and Policy," *Public Opinion Quarterly*, 47, 1 (1983), pp. 16–35; quotation, p. 33.

[24] Lang and Lang, *The Battle for Public Opinion*, pp. 58–59.

[25] Ibid., p. 23.

[26] Ibid., p. 24.

by the symbols used in describing them, such as the Watergate "caper" or the Watergate "scandal."

5. The media link the events to well-known secondary symbols, such as the "Democratic" or the "Republican" positions on the events.

6. The media confer status, prestige, and standing on certain spokespersons who articulate positions on the issues.

In this manner, the Langs state, "The process of agenda-building . . . goes on continuously and involves several feedback loops. The most important of these are (1) the images through which political figures see themselves and their own activities mirrored in the media, (2) the pooling of information within the press corps that fosters similarities in the imagery disseminated, and (3) the various indicators of the public response, especially opinion polling, towards which press and polity alike are oriented."[27] "As for the agenda-setting hypothesis," they note, "the media do play a vital role in calling attention to a problem, but neither public awareness nor public concern suffices to convert a problem into a public issue. It becomes a public issue only when the public can locate it on the political landscape and see reasons for taking sides."[28]

Some researchers have suggested that long-term mass media coverage of certain topics may split a society into segments of knowledgeable and uninformed people. Since not everyone pays the same amount of attention to mass-communicated news and information, it is argued that the more information the mass media gives on a topic over time, the more likely it is that certain kinds of people who pay attention to news and information will learn more about it than the rest of us. Tichenor, Donohue, and Olien have proposed a "knowledge-gap" hypothesis as one possible social consequence of mass-communicated news.[29]

They suggest that one consequence of mass communication coverage is an increase in the knowledge gap between various social strata in the society who are differentially likely to pay attention to the news and to build upon their prior knowledge. (Such differences in communication behavior may occur, for example, between persons contrasted by education, age, gender, or other characteristics.)[30] According to this general hypothesis, one social consequence of continuous mass communication about a social issue (or any topic) might be to divide the public between those who are relatively well informed about it (not merely have heard about it) and those who are not. If this tendency is extended to include a wide variety and large number of important social issues, then the public would be split between those who generally know and those who do not.

While theoretically possible, this development does not necessarily occur, and further research has specified some of the conditions that may modify it.[31]

[27] Ibid., p. 60.

[28] Ibid., pp. 60–61.

[29] Phillip J. Tichenor, George A. Donohue, and Clarice N. Olien, "Mass Media and Differential Growth in Knowledge," *Public Opinion Quarterly*, 34 (1970), pp. 158–170.

[30] For a study exploring the role of interest as related to the knowledge gap, see B. K. L. Genova and Bradley S. Greenberg, "Interest in News and the Knowledge Gap," *Public Opinion Quarterly*, 43 (1979), pp. 79–91.

[31] For one summary of relevant research, see Roberts and Bachen, "Mass Communication Effects," pp. 321–322.

We need to keep in mind, too, that people are not solely dependent on mass communication for learning about social issues (or about anything else). Personal experience and interpersonal communications play important parts. Certain features of the social issue and the community (for example, whether or not there is social conflict) also seem to matter. For example, Tichenor and his colleagues report on their studies of community issues, conflict, and public affairs knowledge conducted in 15 different community areas in Minnesota since 1969.[32] They examined, among other things, whether the gap in knowledge about a social issue between persons relatively high and low in socioeconomic status is greater or smaller on issues perceived as "touchy subjects" involving social conflict.

They report that the knowledge gap appeared to be lower where social conflict was higher. They interpret the findings (along with others from their studies) as suggesting that "High media attention to a local issue, accompanied by high familiarity, frequent interpersonal communication, and a conflict-laden atmosphere may jointly create the conditions under which the knowledge tends to become more equally distributed among persons higher and lower in social status."[33] Thus we are reminded again of the importance of studying mass communication in its social context and together with patterns of interpersonal communication.

Conceptions of Public Reality

A major body of contemporary research and theory deals with the contributions of mass communication—especially news reports and "factual" portrayals—to the public's conceptions of reality, the "facts," concepts, and definitions from which people construct their beliefs about the world in general and about social reality in particular. Interest in this topic is far from new, but recent new case studies have given us some insights into the parts played by mass communication, interpersonal communication, and personal experience in shaping people's concepts of distant events, matters unlikely to be observed firsthand, and complex and abstract topics, such as the state of the economy. Further, they seek to understand how communications contribute to publicly shared conceptions of reality.

The late political columnist Walter Lippmann recognized the significance of reality "construction" (although he did not label it that) in his classic book on public opinion written generations ago.[34] Lippmann distinguishes between "the world outside and the pictures in our heads." He notes "how indirectly we know the environment in which nevertheless we live." Little of what we know about the world and events in it comes from our direct observation and personal experi-

[32] Phillip J. Tichenor, Jane M. Rodenkirchen, Clarice N. Olien, and George A. Donohue, "Community Issues, Conflict, and Public Affairs Knowledge," in *New Models for Communication Research*, ed. Peter Clarke, *Sage Annual Reviews of Communication Research*, 1973, vol. II, pp. 45–79.

[33] Ibid., p. 72.

[34] Walter Lippmann, *Public Opinion* (New York: Harcourt Brace, 1922). See especially chap. 1, "The World Outside and the Pictures in Our Heads," from which the phrases used here are taken.

ence—much more comes from what we are told or shown by other people and by the mass media of communication upon which we have become increasingly dependent. There is, he argues, a "pseudo-environment" that is inserted between the individual and the environment. Human behavior is in response to this pseudo-environment, dependent on the pictures in our heads. These pictures, especially those regarding social life but also other matters, are fictions—not deliberate lies, but rather humanly created, socially constructed representations of the environment of life.

In the many decades since Lippmann's insightful treatise on public opinion, a small but growing body of research has addressed questions of how people come to acquire the pictures in their heads and to construct their concepts of social reality. One of the earliest explorations of television's part in all this is a prizewinning study by sociologists Kurt Lang and Gladys Engel Lang of television's portrayal of a MacArthur Day celebration in Chicago in 1951.[35] The celebration included a major parade and other social ceremonies for General Douglas MacArthur, who had just returned from Korea after being relieved of his command by President Harry S Truman. The Langs compared the events presented on television with accounts made by on-the-spot observers. They report major differences.

The television audience, as might be expected, had a better view of the parade and other events than the people on the street. The camera provided viewers with closeups, with movement from spot to spot to follow the action, and generally put the viewer into the center of more happenings than any one on-site observer could attend. These and other differences between the event as televised and the event as witnessed combined to give the television viewer an image of the parade that was uncharacteristic of the actual ceremonies, yet created a "reality" of its own—literally a set of pictures in the viewer's head.

The telecast conveyed, among other impressions, the sense of a highly dramatic and exciting event, of wildly cheering and enthusiastic crowds. By contrast, eyewitnesses reported far less drama, much standing around, and an orderly audience of spectators rather than an active crowd.

The Langs examine how both the nature of television production (at that time) and the public's prior expectations that the events would be dramatic contributed to the televised version. They then speculate about the social effects of the pictures of "reality" thus constructed. They argue that the dramatic bias of the televised version of the parade, together with seemingly similar presentations elsewhere in the country around the same week or so, created a public image of overwhelming popular sentiment in favor of General MacArthur, whose recent "firing" was controversial. This image, given further credibility by accounts in other mass media and through general conversations, itself became a "reality" that overshadowed the concrete reality of a relatively unexciting public ceremony. The Langs label this impact on public opinion through creating an impression of public sentiments a *landslide effect*, and they attribute it to television.

[35] Kurt Lang and Gladys Engel Lang, "The Unique Perspective of Television and Its Effect: A Pilot Study," *American Sociological Review*, 18 (1953), pp. 3–12.

More recently, Elizabeth Noelle-Neumann has proposed a "spiral of silence" theory that is relevant here. She argues that mass communication helps
to shape people's perceptions of what are the dominant or popular opinions
about social issues and other topics. In turn, persons who favor the apparently
dominant viewpoint speak out on it, while others keep quiet about private views
that seem to be "unpopular." This process makes the original "dominant" views
even more visible—since most of the people who are speaking out on an issue
seem to favor these views, while the opposition is silent. Confronted with the
apparent growing consensus toward the "dominant" views, the opposition becomes even more silent, thus forming a spiral of silence. There is more to the
theory than can be summarized here. Noelle-Neumann tests and refines the theory through survey research findings.[36]

Some interesting original research on mass communication and the construction of reality has been done by British sociologists. As an example, James
Halloran, Philip Elliott, and Graham Murdock present an instructive case study
of the relation between mass media coverage of an anti-Vietnam war demonstration in London and viewers' knowledge about and interpretations of the
events.[37] Among other points, the authors show, through analysis of media coverage prior to and during the march, that the demonstration was previewed as a
dramatic and probably violent event. The media coverage of the event, in turn,
presented it this way for television viewers and for readers. The media did not
present a variety of viewpoints and interpretations focusing on different aspects
of the day's demonstrations, according to the researchers, but rather focused on
one news issue—violence. The authors attribute this image not to the media's
deliberate distortion or falsification of events presented (there was some violence), but rather to the newsmaking processes of selection and interpretation of
events "for their relevance to the basic and predetermined news issue."[38]

As another example, Paul Hartmann and Charles Husband conducted a
major study of how people's conceptions of the racial situation in Britain were
influenced by personal experience with minorities and by information about
them derived from mass communication.[39] The authors conclude that how people felt about minorities was often affected by the immediate social environment
and their personal experiences, but their perceptions of the racial situation as a
social problem were derived from the mass media. Thus whether whites liked or
disliked minority group members was in part influenced by the norms of their
own neighborhood and by their personal contacts with persons from minority
groups. But the public's conceptions of the social issues of minorities and immi-

[36] Elizabeth Noelle-Neumann, "The Spiral of Silence: A Theory of Public Opinion," *Journal of Communication*, 24, 2 (1974), pp. 43–51, and "Turbulences in the Climate of Opinion: Method-ological Applications of the Spiral of Silence Theory," *Public Opinion Quarterly*, 41 (1977), pp. 143–158, and *The Spiral of Silence: Public Opinion—Our Social Skin* (Chicago: University of Chicago Press, 1984).

[37] James D. Halloran, Philip Elliott, and Graham Murdock, *Demonstrations and Communication: A Case Study* (Harmondsworth, Middlesex, England: Penguin Books, 1970).

[38] Ibid.

[39] Paul Hartmann and Charles Husband, *Racism and the Mass Media* (Totowa, NJ: Rowman and Littlefield, 1974).

gration were chiefly shaped by the "facts" people derived from the mass media stories, such as impressions about the number of minority group members there were in the country, whether the numbers were increasing and how fast, and whether there was a shortage of housing and jobs. These were the "facts" that the public shared, the common public definition of the situation, regardless of varying personal experiences.

A more recent example of research on how mass communication and personal communication fit into the social construction of public reality is provided by Josephine R. Holz's case study of the neo-Nazi "march" in Skokie, Illinois in 1978, cited earlier in this chapter.[40] Holz was concerned with how people far removed from the event, and therefore mainly dependent on mass media reports for their knowledge about it, constructed their views and opinions about what was going on. She interviewed samples of residents in and around Philadelphia, Pennsylvania—far from the proposed "march." The study compared views of the event and opinions about it expressed by persons of various social backgrounds, who were likely to differ in their feelings about the event. She also conducted intensive interviews with "networks" of people (family, friends, neighbors, and co-workers) who discussed the issues among themselves as the news stories were developed.

Holz reports that there were expected differences in awareness of the events, personal opinions about them, and frequency of discussions about the issues according to people's social characteristics, such as education and religious background. Nevertheless, people from all walks of life expressed similar concepts and gave similar descriptions of what the event was all about. As she puts it: "While these predictable differences in awareness, interest, and opinions about the Skokie 'march' were found among different subgroups of respondents in this study, what may be equally if not more noteworthy is the extent to which and the areas in which respondents who differed in these respects did *not* differ in their conceptions and beliefs about the march and neo-Nazism."[41]

Nearly all respondents described the proposed event as a "march"; they did not label it a demonstration, gathering, parade or other kind of event. The term "march" was clearly part of the mass media's depiction of the event and had historical connotations of the Nazi marches in Germany prior to and during World War II. Most people, regardless of social background, described Skokie as a largely Jewish community with a high number of Holocaust survivers living there—an image also traceable to the mass media stories.

Other important components of people's conceptions about the event also did not differ systematically among various subgroups in the sample, such as beliefs about the number of neo-Nazis who would march, the size of the neo-Nazi group in the United States, the kinds of people they are, whether or not there would be violence during the march, and who would cause it. "In other words," the author states, "there were important respects in which categories of respondents who differed in their awareness, interest, and opinions about the Skokie

[40] Holz, "Communication About the Skokie 'March.'"
[41] Ibid., pp. 256, 257.

march nevertheless shared common beliefs, assumptions and expectations about the event and about neo-Nazism in general."[42] These were the pictures in people's heads. They were the "reality" that people discussed.

A Comment on the Concept of Effects

By this point, it should be apparent that we speak of the "effects" of mass communication only as a convenient expression. Mass communication does not "cause" status conferral (itself a concept), or any other of the social phenemona in which mass communication is implicated. From our sociological perspective, an analytical model of direct cause and effect is inappropriate and unproductive. These are complex social matters. The processes involved usually are not revealed through standard laboratory experiments. But we are increasingly informed through case studies, surveys, and exploratory investigations in field settings.[43]

The notion of direct mass media "effects" seems intellectually less promising (aside from its popular, social, and political appeal) to some sociologists of mass communication today than it did a few years ago (or than it does today for communication researchers with other general orientations).[44] We seek to understand the kinds of contributions that mass communication and interpersonal communication together make to important social phenemona, including both socially differentiated and commonly shared knowledge, beliefs, and behavior. These are important considerations to keep in mind, since they apply not only to our preceding treatment of the "effects" of mass communication surveillance activities, but also to the discussions about correlation, entertainment, and socialization that we turn to now.

PUBLIC CAMPAIGNS AND MASS PERSUASION IN A DEMOCRACY

Throughout our century, many citizens of the Western world, and especially those in democratic nations, have become increasingly concerned about the political and social power of mass communication for propaganda and mass persuasion. Underneath such concern lies a fear that individuals and society can be manipulated by persons who control, use, or have special access to the mass media. We worry: Are our personal beliefs, values, attitudes, opinions, knowledge, and behavior so vulnerable to what we see on television, read in the newspapers, hear on the radio? In one sense, of course, they are. As we have seen in the preceding sections, much of what we "know" about the world comes

---

[42] Ibid., p. 259.

[43] As examples see ibid., and Colleen Cool, "Communication and the Formation of Beliefs about Economic Recession," paper presented at the Fifth International Conference on Culture and Communication (1983).

[44] For an earlier treatment of mass communication effects that has become a "classic" reference, see Joseph T. Klapper, *The Effects of Mass Communication* (Glencoe, Ill: Free Press, 1960).

through mass communication and, together with our own experiences and interpersonal communications with other people, serves in the social construction of reality about which we form opinions and toward which we direct our actions. But our concern in this section is with more direct attempts at public persuasion.

We focus here on studies of public communication campaigns. Not all such campaigns succeed in affecting the public's knowledge, opinions, attitudes, or behavior. The Cincinnati Plan, mentioned in Chapter 5, provides a good example of how selective exposure by the public undermined an intensive mass information campaign on world affairs. The process of mass persuasion is far from automatic or simple, and the public's role in this process is far from passive. We have a number of studies of successful public campaigns, however, from which lessons can be learned. We will discuss a few of these cases here.

CASE 2:   The Great American Values Test

In 1984 social psychologists and communication researchers Sandra Ball-Rokeach, Milton Rokeach, and Joel Grube reported the results of a unique field experiment designed to study the "cognitive and behavioral effects of a TV program on people who had voluntarily selected themselves to watch it in the privacy of their homes."[45] The researchers produced a special half-hour television program that was broadcast over the air one evening at 7:30 P.M. to residents in a region in the state of Washington. They then assessed the impact of the program by study of the beliefs and behavior of samples of these residents who had or had not watched the program, comparing their views prior to the broadcast with those subsequent to it, and contrasting these results with data on residents from similar communities that could not receive the broadcast.

The experiment built upon prior theoretical development and research findings about people's belief systems and on a dependency theory of mass communications behavior. In previous studies, Rokeach and others had found that people's belief systems (as inferred from their ranking of values on a specially developed values scale) are affected by circumstances that inform a person about his or her own value preferences, allow comparison with those of others, invite a self-confrontation with any discrepancies between the person's current values and those that best fit his or her self-image and self-esteem, and increase the salience of those values that do fit with and support that self-image. In this instance, the target values were freedom, equality, and environmental beauty.

The researchers expected that a television program that could get people to compare their values with those of other people (or average Americans) would reinforce the importance of these three American target values for certain viewers who ranked them high. It also would cause an uncomfortable self-

[45] Sandra Ball-Rokeach, Milton Rokeach, and Joel W. Grube, *The Great American Values Test: Influencing Behavior and Belief Through Television* (New York: Free Press, 1984). I am grateful to the authors for sending me a manuscript copy of their work. The quotation is from p. ix of the book.

confrontation for those viewers who ranked these values sustantially lower than fellow-Americans who served as a reference group for their own self-image and self-esteem. Mindful that people's reactions under laboratory conditions do not necessarily occur under more natural social circumstances, the researchers tried to reach television viewers in their homes, under normal viewing conditions. Hence the decision to broadcast the program rather than to test its effectiveness on an experimental group in a laboratory.

Dependency theory suggests that, given the choice, people who are more dependent on the mass media for fulfilling certain needs and for supplying certain gratifications should be more likely to view the program and to be influenced by it than others. To test these ideas, the researchers produced a television program, "The Great American Values Test," hosted by a television star, Ed Asner, and an anchorperson of ABC's television program "Good Morning America," Sandy Hill. The program presented data and a discussion of how various kinds of Americans have fared in studies of their values, and it invited the viewer to consider his or her own beliefs. Particular attention was given to the three target values of freedom, equality, and environmental beauty. The television program reached about 26 percent of the people in the experimental city, comprising about two-thirds of those people who were watching television at 7:30 on the night of the broadcast.

What were the results? Comparisons between the total intact samples of residents in the experimental city and those in the control city showed no statistically significant differences in values and attitudes between them either before the program or in the posttest measurements six weeks following it. Nevertheless, the researchers report, those people within the experimental city sample who watched the show from beginning to end raised their rankings of two of the three values (freedom and equality) to a statistically significant degree, and also raised the ranking of the third value somewhat between the pretest and and posttest measurements. People who did not see the program, however, and those who saw only part of it because something interrupted their viewing did not change their value priorities.

Measures were made too of people's attitudes toward black people and toward women (attitudes considered to be related to underlying values about equality). Again, while the experimental and control cities were not different, viewers who saw the entire program expressed more favorable attitudes (less racially prejudiced or sexist) six weeks after the program than prior to it (even though initially they were less favorable than others). Attitudes of nonviewers or interrupted viewers did not change.

Finally, the researchers examined certain possible behavioral consequences of the program two to three months later. They studied whether or not people responded to subsequent mail appeals for support or financial contributions from each of three voluntary associations whose causes seemed relevant to the three target values of the program. The researchers report that people who viewed the program fully were more likely than others to respond favorably to these requests and contributed more money, on average, than either nonviewers or interrupted viewers.

As for dependency theory, viewers were more likely than others to score high on media dependency (as measured by questionnaire items), especially depending on the media for gaining social and self-understanding. In turn, the program had more impact on those uninterrupted viewers who scored high on these media dependency measures (but not on two others, dependency for action orientation or for play). Thus the concept of mass media dependency proved useful in specifying certain kinds of audience members more likely to be influenced than others. The authors conclude: "A TV program designed to conform to certain theoretical considerations can significantly affect the beliefs and behavior of large numbers of people for at least several weeks or months afterwards."

The study specifies some of the communication conditions leading to the program's impact, such as content that challenges the self-image and self-esteem of some viewers, and identifies certain kinds of people most vulnerable to such mass communication influence. These are important lessons to keep in mind. And the authors raised serious ethical questions about the power of the media for mass persuasion; for good or evil purposes. just in time for publication in Orwell's 1984!

CASE 3:   Mass Persuasion

The public's susceptibility to mass persuasion under certain circumstances was powerfully illustrated and examined in a now classic case study, *Mass Persuasion*, by Robert K. Merton and his research associates.[46] They analyzed how a popular entertainer of the times, singer Kate Smith, managed to persuade radio listeners to pledge, through telephone calls to CBS, to buy millions of dollars worth of government war bonds during an eighteen-hour radio marathon during World War II.

The study combined a content analysis of the broadcast's themes, detailed focused interviews with a sample of the program's listeners (some of whom had pledged to buy bonds), and a sample survey of 1,000 New Yorkers. The researchers found the broadcast effective because of a combination of factors. Among them were the format of the show (a radio marathon broadcast), the public's image of Kate Smith (as a sincere, patriotic person), the themes employed (mainly patriotic), the favorable predispositions of the audience, and the social climate during wartime.

Content analysis could classify the variety of themes used, but focused interviews with listeners were needed to help assess the themes' effectiveness. Listeners' responsiveness to one or another theme seemed to differ according to each person's predisposition toward war bonds in general and their initial intention to buy bonds during the immediate War Loan Drive. Some listeners were fairly sentimental and emotional about buying bonds (to help win and end the war). Some people fully intended to buy one or more bonds sometime during the Loan Drive (of which the radio program was a part); others did not. Classifying

[46] Robert K. Merton, Marjorie Fisk, and Alberta Curtis, *Mass Persuasion: The Social Psychology of a War Bond Drive* (New York: Harper & Brothers, 1946).

people according to these predispositions resulted in a typology of people that related to their response to particular themes during the broadcast. For example, persons emotionally supportive of bond purchases who also intended to buy a bond sometime during the drive seemed to respond to the "facilitation" theme (just pick up the telephone and pledge), thus channeling their intentions into a purchase during the broadcast by Kate Smith. Other themes appealed to persons with different predispositions.

Although relatively few in number, one type, labeled the susceptibles, warrants special consideration here. Of special interest is the process by which they seem to have been persuaded, because it suggests how an effective communicator can momentarily change people's views about social norms, work on their self-image and self-esteem, and thereby get them to do something they hadn't intended. Do not assume that because the example comes from the past that it need not apply today. Each of us may be vulnerable to such persuasion by mass communicators under the right (or, if you prefer, wrong) circumstances. We can learn from the example and be on our guard.

The susceptible audience members, in this instance, were people who were emotionally supportive of the war effort and favored buying bonds to help the country, but who had no intention of buying a bond at the time of the broadcast. Why not? Because they believed they were already doing their share through systematic purchase of war bonds through payroll savings plans or some other means. These good citizens had done their part and felt good about it. They tuned in and listened to the marathon broadcast as spectators, perhaps pleased that Kate Smith was trying to persuade others, who seemed to need urging, to do their share too. Then a strange thing happened to some of these observers—they themselves were persuaded to buy more bonds during the broadcast!

By taking some liberties with Merton's analysis and drawing additional clues from the recent study by Ball-Rokeach et al., we are able to suggest the apparent strategy through which any of us might be influenced by a mass communicator who addresses a topic that touches our emotions, self-image, and self-esteem. We list them as steps to be aware of, as follows:

1. The communicator presents information about the behavior of members of the group that surpasses what the audience member thinks is the social norm. (Smith told stories about the wartime sacrifices of soldiers and civilians.)
2. The communicator evaluates this extraordinary behavior as good and praiseworthy, preventing the audience from regarding it as too extreme. Thus Smith called certain actions "the supreme sacrifice."
3. The audience member is invited to compare his or her own conduct with that in the ideal cases cited by the communicator. (Smith's question to the listener, "What are you doing compared with what this mother has done?" Such self-confrontation was an essential part of the Great American Values Test too.)
4. The communicator invites judgment of his or her own behavior in the relevant area, thus establishing a right to speak as a moral leader for the moment. (Smith's personal sacrifice in doing the exhausting marathon was made evident to the listeners.)

5. The audience members who once felt pretty good about themselves and their conduct now take a second look and some, finding themselves not living up to their
   prior self-image as good citizens, feel guilty and want to improve that image. What
   should they do? The communicator, as moral leader of the instant, provides an answer by formulating the new, acceptable norms and by prescribing the new behavior that will raise one's self-esteem again and reduce guilt feelings (to contribute
   beyond your normal plans, to buy, in a sense, a *sacrifice bond*, the one that hurts—
   but makes you feel good again).
6. The persuader provides a mechanism for immediate compliance with the new
   norm (call in by telephone).
7. The communicator rewards the new behavior in some way, thus making it seem to
   be the new norm that all good people are following, such as through direct praise,
   reports about the success of the campaign or mission, criticisms of the "deviants"
   in the audience who are not doing their share.

As mentioned, we have taken liberties in constructing these steps in mass
persuasion. The number of "susceptible" listeners in Merton's study was small
and analysis of their behavior played only a small part in the total study. Our
reformulation here is meant to suggest some of the communication processes
that seem to be involved. These processes, in my opinion, transcend the historical moment of the singular yet instructive case of the wartime radio marathon.

Can such things happen today in our sophisticated modern world of television, jet travel, and high tech? Are we less susceptible to mass persuasion than in
the past? One wonders.

One thing that is missing from our analysis thus far is consideration of the
role of personal influence in the process of mass persuasion. Our understanding
of the *social* processes that enhance or limit a program's impact would be
enriched by information about the social context within which people receive
the program and their conversations about it then and later with family, friends,
neighbors, and others. We turn next, therefore, to some recent studies that
touch upon the role of both mass media and interpersonal communications in
public campaigns.

MASS MEDIA AND INTERPERSONAL
COMMUNICATION IN MASS PERSUASION

Practical experience and research on new information campaigns have advanced
our knowledge about what the mass media and interpersonal communication together can accomplish during public campaigns. A broad range of contemporary
experiences and research results was assembled and presented at a national conference on communication strategies in the 1980s. These accounts evaluate a
diversity of results from public campaigns against smoking, for the prevention of
heart disease, for family planning, for the prevention of wildfires, and for the
conservation of energy—to mention some of the topics covered.[47] In this section
we will present a few examples from these studies.

[47] Ronald E. Rice and William J. Paisley, eds., *Public Communication Campaigns* (Beverly Hills,
CA: Sage, 1981).

Alfred McAlister, for example, drawing upon research on antismoking campaigns, argues that communication campaigns must first inform people about the consequences of undesirable behavior (undesirable from the campaign's perspective), persuade them to cease or avoid such behaviors, and train them in the skills necessary to do so. He states that while antismoking campaigns have been successful in the past in providing information and even in persuading people about the "right" thing to do, only recently have they studied how to include some training for maintaining partial or total abstinence. He points out the importance of interpersonal support (presumably through interpersonal communication) to this maintenance. "Mass communication media," he argues, "may effectively inform, persuade, and train their audiences, but lasting change will not be achieved in the absence of a supportive social environment. . . . researchers now realize that campaign effectiveness may depend upon the creation of opportunities for interpersonal communication, participation, and social reinforcement. This has led to attempts to efficiently integrate mediated and interpersonal communications and thus further progress toward the indentification of potentially effective strategies for discouraging and reducing smoking."[48]

Another example of different contributions by mass communication and interpersonal communication comes from studies of family planning campaigns. Shahnaz Taplin's review of research on national family planning programs in several countries leads to the general conclusions that "(1) The mass media can increase the level of knowledge (especially awareness) about family planning among the target audience but that (2) communication from family planning field workers, peers, and others is more effective in changing attitudes toward family planning which motivate adoption and continued use."[49] Taplin notes that one direction national family programs have taken recently is to utilize traditional channels of communication in various countries, such as singing poets, theater plays, and folk theater.

CASE 4:   The Stanford Heart Disease Prevention Program

Special effort to evaluate the relative contributions made by campaign-initiated mass communication and interpersonal communication were reported in accounts of the Stanford Heart Disease Prevention Program, a large-scale, relatively long-range program aimed at getting people to take steps that might reduce their risk of heart disease. A three-year campaign and an evaluation research project were conducted to compare three communities in California in the 1970s. The study was designed to assess, among other things, how much the campaign had achieved in one community (Gilroy) by using only mass media

[48] Alfred McAlister, "Antismoking Campaigns: Progress in Developing Effective Communications," in Rice and Paisley, *Public Communication Campaigns*, pp. 91–104; quotation, p. 92.

[49] Shahnaz Taplin, "Family Planning Communication Campaigns," in Rice and Paisley, *Public Communication Campaigns*, pp. 127–142; quotation, p. 129.

tactics and how much in another community (Watsonville) by using mass media and interpersonal communication (in the form of face-to-face instruction with some of the population). Results from these two communities were compared with data gathered in a third community (Tracy) that received neither form of the campaign.

The general purpose of the Stanford Heart Disease Prevention campaign was to bring about changes in information, attitudes, and risk-related behavior—changes expected to reduce the overall risk of heart disease. More specifically, it aimed at getting each person to achieve his or her ideal weight, to stop smoking or at least to cut down, to increase physical activity, and to control his or her consumption of alcohol, refined sugar, salt, cholesterol, and saturated fats. The strategy was based upon generalizations derived from the research literature on communication, persuasion, and behavior change. This strategy called for drawing a specific health issue to the public's attention, providing information that makes the issue relevant to individuals, motivating individuals to change their behavior and encouraging the new behavior, providing training to develop the skills necessary to adopt the new behavior, and teaching techniques for keeping up the new behavior through one's own self-control.

The mass media campaign was extensive and varied, consisting of such specially produced materials as one hundred radio spots, fifty television spots, several hours of radio and television programming, newspaper columns and advertisements, billboards, direct mail literature, and other materials, in English and in Spanish. These prepackaged campaign materials were sent to local mass media for use in the public interest.

To summarize the study design: Citizens in two communities, Gilroy and Watsonville, were able to receive whatever components of the mass media campaign the local mass media carried. In addition, some residents of Watsonville who were statistically relatively higher risks for heart disease were approached for interpersonal face-to-face instruction about how to change certain habits (such as heavy cigarette smoking) that might contribute to their personal risk of heart disease. This combination of mass media campaign and interpersonal instruction was to set the standard against which the results of the media-only campaign would be compared. Gains in both communities, however, could be compared also to data on behavior in the third community, which received no campaign.

Did the campaign work? Very well, according to the summary review by Nathan Maccoby and Douglas Solomon.[50] Changes in knowledge, attitudes, behavior, and physiological measures were most likely to occur in Watsonville, where both mass media and personal intervention were used. But there was also improvement in Gilroy, where the mass media campaign was used alone. The research results help specify how the mass media and interpersonal communications complemented each other during public communication campaigns. Some campaign tasks, such as placing an issue on the public's "agenda" of salient concerns or making information available to widespread audiences, can be tack-

[50] Nathan Maccoby and Douglas S. Solomon, "Heart Disease Prevention," in Rice and Paisley, *Public Communication Campaigns*, pp. 105–126.

led by means of the mass media with some success. Other campaign tasks, such as helping people to develop the skills necessary to keep up a new resolution (such as not to smoke any more) may also require direct intervention on a personal level to be successfully accomplished (although the researchers state that the mass media can contribute here too). The results of this three-community study, Maccoby and Solomon conclude, "provide evidence that behavior change for better health can be accomplished through sustained community-based education, but we have only begun to define the optimal strategy for conducting that education."[51]

Encouraged by the results of the first study, the Stanford Heart Disease Prevention Program launched a major five-community study in 1979, intended to run for a period of five to eight years. The communities are larger than those studied before, and the campaign will try to reach people from a wider range of ages than before, including youths. Campaign materials are being produced and modified on the basis of research and on-the-spot pretesting with members of the communities. Various community organizations are playing active roles in the campaign. The campaign employs a variety of communication channels and content.

One major conclusion that can be drawn from many of the studies we have reviewed in this section is that mass communication and interpersonal communication, *together*, contribute to the success and failure of public communication campaigns. Each mode of communication has particular strengths and limitations from the perspective of a specific campaign, and each modifies the other's role. Consideration of both interpersonal communication and the mass media is necessary for fuller understanding of the role of mass communication in public persuasion.

[51] Ibid., p. 115.

CHAPTER 8

Social Consequences of Mass Communication: Public Concern Over Mass Entertainment

Everyone, it seems, has strong views about the harmful effects of mass-communicated entertainment. Charges, denials, and countercharges appear in public and private, in discussions about media effects among concerned parents, in public testimonies before congressional committees, in newspaper editorials, in essays in popular magazines, on radio and television talk shows. The alleged harmful effect of media content worries people, who are especially concerned about the showing of violence, sex, crime, and other touchy subjects on television programs, in the movies, and elsewhere. At the same time, some people hope that a particular television program or other media content will have social benefits, that the television docudrama "Roots," for example, would reduce racial prejudices. Arguments can be found in the literature asserting that mass media entertainment has "bad effects," "good effects," or no effect at all on public taste, morals, social behavior, and other matters.

Why is there so much public concern and controversy about the effects of mass entertainment? For one thing, there is a sense of urgency about solving the social problems that many people fear are intensified by, even caused by, mass entertainment. People are anxious about crime, delinquency, terrorism, public morality, and other perceived social problems. Those people who think that our mass communication contributes to these problems want something done about it now, and they express their opinions with conviction and sometimes passion. Other people, often less convinced of these alleged effects, are equally passionate about protecting people's rights to freedom of information and entertainment. Hence the public concern.[1]

For another thing, we would like simple, direct, and quick answers to our questions about media effects. Scientific research findings are often slow in unfolding and are subject to different theoretical interpretations. That's how a dis-

[1] Lazarsfeld and Merton suggest four reasons why the public and social critics are concerned about the mass media: (1) alarm over the ubiquity of the mass media and their alleged power to manipulate people; (2) fear that the power elite in a society will use the mass media to reinforce the status quo, discourage social criticism, and impede beneficial social change; (3) belief that mass entertainment lowers esthetic tastes and standards for popular culture in its effort to attract and hold the largest possible audiences; and (4) belief that mass media entertainment wastes our leisure time, time that could be better spent on self-improvement or on other worthy activities. See P. F. Lazarsfeld and R. K. Merton, "Mass Communication, Popular Taste and Organized Social Action," in L. Bryson, ed., *The Communication of Ideas* (New York: Harper, 1948), pp. 95–118.

cipline grows and adds to our knowledge about the world. But some people are impatient and press for immediate, practical results and unambiguous interpretations (usually favoring their point of view). Furthermore, for some people, the concern about harmful media effects is a moral issue, not addressed by the seemingly objective, disinterested, and dispassionate scientific approach. Hence the public controversy.

In this chapter we will review a few of these public concerns and give examples of mass communication research and theory that addresses some of the major issues. Much of the current research on mass entertainment focuses on television programs, reflecting that medium's mass popularity and the public concern over its influence. The fact that many of our research examples, then, are taken from television research is understandable. Nevertheless, it is good to keep in mind that mass entertainment is found in other media as well, in newspaper features and comics, comic books, radio's popular music and talk shows, motion pictures, magazines, and books.[2] At various times in our modern history the public has been concerned about the content of these and other channels of communication.

The social influence of motion pictures, for example, was the subject of much attention during the 1930s, resulting in a set of studies on the effects of movies on children. Special attention was given to the movies' impact on children's knowledge, behavior (including sexual behavior), crime, delinquency, attitudes toward significant social concepts, standards and ideals, health and emotions.[3] Years later, people worry about the effects of "adult" movies. Radio programs, especially soap operas and popular entertainment, were matters of concern and social research in the 1940s, with critics wondering what gratification people got from such entertainment and what effects it had on them.[4] Later there was concern about the lyrics of rock-and-roll music and its alleged effects on young listeners.

The content of popular comic books, especially scenes and stories of sex and violence, worried parents and others. (One of the earliest publicized reforms of the comic book industry under its first "czar" was a regulation against exaggerated drawings of women's breasts and other physical features on comic book covers.) Antipornography crusades have been directed against sexually explicit mass media materials such as "adult" movies, books, and

---

[2] The study of popular culture has become a specialty in its own right. At least two scholarly journals carry essays and research findings by social scientists and humanists: *The Journal of Popular Culture* and *The Journal of Popular Film and Television*, both publications of Bowling Green University, Ohio, the home of the Center for the Study of Popular Culture. For example, see Ray B. Browne, ed., *Rituals and Ceremonies in Popular Culture* (Bowling Green, OH: Bowling Green University Popular Press, 1980), and Ray B. Brown, Marshall Fishwick, and Michael T. Marsden, eds., *Heroes of Popular Culture*, 1972. For a set of essays commenting on popular culture, see Arthur Asa Berger, *Television as an Instrument of Terror: Essays on Media, Popular Culture, and Everyday Life* (New Brunswick, NJ: Transaction Books, 1980).

[3] See W. W. Charters, *Motion Pictures and Youth: A Summary* (New York, Macmillan, 1934). For modern work, see Bruce A. Austin, "Film Audience Research, 1960–1980," *Journal of Popular Film and Television*, 8, 2 (1980), pp. 53–60.

[4] For one classic example, see Herta Herzog, "What Do We Really Know About Daytime Serial Listeners," in Paul F. Lazarsfeld and Frank Stanton, eds., *Radio Research 1942–1943* (New York: Duell, Sloan and Pearce, 1944), pp. 3–33. For a modern look, see Muriel G. Cantor and Suzanne Pingree, *The Soap Opera* (Beverly Hills, CA: Sage Publications, 1983).

magazines.[5] So it might be said that in this area, the medium is not the focus. Rather, it is the content of mass-communicated entertainment that people fear might harm the audience, or hope might be of social benefit.

The issues selected for brief treatment here concern research or theories about mass entertainment involving violence, sex and pornography, expressions of prejudice or antiprejudice toward minorities, and various social and cultural values.

VIOLENCE

Many people are concerned, even anxious, about violence and sexual activities portrayed by the mass media, especially in entertainment. This content offends some people's standards of morality or good taste. Public concern also reflects people's fear and belief that "bad" content has harmful social, psychological, and moral effects (especially on young persons) and leads to antisocial behavior.

Public opinion about the effects of violence in mass media content is divided, but most people believe that it is harmful, especially to children. Gallup polls taken in the mid-twentieth century found that about seven of every ten Americans believed juvenile delinquency can be blamed at least partially on crime comic books and television and radio programs. This concern has been translated into public efforts to get more "facts" about what harmful attitudes and behavior are "caused" by what is seen or heard in the movies, on television, or in other forms of popular entertainment.

Media presentations of sex and violence have been the subjects of several federally sponsored commissions on the effects of mass communications, in addition to numerous other less programmatic investigations. The secretary of health, education, and welfare authorized the formation of a surgeon general's Scientific Advisory Committee on Television and Social Behavior to investigate scientifically the harmful effects, if any, of televised crime and violence, particularly in leading to antisocial behavior and especially by children. The results of this investigation, reported in six volumes, were published in 1972, amid some controversy about their meaning. The committee summarizes its interpretation of the numerous studies it commissioned or reviewed as follows:

> A preliminary and tentative indication of a causal relation between viewing violence on television and aggressive behavior; an indication that any such causal relation operates only on some children (who are predisposed to be aggressive); and an indication that it operates only in some environmental contexts.[6]

Since the publication of this report, and partly because of its impetus, there has been an enormous amount of new research on television and social behavior.

---

[5] For one study, see Louis A. Zurcher, Jr., and R. George Kirkpatrick, *Citizens for Decency: Antipornography Crusades as Status Defense* (Austin: University of Texas Press, 1976).

[6] Surgeon General's Scientific Advisory Committee on Television and Social Behavior, *Television and Growing Up: The Impact of Televised Violence* (Washington, DC: U.S. Government Printing Office, 1972), p. 11. Also see the other five volumes issued under the title *Television and Social Behavior*.

In 1982 a follow-up report reviewed the preceding decade of research on television and behavior, noting that more than 2,500 research publications on television's influence on behavior had appeared in those years.[7]

Most of this research is psychologically oriented, focusing on the effects of television on the individual. Most studies through the early 1970s were designed to test whether or not some specific content, such as violence, has an impact on attitudes and behavior. The general communication model used was a psychological one of stimulus-response. During the latter 1970s, earlier stimulus-response models were put aside by some researchers in favor of other approaches. Psychologist Jerome Singer, for example, comments that "A major advance in the research approaches to television in the 1970s has been reflected in the increasing recognition that this medium must be understood more broadly in relation to the natural cognitive and affective development of the growing child."[8] Nevertheless, the approach remains essentially psychological.

Some of these recent studies report a statistical relation between the amount of violence watched on television and aggressive attitudes or behavior, which the reviewers interpret as causal—that is, that watching televised violence leads to aggression. But other studies have not found this relationship, or found only weak or modest statistical relationships.[9]

There are differences of opinions, then, as to whether there is any meaningful, significant connection between people's usual exposure to violence in the mass media (television and other media) and their subsequent aggressive, even delinquent, behavior. Furthermore, if there is such a connection, can it be interpreted as causal, contributory, or even deterrent?

Some authorities have argued that certain mass media content has harmful effects that are so obvious as to be self-evident. For example, Fredric Wertham, a well-known psychiatrist, comments in his analysis of certain crime comic books in the mid-1950s (entitled *Seduction of the Innocent*) that:

> They contain such details as one girl squirting fiery "radium dust" on the protruding breasts of another girl ("I think I've discovered your Achilles heel, chum."); white men banging natives around; a close up view of the branded breast of a girl; a girl about to be blinded. Whenever I see a book like this in the hands of a little seven-year-old boy, his eyes glued to the printed page, I feel like a fool to have to prove that this kind of thing is not good mental nourishment for children![10]

Nevertheless, he went on to support his ideas with research through a combination of content analyses, clinical case histories of children, and psychological tests.

Other authorities, who have reservations about the importance of mass

[7] See *Television and Behavior: Ten Years of Scientific Progress and Implications for the Eighties*, vols. 1 and 2, eds. David Pearl, Lorraine Bouthilet, and Joyce Lazar (U.S. Department of Health and Human Services, Washington, D.C.: U.S. Government Printing Office, 1982). Much of this report deals with psychological studies of television and the growth and development of children and therefore falls beyond the scope of our book.

[8] *Television and Behavior*, vol. 2 (1982), p. 2.

[9] For one review, see F. Scott Andison, "TV Violence and Viewer Aggression: A Cumulation of Study Results, 1956–1976," *Public Opinion Quarterly*, 41 (1977), pp. 314–331.

[10] Fredric Wertham, *Seduction of the Innocent* (New York: Rinehart and Company, 1954), p. 31.

media's contribution (if any) to delinquent behavior, have expressed concern lest a focus on mass communication as "cause" might divert attention from other possible factors in delinquency, such as disturbed family relationships, the influence of neighborhood gangs, and other contributors. *Television and Growing Up*, the 1971 summary report for the U.S. surgeon general, states:

> The real issue is once again quantitative: how much contribution to the violence of our society is made by extensive violent television viewing by our youth? The evidence (or more accurately, the difficulty of finding evidence) suggests that the effect is small compared with many other possible causes, such as parental attitudes or knowledge of and experience with the real violence of our society.[11]

One alternative view is that communication content that to the observer seems harmful actually might be serving as a deterrent to delinquency—permitting youth to work off their aggressions vicariously, for example, as they watch scenes of violence on television or in the movies. This viewpoint was tested in studies by psychologists Seymour Feshbach and Robert Singer and described in the 1971 report to the surgeon general. Other researchers, however, have challenged the "catharsis" hypothesis, and a review in the 1982 report states that "the wealth of evidence demonstrating that violence viewing and aggression are positively related contradicts the catharsis hypothesis" in the judgment of that reviewer.[12]

One viewpoint shared by many professionals is that whatever the "effects" of violent content may be, if any, they will vary among different kinds of people. For example, the average adolescent may be unharmed by scenes of violence, but an emotionally disturbed youngster or a gang may be stimulated by them. Thus the first report to the surgeon general states that any causal relation between television violence and aggressive behavior operates only on some children who are predisposed to be aggressive.

That 1971 report, as noted earlier, was not without its own critics. Some believed that the evidence warranted a stronger, positive statement about a causal link between violent programs and juvenile aggression. Others suggested that the inquiry never addressed the most socially meaningful questions. Sociologist Leo Bogart, for example, charged that the committee's underlying question, "Does exposure to TV violence lead children to specific acts of antisocial behavior?" does not reflect the most fruitful social and sociological approach to the problem, couched as it is in a stimulus-response paradigm.

In real life, he argues, "communications do not work that way. The entire history of mass communication research has shown the tremendous difficulty of teasing out specific effects from the tissue of surrounding social influences. . . . The 'invisible' effects of individual incidents of TV violence might add up to patterns that would leave their traces upon the culture even when specific episodes could not be related to specific effects." The significant questions, he suggests, "go beyond the short-run relationship between television violence and aggressive behavior in children. They concern the long-run influence of the mass

---

[11] *Television and Growing Up*, p. 4.
[12] L. Rowell Huesmann, "Television Violence and Aggressive Behavior," in *Television and Behavior*, 2 (1982), pp. 126–137.

media in shaping our national character."[13] The detection of patterns and long-run influences is beyond the scope of most of the experimental studies in the report. Their study remains a challenge today.[14]

CULTIVATION STUDIES

Cultivation analysis is the method by which George Gerbner, Larry Gross, and their associates link their content analyses of television programs (the cultural indicators project described in Chapter 6) to the study of mass communication effects.

According to cultivation theory, television contributes to viewers' conceptions of social reality in ways that reflect its "messages" about the world. Cultivation analysis compares the answers given by frequent television viewers and by relatively light viewers to survey questions about social reality (for example, about crime). It expects that frequent viewers will be more likely to give the "television" answer—that is, the one that reflects television's picture of the world, as detected through content analyses. They will be less likely to give answers closer to the real world (as reflected, for example, in official crime statistics or by census data).

The spread between the percentage of heavy and light viewers who give such a "television" answer is called the *cultivation differential.* It is interpreted by the researchers as a sign of television's cultivation of common perceptions of social reality among viewers. Television's cultivation of viewers' outlooks, it is argued, has significant personal and social consequences.

For example, the relatively high frequency of violent crime and police drama on television should make heavy viewers of television more likely than light viewers to overestimate such matters as the rate of such crimes in real life, the number of people working in law enforcement, and the viewer's own chance of becoming a victim. The researchers report that in a number of studies of both children and adults, heavy viewers are more likely than light viewers to give answers closer to television's picture of reality.

The tendency of heavy viewers to see the world in TV's terms has social implications beyond the impact of a single television episode or portrayal of violence, according to cultivation theory. It leads, for example, to a widespread fear of crime among the general public (who are heavy viewers) and especially among the kinds of people usually shown as victims in television drama (such as the elderly). Such fears, it is argued, can lead people to be more receptive to government actions (perhaps authoritarian, even antidemocratic) that promise to protect the citizen from crime and to make life more secure, but that may affect our civil rights and civil liberties. Or some people may take extraordinary steps for self-protection (moving out of the city, or locking themselves indoors day and night, or buying weapons) that have further social consequences.

[13] Leo Bogart, "Warning: The Surgeon General Has Determined That TV Violence Is Moderately Dangerous to Your Child's Mental Health," *Public Opinion Quarterly,* 26 (1973), pp. 491–521.

[14] For one example, see J. Ronald Milavsky, Horst Stipp, Ronald Kessler, and William S. Rubens, *Television and Aggression: A Panel Study* (New York: Academic Press, 1982).

Cultivation theory has been subjected to criticism and debate in the literature.[15] Several communications analysts have questioned cultivation analysis and its interpretation. Some researchers cite findings that apparently fail to replicate the cultivation studies and that do not support the theory. Others have raised methodological criticisms. It has been argued, for example, that the main statistical differences in beliefs and opinions expressed by heavy television viewers and light viewers are more likely to be the result of other differences between them, such as differences in educational background. Sociologist Paul Hirsch, among others, argues that important differences in answers between heavy and light viewers do not hold up as predicted by the theory once one controls simultaneously for several such demographic or social characteristics that could account for them. In rebuttal, Gerbner and his associates argue that the preponderance of evidence from years of research by themselves and others, conducted under a variety of circumstances, all converges to support their theory.[16]

Whatever the outcome of the debate about the theory and methods of cultivation analysis, it provides a good example of mass communication research that looks beyond the immediate psychological impact of a single television program or story on the individual. In doing so, it addresses important questions about the social consequences of mass-communicated entertainment for the social order and for social control.

SEX AND PORNOGRAPHY

Public opinion is divided about the presumed effects of viewing or reading mass-communicated erotic entertainment. Surveys in the 1970s and 1980s report that more than half of American adults at that time believed that erotic media content led people to commit rape. Around a third of the public believed that sexual materials in mass communication make people "sex crazy." Two-thirds of American adults agreed that erotic materials get people excited. At the same time, six of every ten adults say that mass-communicated sexual materials

[15] For example, see Paul Hirsch, "The 'Scary World' of the Nonviewer and Other Anomolies: A Reanalysis of Gerbner et al.'s Findings on Cultivation Analysis," *Communication Research*, 7 (1980), pp. 403–456, and "On Not Learning from One's Own Mistakes: A Reanalysis of Gerbner et al.'s Findings on Cultivation Analysis, Part II," *Communication Research*, 8 (1981), pp. 3–37. Also see a rebuttal by Gerbner and his associates, "A Curious Journey into the Scary World of Paul Hirsch," *Communication Research*, 8 (1981), pp. 39–72; and a rejoinder by Hirsch on pp. 73–96. For one review of the issues and various findings, see "Television's Influence on Social Reality," by Robert P. Hawkins and Suzanne Pingree, in *Television and Behavior*, vol. 23, pp. 224–247. Also see Thomas D. Cook, Deborah H. Kendzierski, and Stephan V. Thomas, "The Implicit Assumptions of Television Research: An Analysis of the 1982 NIMH Report on Television and Behavior," *Public Opinion Quarterly*, 47, 2 (1983), pp. 161–201, esp. pp. 173–179.

[16] Gerbner and his associates have suggested two cultivation processes—"mainstreaming" and "resonance." *Mainstreaming* is defined as the sharing of common television-cultivated outlooks about the world among heavy viewers from demographic groups that would not ordinarily share the "mainstream" views found in television. *Resonance* means that the cultivation differentials are amplified under certain circumstances when heavy viewers' life experiences seem congruent with the views cultivated by television. See George Gerbner, Larry Gross, Michael Morgan, and Nancy Signorielli, "Charting the Mainstream: Television's Contributions to Political Orientations," *Journal of Communication*, 32, 2 (1982), pp. 100–127.

are informative; about half think that they improve marital relations; more than half say that they provide people an outlet for bottled up impulses.[17]

Further analyses indicate that public opinion in most American communities is divided concerning whether explicit sexual content in movies or in print should be available to anyone who wants it, or to adults only, or to no one. In general, more urbanized communities were less restrictive.[18] In some communities, concerned citizens have organized crusades against the commercial showing of sexually explicit communication content that they regard as offensive or harmful or both.

To study the issues, the U.S. Congress created a Commission on Obscenity and Pornography, which reported to the president and to the Congress in 1970. The commission established an Effects Panel to review and evaluate existing research on the effects of exposure to sexual stimuli from the mass media, to design and implement a program of new research, and to summarize and evaluate the total findings for the commission. The panel's investigation included a variety of studies.

The panel concluded that there is reason to doubt that erotica is a determinant of the extent or nature of people's habitual sexual behavior. It said that findings also suggest that exposure to erotica had no independent impact upon character and that research "provides no substantial basis for the belief that erotic materials constitute a primary or significant cause of the development of character deficits or that they operate as a significant determinative factor in causing crime and delinquency."[19] On the basis of these and other considerations, the commission recommended the repeal of "federal, state, and local legislation prohibiting the sale, exhibition, or distribution of sexual materials to consenting adults. . . ."[20] They favored and recommended legislation to protect young persons and others from having sexual materials thrust upon them without their consent through the mail or through open public display.

The commission's conclusions themselves were controversial; only twelve of the eighteen members subscribed to the recommendations. Some members remained unconvinced that erotic materials have no harmful social effects; others felt that there was no support for any restrictions on such media content, even for the young. Hence the public controversy continues.[21]

The public remains concerned about the social impact of sexual materials (pornographic or not) available through mass-communicated entertainment or elsewhere—about content that links sexual behavior and violence, for example, and about the treatment of humanity in these and other sexual contexts. Recent

[17] Commission on Obscenity and Pornography, *Report* (Washington, D.C.: U.S. Government Printing Office, 1970).

[18] Marc B. Glassman, "Community Standards of Patent Offensiveness: Public Opinion Data and Obscenity Law," *Public Opinion Quarterly*, 42, 2 (1978), pp. 161–170.

[19] Commission on Obscenity and Pornography, *Report*, pp. 286–287.

[20] Ibid., p. 57.

[21] In 1985 the U.S. Attorney General named a commission to study the effects of Pornography and recommend ways to control it. Its impact may have increased since the previous report, he said, due to changes in content (violence) and easier access at home through videorecorders and cable TV.

studies also have examined the depiction of sexual activities in ordinary (not pornographic) mass-communicated entertainment, especially television programs. They present content analyses reporting the variety and frequency of acts, explicit or implicit in the programs, that the researchers classify as sexual (hugging, kissing, touching, intercourse). Accounts can be found in the 1982 NIMH report to the surgeon general.[22]

PREJUDICE? "ARCHIE BUNKER" AND "ROOTS"

Sometimes a particular entertainment event seems so unusual that it raises public hopes or fears that it will have singularly beneficial or harmful effects. Two examples from American television are the original comedy series "All in the Family," and the 1977 docudrama "Roots."

The central character in "All in the Family," Archie Bunker, was portrayed as a bigot. Bunker's "humor" frequently consisted of racial, ethnic, and sexist slurs. The situation comedy was presented as a form of satire on racial prejudice and bigotry, openly violating previous television norms against expressions of racial and ethnic slurs. Defenders of the program praised it as a form of successful entertainment that could have the beneficial social effect of reducing prejudice by poking fun at bigotry and by making viewers aware of their own undesirable prejudices. Critics feared that the show might be encouraging racism and prejudice and could be especially harmful to impressionable children. Neither side offered much evidence at the time.

In 1974 social psychologists Neil Vidmar and Milton Rokeach recast the issue in terms of the possibility that prejudiced and unprejudiced persons were unequally likely to watch the show, and when they did see it, each would interpret it in line with predispositions. In order to test for such selective exposure and possible selective perception, the researchers studied a sample of adolescents in Illinois and adults in Ontario, Canada.[23] Respondents were classified as relatively high or low in prejudice on the basis of responses to questionnaire items, and then comparisons were made of their reactions to the program.

Frequent viewers of "All in the Family" among the adolescents from Illinois (but not among the adults from Canada) were more likely than infrequent viewers to be relatively high in prejudice, to admire the bigoted Archie more than his "liberal" son-in-law, Mike, and to condone Archie's ethnic slurs. The researchers conclude that highly prejudiced adolescents were more prone than less prejudiced ones to watch the show, a demonstration of selective exposure.

Some patterns of response among these modern television viewers are strikingly similar to those found in the pretelevision study of Mr. Biggott cartoons a quarter of a century earlier. Vidmar and Rokeach found that highly prejudiced

[22] See Elizabeth J. Roberts, "Television and Sexual Learning in Childhood," in *Television and Behavior*, vol. 2, pp. 209–223; L. Theresa Silverman, Joyce N. Sprafkin, and Eli A. Rubinstein, "Physical Contact and Sexual Behavior on Prime-Time TV," *Journal of Communication*, 29, 1 (1979), pp. 33–43.

[23] Neil Vidmar and Milton Rokeach, "Archie Bunker's Bigotry: A Study in Selective Perception and Exposure," *Journal of Communication*, 24 (1974), pp. 36–47.

persons were more likely than less prejudiced ones to admire Archie, to perceive him as making more sense (although relatively few viewers seemed prone to say so), and to see him as winning at the end of the program. The authors interpret such differences as supporting the hypothesis of selective perception. The study serves to remind us once again not to presume mass communication effects simply on the grounds of a program's apparent content and "intended message." We need to consider the social and social psychological processes that come into play.

"Roots" was the first extraordinarily long television docudrama (a mixture of history and fiction), broadcast for eight consecutive nights—a total of twelve hours. Based on the novel by Alex Haley, "Roots" told a dramatic story about black people in the United States and about black slavery in our history. Some critics praised the program and believed that its portrayal of the early treatment of black slaves in America would help to reduce race prejudice among contemporary white viewers. Other people condemned the program for its lack of historical accuracy and feared that the dramatic portrayal of white characters as brutal and blacks as sympathetic victims would stir up racial tensions and increase prejudice, especially among black viewers. Neither side offered much evidence at the time.

Within three months after the final episode of "Roots," no less than six communication studies of people's reactions to the program were published. A summary review of findings from five of these studies (one national and four local surveys) concludes that most people who viewed "Roots" enjoyed it, and that many believed it would leave white viewers with more sympathy, empathy, and tolerance for blacks, having seen what their race endured under slavery. A sizable minority of respondents believed the program would leave black viewers with increased hostility toward whites. But "when actual racial attitude is tapped," the reviewer states, "very little evidence of movement is detected. Obviously, one series of programs will not result in massive attitude change; however, many people in the general population were actually expecting this type of effect."[24]

At least one of the studies, a survey in Cleveland by Kenneth K. Hur and John P. Robinson, suggests that selective exposure and selective perception affected the program's influence on white respondents (although another study by Hur did not report selective exposure among adolescents). Hur and Robinson conclude that their data "hardly suggest that 'Roots' had the influence on the racial attitudes of whites that was widely attributed to it by media critics and observers."[25] They suggest "that the possible effects of 'Roots' on the perceptions of the hardships of slavery were mainly felt by those whites already sympathetic to the program's content." And they interpret their data as "consistent with both selective-exposure and perception hypotheses being at work among our white sample. In contrast to the assumptions of most media analysis and commentary, while a majority of our white sample did watch 'Roots' and most

[24] Stuart H. Surlin, " 'Roots' Research: A Summary of Findings," *Journal of Broadcasting,* 22, 3 (1978), pp. 309–320; quote, p. 318.

[25] Kenneth K. Hur and John P. Robinson, "The Social Impact of 'Roots,'" *Journalism Quarterly,* 55 (1978), pp. 19–24, 83; quotes, pp. 24, 83.

thought it historically informative and accurate, there is little evidence of it producing conversions in racial attitudes."

"Most thought it historically informative and accurate . . ."—there's a finding with latent social implications! All six studies of "Roots" report, in one detail or another, that the majority of people interviewed said they thought that this television docudrama—an entertainment cross between documentary and fiction—was informative, that they learned from it, that it presented accurate portrayals of the historical times, of slavery, of black history, and of the parts played by black and white people in that history. Although none of the studies (concerned as they were with the program's possible effects on racial attitudes) draw this conclusion, it may be that the docudrama is another vehicle through which mass-communicated entertainment contributes to people's views of social reality and to publicly shared beliefs about that reality—in this instance a historical one.

For many people, the television docudrama may be a major, perhaps the main, source of "information" about certain contemporary and historical events, such as the Great Depression of the 1930s, the Holocaust, and the Skokie "march." Even people who have other knowledge about the event may add details or impressions from the docudrama that come, over time, to be blended into their "knowledge" of what happened. Therefore the docudrama, as sociologist Jerry M. Lewis puts it, is a television format that "makes special truth claims that need to be rigorously evaluated."[26]

As an example, Lewis evaluated the docudrama film "Kent State" made for NBC television in 1981. The film was about the tragic events at Kent State University in May 1970, when National Guardsmen fired at students during a confrontation on campus, killing four people and wounding a number of others. In Lewis's judgment, the film was visually accurate and mainly chronologically correct, but it contained a number of factual errors or misimpressions about certain major events, such as that students sang "Light My Fire" as the campus's ROTC building burned to the ground (which Lewis says did not happen; he was there). Lewis suggests that this and other "errors" may lead to "a public conception of fact about what happened at Kent State which is based on error and a distortion of reality."[27]

SOCIAL VALUES AND CULTURAL INFLUENCE

Just as some people fear that young and adult viewers are led to aggressive and antisocial behavior by the violence shown on television, others hope that viewers can be led to prosocial behavior by "nice" television content. Research testing

[26] Jerry M. Lewis, "*Kent State*—The Movie," *Journal of Popular Film and Television*, 9, 1 (1981), pp. 13–18; quote, p. 13.

[27] Ibid., p. 18. As another example, people in Atlanta, Georgia, were concerned that a 1985 television docudrama, "The Atlanta Child Murders," might be misconstrued by the public as a documentary. The network then agreed to broadcast "advisories" informing viewers that the program was not a documentary and that dramatic license had been taken. See Joe Logan, "Atlanta angered by docudrama on child killings," *The Philadelphia Inquirer* (February 7, 1985), pp. 1E, 6E. Also see *Time*, 125, 6 (February 11, 1985), p. 99.

this idea mainly follows the same psychological experimental paradigm that is found in research on the effects of television violence. The results of these experiments are summarized and interpreted in the 1982 report to the surgeon general as "demonstrating that television and film programs can modify viewers' social behavior in a prosocial direction."[28] But since this conclusion is drawn mainly from experimental studies in the laboratory or under other contrived conditions, its applicability to people watching or listening to mass entertainment under ordinary social conditions needs further testing. (The field experiment on The Great American Values Test, described in Chapter 7, is an exception.)

Some authors argue that mass entertainment has important social consequences when it crosses national boundaries.[29] They maintain that the cultural values and messages contained in imported mass-communicated entertainment (and in news and information) can pollute and displace local culture, especially in small or developing countries. Even the very style of the supplier's mass communication production, its technology and values, influences the communication systems of these countries.

Communication scholar Herbert I. Schiller, for example, argues that mass communication has become a mechanism for the cultural dominance of Third World nations by multinational corporations (mainly Western) seeking world markets for their goods and services. To that end, he asserts, they export mass-communicated news and entertainment that supports a value system essential to their commercial purpose. He states too that ruling groups in some Third World countries collaborate in this venture by importing Western goods, services, technology, and communication programs and techniques. He calls the process *cultural imperialism.*[30]

Other authors also have expressed concern that mass communication from abroad may endanger the cultural values of a society and its members. Most criticism seems directed at the apparent mass communication dominance of Western societies (especially the United States) and other capitalistic nations. But concern can be raised also about the impact of mass communication exported from the Soviet Union and other Communist societies. Their news, information, and entertainment reflect the Communist view and also threaten the culture of societies that import them. "Cultural invasion," if such there be, can come from many political directions.

Commenting on this situation in a recent work on basic issues in mass communication, Everette Dennis asserts:

It is said that media imperialism results in cultural imperialism and implants Western ideas and values, thus upsetting natural, evolutionary development. At its core, this argument is ideological. Those on the Left decry the existence and impact of cul-

---

[28] *Television and Behavior*, vol. 2, p. 255.

[29] For example, see Jeremy Tunstall, *The Media Are American: Anglo-American Media in the World* (New York: Columbia University Press, 1977). For another discussion, see Elihu Katz, George Wedell, Michael Pilsworth, and Dov Shinar, *Broadcasting in the Third World* (Cambridge, MA: Harvard University Press, 1977).

[30] Herbert I. Schiller, *Communication and Cultural Domination* (White Plains, NY: M. E. Sharpe, Inc., 1976).

tural imperialism and those on the Right defend the contributions of Western communications enterprises in developing countries. [He adds] The reasons for the dominance of American content are obvious. We produce more programming and make
it available more economically than any other nation in the world. . . . Unfortunately
there is little research on questions of impact, effects, and influence, so we are left
with much speculation.[31]

The public fear of cultural invasion and subsequent cultural pollution, perhaps even cultural dominance, has itself had social consequences, as in laws restricting the amount of foreign programs that can be broadcast by domestic
television stations, restrictions on foreign ownership of magazines and other
mass media, censorship of imported motion picture films, and other measures.
Such concern also lies behind some of the issues surrounding reactions to the
possibility of international direct satellite broadcasting and nations' rights to
control the flow of information and entertainment within their borders versus
beliefs in the right to a free flow of information and communication throughout
the world.

It is not a simple matter, as we have seen, to establish the social effects of
mass entertainment and information. The possibility suggested by some of the
works cited in this chapter is that people, both children and adults, learn something about society's values, about life and how to cope, from what they see and
hear through mass communication. To understand this better, we need to direct
our attention to the topic of socialization and to examine the part that mass
communication and interpersonal communication play in this social process.
We consider this next.

[31] See Everette E. Dennis and John C. Merrill, *Basic Issues in Mass Communication: A Debate*
(New York: Macmillan, 1984); quotes, pp. 183, 184.

CHAPTER 9

Social Consequences of Mass Communication: Mass Communication and Socialization

Socialization is the social process by which individuals come to belong to a society and acquire some of its values, beliefs, perspectives, knowledge, social norms, and preferences—in short, its culture.[1] People are thereby more or less assimilated into the social system. This happens throughout life—as, for example, babies learn how to communicate, children are instructed to know "right from wrong," individuals are groomed for particular occupational roles and other social statuses, and immigrants become accustomed to their new country. It happens in many social transitions involving real or anticipated changes in social status.

Through socialization we acquire some of the culture of our social group and internalize (in some measure) its concepts and social norms, thus coming to take into account the social expectations of others. Through our social membership we are protected as infants and subsequently equipped with the tools for survival and growth—language, ideas, knowledge, skills, and other pieces of our culture.

Socialization is never "total." No one can know or be responsible for the total normative system of any society. But we are accountable for those norms appropriate to the social roles that we play. Socialization is also an ongoing pro-

---

[1] Socialization is a subject of interest to scholars from many disciplines, especially sociology, social psychology, anthropology, and psychology. The term *socialization* has a variety of meanings among these scholars. Some authors use it to refer to psychological changes within the individual (as in beliefs or knowledge) that are in accord with the society's or group's approved views. Used in this way, socialization sometimes is regarded as a form of personal learning, development, or adjustment. Others use the term to refer to the social processes by which an individual is introduced into the society's or group's culture. For others, the term refers to the institutionalized ways that society inducts persons into membership. Other meanings are possible. I will try to make clear the particular meaning being used by an author or by myself throughout this chapter. We exclude studies on the deliberate use of mass communication or mass media technology for educational and instructional purposes in scholastic matters, such as in classrooms or televised courses. Educational communication is an important topic in its own right, but it falls ouside the focus of this book. For some contemporary social psychological perspectives on socialization, see Diane M. Bush and Roberta G. Simmons, "Socialization Processes over the Life Course," in *Social Psychology: Sociological Perspectives*, eds. Morris Rosenberg and Ralph H. Turner (New York: Basic Books, 1981), chap. 5; Viktor Gecas, "Contexts of Socialization," Ibid., chap. 6; and Jerold Heiss, "Social Roles," Ibid., chap. 4. For insights into communicational aspects of socialization, see Ray L. Birdwhistell, *Kinesics and Context* (Philadelphia: University of Pennsylvania Press, 1970).

cess, from childhood through old age. We are usually socialized about some behavior while we are young; we acquire, for example, basic norms about proper eating behavior. But socialization about other roles, adult sexual conduct, for example, may be postponed until later. We participate in continuous socialization and resocialization throughout life as society's norms change or our own social circumstances change—as we move, for example, from civilian status to military life and back, or simply grow up and move through life.

Major responsibility for socialization sometimes rests with different persons or social organizations, depending on the normative area involved, but others also may contribute to the process. In our society, as examples, early childhood toilet training is usually the parents' responsibility, whereas occupational training is given on the job by other members of the occupation or by specialists in a vocational or professional school. Some socialization involves deliberate training, but some also occurs less formally, even apparently inadvertently, when a person picks up cues about proper behavior and social norms without explicit instruction.

Mass communication plays a part in this complex process of socialization, especially in societies such as ours where the mass media are ubiquitous. At various times in our lives we learn about some social norms from the mass media. But learning about social norms is not the same things as being socialized, which requires that we make these norms part of our own social and personal code (or feel appropriately guilty if we don't).

Usually socialization requires interaction with others who are significant in our lives or important at the time. These are the persons whose power and influence over us during social interaction induces us, bit by bit throughout our lifetimes, to subscribe to pieces of our culture. They lead us, through social interaction, to want to behave as expected by themselves, by other "right-thinking" members of the society, and ultimately by ourselves. Since there is no real social interaction between ourselves and the mass media, they possess none of the seductive or coercive powers of interpersonal communicators during socialization.[2] Nevertheless, it would be a mistake to dismiss mass communication as irrelevant to the socialization process. There is a growing body of communications research, much of it recent, that bears upon this topic.

MASS COMMUNICATION AND EARLY SOCIALIZATION

The role of mass communication in the socialization process probably is not uniform throughout one's lifetime. We have more research information about this role for some ages than for others. Not much is known about it in infancy, for example, despite anecdotal observations that some parents "prop up" the baby in front of the family television set, as a kind of visual pacifier. Sociologists have not been very concerned with studying what role mass communication plays in

[2] But the mass media sometimes give the illusion of social interaction with familiar persons presented on television, radio, motion pictures or in print, an illusion that has been labeled *parasocial interaction* by Donald Horton and R. Richard Wohl in "Mass Communication and Para-Social Interaction," *Psychiatry*, 19 (1956), pp. 215–229.

our socialization as infants, probably because of the much greater importance attached to the communication roles of parents and other people surrounding the very young child.

It has been suggested by Herbert Hyman and others that mass communication plays an indirect role in children's socialization by providing parents with information and advice about the proper care and training of infants and children. This "secondary" socialization "works specifically and strategically upon the ways in which a socializer handles his or her role." Hyman quotes Davison and Yu's comment that "Syndicated newspaper columns and popular magazine stories on how to bring up children, directed to parents, may have greater effects than all the TV programs directed to children. The same may be true of popular 'baby-care books,' which circulate in millions of copies."[3]

Considerable research has been addressed to the role of mass communication in the socialization of children beyond infancy—from preschool through adolescence. Much of this research is psychological in its approach, studying mass media's apparent effects on the individual child and paying less attention to the social processes involved in socialization.[4] These studies often begin with a model of the communication process in which mass communication content is treated as a direct stimulus to which each individual child responds.

Studies in this psychological tradition are likely to ask, for example, whether children who watch a lot of television, or who see some particular televised content, are more likely than others to express certain social opinions and to have more stereotypical views about social behavior. These studies often contribute to our knowledge by determining whether a statistical relationship exists between a person's mass communication behavior and his or her social views.

Once a statistical relationship has been determined, we would like to be able to interpret it, to study the conditions and circumstances under which it might be stronger or weaker, and to understand how it came about, especially the underlying social processes. Thus some sociological or social psychologically oriented studies are concerned with how the associations that have been demonstrated between individual's mass communication behavior and their expressed beliefs, opinions, and other views are modified or conditioned by specific social factors. In so doing, these studies go beyond earlier communication models of a simple direct stimulus-response connection between mass communication con-

---

[3] Herbert H. Hyman, "Mass Communication and Socialization," in *Mass Communication Research*, eds. W. Phillips Davison and Frederick T. C. Yu (New York: Praeger, 1974), chap. 3; quotation, p. 60.

[4] Most of this psychological research, while interesting and instructive, falls outside our sociological focus here. For an account of studies on how children of different age groups view, interpret, and react to television's form and content, see Jennings Bryant and Daniel R. Anderson, eds., *Children's Understanding of Television: Research on Attention and Comprehension* (New York: Academic Press, 1983). For an account of research on television and child development, see Hope Kelly and Howard Gardner, eds., *Viewing Children through Television* (San Francisco: Jossey-Bass, 1981). For a series of papers addressing a special issue, see Gordon L. Berry and Claudia Mitchell-Kernan, eds., *Television and the Socialization of the Minority Child* (New York: Academic Press, 1982). For an account of an attempt to reduce children's sex-role stereotyping through television programming, see Frederick Williams, Robert LaRose, and Frederica Frost, *Children, Television, and Sex-Role Stereotyping* (New York: Praeger, 1981). For an overview, see Donald F. Roberts and Christine M. Bachen, "Mass Communication Effects," *Annual Review of Psychology*, 32, pp. 307–356 (Palo Alto, CA: Annual Reviews, Inc., 1981).

tent and the individual's reaction. An example of this contemporary approach can be found in a complex series of studies by Bradley Greenberg, Charles Atkin, and their associates. We will focus here on their findings about how a statistical relationship between children's television viewing and their ideas about normal family roles was strengthened (or reduced) depending on the parents' behavior.[5]

First, Greenberg and his colleagues analyzed the content of three years' worth of "family" television programs broadcast during prime time. They classified the interaction among the television family members as "going toward" one another (being supportive), "going away" (evading one another), or "going against" one another (opposing one another). The content analysis was more complex than this, but we simplify its description for our purposes here. In a related study, the researchers found that family television shows from different genres (situation comedies or drama) had different rates of physical and verbal aggression in them.

In a third study, the researchers collected data from more than 600 children from the fourth, sixth, and eighth grades in schools in predominantly working-class neighborhoods in Detroit and San Jose and South Berkeley, California. They measured how much each child watched various family television programs classified into types developed out of the previous content analyses. Four measures were used: viewing programs showing a lot of affiliative behavior ("going toward") among family members, viewing programs showing relatively little such affiliative behavior, viewing programs showing a lot of conflict behavior ("going against") among family members, and total viewing of family-type programs, whatever their content. The researchers then examined the extent to which children's ideas about real family behavior varied according to their viewing of different kinds of family programs on television. Such variation, they reasoned, might imply that children were learning about family roles from television.

The differences in ideas about family life expressed by children contrasted by their television viewing were small but statistically significant: that is, not likely to have occurred by chance if there were no real differences in ideas held by the contrasted groups. Children who watched relatively more television than others were more likely to express beliefs that real-life family interaction is affiliative in nature. This association held regardless of the kind of family shows watched (but it should be noted that family shows portrayed mainly affiliative behavior; there were relatively few conflict portrayals for children to see). Children who frequently watch television's family programs are more likely than others to "appear to believe that family members in real life show support and concern for each other."[6]

These statistical associations, however, need not mean that television view-

[5] See Nancy L. Buerkel-Rothfuss, Bradley S. Greenberg, Charles K. Atkin, and Kimberly Neundorf, "Learning about the Family from Television," *Journal of Communication*, 32, 3 (1982), pp. 191–201. For details on the content analysis, see Bradley S. Greenberg et al., *Life on Television* (Norwood, NJ: Ablex, 1980).

[6] Buerkel-Rothfuss et al., "Learning about the Family," p. 197.

ing led to the formation of these beliefs. Other explanations are possible. (One alternative, among others, is that children who think that family life is nice and supportive are more likely to choose to watch family shows than are children who have a more negative image of family life.)

What about the role of parents in all this? The researchers examined the extent to which the original associations between children's television viewing and their ideas about real families were modified when parents seemed to intervene in various ways. They considered, for example, what happened to these associations when parents controlled their children's television viewing, provided guidance as to what programs to watch, watched family shows along with their children, made comments about the shows, and talked with their children about family roles.

In general, each of these kinds of family intervention seemed to strengthen somewhat (although not greatly) the original statistical associations between television viewing habits and children's beliefs that family life tends to be positive, supportive, and affiliative. The authors infer that "The control parents exert over viewing, the shows they guide their children to watch, the comments they make about television families, the shows they watch with their children, and the amount of time they spend talking and interacting with their children can all make a difference in the beliefs those children hold about how family members behave in the real world."[7]

Recent communications research has been concerned also with the mass media's possible influence on children's views of social roles other than those in the family. Most current research has focused on the influence of television. A comprehensive review of some recent findings about television and "role socialization" appears in a report on television and behavior delivered to the National Institute of Mental Health in 1982. The review covers research on five "social roles" centered on family, sex, race, occupation, and age.

Most communications research on such matters, according to the reviewer (Bradley Greenberg), consists of content analyses of how television depicts family members, men or women, black or white characters, occupations, and age cohorts. These accounts may provide the basis for informed speculation about television's contribution to learning about these roles. But few of them attempt to show empirically a connection between specific mass media content and socialization. Studies otherwise dealing directly with evidence of television's "effects" on role socialization also are scarce. Greenberg comments: "Proof of impact . . . has not been pursued with much vigor."[8] Most of the studies on the effects of mass communication content on role socialization are correlational in nature (as discussed above), showing relationships between television viewing and ideas expressed about sex roles, occupational roles, and the like.

---

[7] Ibid., pp. 200–201.

[8] Bradley S. Greenberg, "Television and Role Socialization: An Overview," in *Television and Behavior: Ten Years of Scientific Progress and Implications for the Eighties,* Vol. 2, eds. David Pearl, Lorraine Bouthilet, and Joyce Lazar (National Institute of Mental Health, Washington, DC: U.S. Government Printing Office, 1982), quotation, p. 188.

Early Political Socialization

Research on the socialization of children and adolescents into political behavior and orientation has expanded greatly since 1959, when the concept of *political socialization* was coined by Herbert Hyman in his pioneering work on the subject. Hyman called for the study of those differential childhood experiences through which members of various social groups learn about politics. Knowledge about these experiences, he argues, will help us to understand continuities in patterns of adult political behavior, such as regularities in individual adult political behavior and stable differences between groups of adults. He directs attention more specifically "to the *socialization* of the individual, his learning of social patterns corresponding to his societal positions as mediated through various agencies of society."[9] The agency receiving first, but by no means the only, consideration in his early work was the family.

The original concept of political socialization has been broadened considerably over the years, as we will see in a moment. This breadth is nicely demonstrated in a recent statement by communications researchers Charles Atkin and Walter Gantz, who define it as "a developmental process by which children and adolescents acquire cognitions, attitudes, and behaviors relating to their political environment."[10]

Around the early 1970s, mass communication theorists and researchers interested in understanding political behavior suggested that the mass media deserved to be examined as possibly important agencies for political socialization in our society. Since then, a number of studies of the mass media's role in political socialization have related the individual youth's use of the mass media to his or her political knowledge, beliefs, attitudes, opinions, and behavior.

Several studies have demonstrated statistical associations between political knowledge and reading newspapers and watching television, for example. Others have examined statistical associations between young people's media use and their interest in political affairs, attitudes toward political leaders, and other so-called affective traits. Atkin suggests that the use of the mass media, especially the news media, significantly influences some of these political expressions—for example, increasing political interest, affecting attitudes toward political leaders, and influencing political opinions. But "more basic dispositions such as political efficacy and party identification appear to be resistant to change."[11]

Studies have related young people's media use, especially paying attention to printed news and to public affairs broadcasts, to such political behavior as electioneering, attending political rallies, and joining political organizations. One obvious difficulty in interpreting such statistical associations is that following political news in the mass media may itself be a form of political behavior, like

[9] Herbert H. Hyman, *Political Socialization: A Study in the Psychology of Political Behavior* (Glencoe, IL: Free Press, 1959), quotation, p. 25.

[10] Charles K. Atkin and Walter Gantz, "Television News and Political Socialization," *Public Opinion Quarterly*, 42 (1978), pp. 183–197; quotation, p. 184.

[11] Charles K. Atkin, "Communication and Political Socialization," in *Handbook of Political Communication*, eds. Dan D. Nimmo and Keith R. Sanders (Beverly Hills, CA: Sage, 1981), chap. 11, pp. 299–328; quotation, p. 316.

electioneering. It is also difficult to determine which behavior—media use or political behavior—comes first, since either one could stimulate the other. Probably they are interrelated.

The same difficulties arise in interpreting statistical associations between following political news in the mass media and holding political conversations with parents and friends. Adolescents who are interested in politics (for whatever reasons) are likely both to follow politics in the mass media and to talk about them; they also are politically active in other ways.

The measures of political socialization used in some studies, such as adolescents' knowledge about political news, are interesting, but may not capture the central and enduring features of political socialization. Socialization that sets patterns of adult political behavior involves more than conveying a few facts. Socialization for citizenship in a democracy (or in another form of society) implies more enduring lessons about one's place in society, political identity, social values, social norms about political rights and duties, and one's civic roles—to mention but a few matters.[12] Fortunately, recent communications research is reaching out to examine some of these factors.

The study of mass communication's influence on young people's political behavior seems a promising direction. Participation in political organizations, campaigns, discussions, and other such activities provides precisely the context within which young people might be socialized into future political and civic roles. Mass communication may encourage or discourage such participation, by portraying political activity or inactivity as appropriate behavior for young people of various social classes, ethnic, or other backgrounds. Furthermore, it may turn out that persons who are socializing the youth about political behavior—whether in organizations, in the family, in the classroom, or elsewhere—use mass communication in the process.

Parents' Mediation in Early Socialization

The mass media's role in socialization, as Frederick Elkin and Gerald Handel put it in their book on children's socialization, cannot "be considered in isolation. They are ordinarily seen or heard in group settings, and the family and peer group have a considerable influence in guiding exposure to, and generally defining, their content."[13] We have seen this to be true for television, for example, in many settings. Studies of preschool children's use of television in Great Britain and Ireland, to mention but one example, report that mothers play an active role in encouraging and discouraging children's television viewing and in discussing programs with them.[14]

[12] For a research example, see Herbert H. Hyman, Charles R. Wright, and Terence K. Hopkins, *Applications of Methods of Evaluation: Four Studies of the Encampment for Citizenship* (Berkeley and Los Angeles: University of California Press, 1962).

[13] Frederick Elkin and Gerald Handel, *The Child and Society*, 3rd ed. (New York: Random House, 1978), p. 161.

[14] This study was conducted by James D. Halloran. For a summary, see Erentraud Homberg, ed., *Pre-school Children and Television: Two Studies Carried Out in Three Countries* (New York: K. G. Saur Publishing, 1978).

Adults also play a role in children's use and interpretation of other mass media. As the authors of a recent report on television and pre-school children in Sweden aptly point out, "In using other mass media, pre-school children require even more support from adults than when watching television and listening to the radio. They cannot read by themselves, they cannot operate a record player or a tape-recorder alone, and they also need an older person to accompany them to the cinema."[15] While older children may be less dependent on adults than these preschool children, the family and others (including other children) nonetheless play a role in affecting mass communication's contributions to socialization.

Communications research has explored how parents talk about television stories with their children, interpret the stories, and draw upon them for examples and illustrations to help socialize their children. Our example here comes from the work of communications researcher Paul Messaris. Messaris conducted exploratory, open-ended interviews (that is, interviews during which the respondent can speak at length and in detail about the topic) with a sample of approximately 100 mothers of young children in Philadelphia. These mothers spoke of the variety of ways in which they had turned television incidents into occasions for socialization.[16]

The practices reported include teaching the child the distinction between what happens on television and "real life," distinguishing among types of television programs (fiction and news), discussing the degrees of accuracy and representativeness of television's apparent realism, supplying additional information about topics that appeared on television, evaluating conduct and events shown on television, and encouraging the child to imitate or not to imitate televised behavior. Such informal, seemingly casual discussion about television occurs as part of the day-to-day interaction between mother and child, and often reinforces points being made through socialization on other occasions and by other means.

Messaris cites a number of examples and comments from the mothers. One, for instance, used a television program as an opportunity to instruct her young son and warn him about real dangers and risks in life:

> ". . . this thing they had on the runaway kids. We had a big discussion about that because I told him that, you know, the kids . . . they do run away, they do get in trouble, and . . . they get in things like this white slavery stuff."[17]

Other examples include instances in which mothers explained to children that in real life (apparently in contrast to televised cartoons), one doesn't bounce back up again if "flattened like a pancake"; that persons who seem to die in television drama are only actors or actresses pretending, but death in televised news ac-

---

[15] The study was directed by Leni Filipson. For a summary, see Homberg, *Pre-school Children and Television;* quotation, p. 75.

[16] See Paul Messaris, "Parents, Children, and Television," in *Intermedia,* 2nd ed., eds. Gary Gumpert and Robert Cathcart (New York: Oxford University Press, 1982), pp. 580–598; Paul Messaris and Carla Sarett, "On the Consequences of Television-Related Parent-Child Interaction," *Human Communication Research,* 7 (1981), pp. 226–244.

[17] Messaris, "Parents, Children, and Television," p. 586.

counts about war are for real; that witches are only make-believe; that real jobs are seldom so glamorous and adventurous as portrayed on television; that normal family life is not the way its presented on certain television family dramas.

Mothers discussed such topics with their children (in connection with something seen on television) as the nature of American westward migration, slavery, and the meaning of the Jewish Seder. Messaris's study is exploratory and limited to the experiences of the mothers he interviewed—but what a rich variety of experiences they report! The findings clearly demonstrate the need to take into account the active role of people such as parents, friends, siblings, teachers, and others in mediating mass communication content during socialization.

In a further, systematic analysis of the interview reports, Messaris and Sari Thomas (also a communications researcher) address the sociologically interesting question of whether mothers in different social classes differed also in the kinds of comments they made to their children when referring to television in socialization.[18] Comparisons were made between the experiences reported by mothers in households that the researchers classified (for purposes of this study only) as relatively upper-middle or lower-middle class. The former usually were households where the breadwinner was in business or a profession; the latter usually were households where the breadwinner was employed in sales, clerical, or blue-collar occupations.

A majority of mothers from both social classes said that they gave children additional information about some topic shown on television and explained to them that television shows are not real life or representative of it. At the same time, lower-middle class mothers were more likely than upper-middle class ones to have confirmed for their children the realism of television stories that gave a negative portrayal of crime or other undesirable behavior in order to discourage children from possibly being tempted by such life styles.

A sizable minority of mothers said that they made evaluative comments about television characters and their behavior to encourage the child to imitate certain behaviors and to discourage imitation of certain others. Mothers in lower-middle class families were more explicit about these directions. Upper-middle class mothers seemed more likely to make nondirective comments about the televised behavior, making clear their own personal evaluation of it, but leaving the child to work out the implications for his or her own behavior. The authors interpret this finding as compatible with social research that suggests there is a norm of relative "autonomy" in the socialization of children in upper-middle class families, who are expected to fill managerial, professional, or entrepreneurial occupations when they grow up.

One needs to take care, as the authors note, not to make too much of these findings. The data do not permit generalization beyond the specific families studied. Nevertheless, they suggest the importance of considering social class and other social structural factors when studying parents' discussions about tele-

[18] Paul Messaris and Sari Thomas, "Social-Class Differences in Mothers' Comments about Television." I wish to thank Professors Messaris and Thomas for making an unpublished report of this study available to me; the account in this chapter is based on that report.

vision with their children and the ways in which such discussions link mass communication into the socialization process.

GROWTH AND THE SEARCH FOR GUIDANCE

Throughout our lifetime, the parts played in the socialization process by the mass media, various social institutions, other people, and ourselves are likely to change. For example, parents are probably less likely to interpret the moral lessons of television programs for adolescents than for very young children. Adolescents and adults, in turn, take an increasingly more active part in initiating their own socialization after childhood, sometimes anticipating their movement into new social roles.[19]

People sometimes refer to the mass media for guidance about social norms when anticipating new social roles or for guidance about current roles. A few studies illustrate this tendency. Research in the heyday of radio soap operas, for example, found that some listeners believed they could get "prescriptions" for handling some of life's problems from such daytime radio serials.[20] The more or less self-conscious use of the mass media for getting clues about certain social norms varies with one's social situation. Brenda Dervin and Bradley Greenberg report, for example, that low-income black adults were more likely than middle-class white adults to say that people watch television because they can learn from the mistakes of others, that television shows how other people solve the same problems they have, and that they can learn a good deal from it.[21] Walter Gerson, in a frequently cited study of black and white adolescents, reports that black youths were more likely than whites to say that they used the mass media to learn about or to verify social norms about "dating."[22]

The counseling activities of the mass media may become formalized and institutionalized, as for example in the *bintelbrief*, a regular publication of questions and advice in Jewish newspapers read by many immigrants to America earlier in the century. And we are familiar with contemporary letters for advice written to newspaper columnists.[23]

These examples demonstrate that people do, under various conditions, turn

[19] See J. T. Mortimer and R. G. Simmons, "Adult Socialization," in *Annual Review of Sociology* (Palo Alto, CA: Annual Reviews, Inc., 1978), vol. 4, pp. 421–454; Orville G. Brim, Jr., and Stanton Wheeler, *Socialization after Childhood* (New York: Wiley, 1966); Robert K. Merton, *Social Theory and Social Structure*, rev. ed. (Glencoe, IL: Free Press, 1957), pp. 265–271; and Herbert H. Hyman, "Mass Communication and Socialization," pp. 50–54.

[20] Herta Herzog, "What Do We Really Know about Daytime Radio Serial Listeners?" in *Radio Research, 1942–1943*, eds. Paul F. Lazarsfeld and Frank Stanton (New York: Duell, Sloan and Pearce, 1944), pp. 3–33; also see John C. Sutherland and Shelley J. Siniawsky, "The Treatment and Resolution of Moral Violations on Soap Operas," *Journal of Communication*, 32, 2 (1982), pp. 67–74; and Muriel Cantor and Suzanne Pingree, *The Soap Opera* (Beverly Hills, CA: Sage Publications, 1983).

[21] Brenda Dervin and Bradley Greenberg, "The Communication Environment of the Urban Poor," in *Current Perspectives in Mass Communication Research*, vol. I, eds. F. Gerald Kline and Phillip J. Tichenor (Beverly Hills, CA: Sage Publications, 1972), chap. 7.

[22] Walter Gerson, "Mass Media Socialization Behavior: Negro-White Differences," *Social Forces*, 45 (1966), pp. 44–50.

[23] See Hyman, *Political Socialization*, p. 63.

to mass communication for guidance. It contributes in some manner, along with other sources of social norms such as the family, school, and peer group. We can learn something about the relative weight people give to the mass media as normative guides from what people say about them, although these statements cannot be taken alone as evidence of the media's actual significance. People may be unable to assess the relative importance of the mass media, family, friends, church, school, or other forces for shaping personal ideas, views, opinions, and beliefs. But when asked to do so in a survey, the ubiquitous mass media seem the popular first choice. As an example, Steven Chaffee, L. Scott Ward, and Leonard Tipton report that a sample of high school students in Wisconsin rated the mass media as the most important sources of information and opinions about current affairs, in comparison with such alternative sources as parents, friends, and teachers.[24]

A rare example of a direct inquiry into the relative priority that adolescents would give to different sources of advice about social behavior is found in an interesting study by Raymond Forer of reactions to a radio program called "Mind Your Manners." The program featured a panel of "typical" teenagers who discussed personal problems submitted by listeners and then gave advice. Forer surveyed several thousand high school students in Connecticut. Listeners to the program were asked, among other things, whether they followed the advice given by the teenage panel and what would happen if this advice conflicted with norms prescribed by family, friends, or other sources.

Most of the listeners thought that the advice given on the program was very good and that they would ordinarily follow it. But most of them said they would not follow the program's advice if it conflicted with the advice of their parents or siblings, religious leaders, older friend, grandparents, aunt, or uncle. Thus, to the extent that we can take the students' answers at face value, the family's version of social norms would seem to take priority.[25]

In a study during the Vietnam war, Neil Hollander asked high school seniors in two schools in Washington a set of questions about their thoughts concerning war. He then asked them to indicate which of eighteen possible sources of information they thought they had used in arriving at each of their own views about war. These students mentioned the mass media, especially television, more frequently than such other sources as church, family, friends, and school.[26]

Another study from the same era, using replies from more than 2,600 elementary and junior high school students in three eastern states, also compared the mass media, family, schools, and church as sources of influence on youth's ideas about war. Statistical associations were taken as signifying that mass media (or other source) played a role in socialization (an interpretation discussed earlier in this chapter). Children who were relatively heavier users of the mass media (mainly television and newspapers, in this instance) were more informed about

[24] Steven Chaffee, L. Scott Ward, and Leonard Tipton, "Mass Communication and Political Socialization," *Journalism Quarterly*, 57 (1970), pp. 647–659, 666.

[25] Raymond Forer, "The Impact of a Radio Program on Adolescents," *Public Opinion Quarterly*, 19 (1955), pp. 184–194.

[26] Neil Hollander, "Adolescents and the War: The Sources of Socialization," *Journalism Quarterly*, 58 (1971), pp. 472–479.

the war in Vietnam. But there was no significant association between the amount of television viewing or newspaper reading and the children's opinions about the Vietnam war or attitudes toward war in general.

The investigator, Howard Tolley, Jr., suggests that "Personal contacts at home, school, or in the community undoubtedly determine the child's first ideas and encourage attention to publications which confirm that viewpoint," and that "the impact of both the press and the broadcast media depend to some extent on socializing agents more directly and personally responsible for educating the young." He concludes: "Children's outlook on war in general varies according to their parents' attitudes on Vietnam and the types of school they attend, but has little relation to reading or viewing habits."[27]

These studies, then, underscore the need to see mass communication, together with interpersonal communication, as an integral part of the total process by which young people become socialized into our culture. We turn our attention now to the socialization of adults.

MASS COMMUNICATION AND ADULT SOCIALIZATION

Ordinarily, most adults have had many more years of socialization into their particular culture than children have had. For them, further socialization usually involves reinforcement and elaboration of previously learned social norms, or their modification, and learning some new ones. Exceptions occur when there is a major shift in social roles, as in the case of adult immigrants who have been socialized in another culture. When relatively major changes in values, norms, and behavior are expected of adults, the process of socialization is called *resocialization*. It implies giving up some important old social norms and replacing them with new ones. Total resocialization is rare, perhaps never happens, but under certain circumstances a large amount of a person's previously acquired sets of beliefs, values, ideas, and norms may be replaced by new ones—or at least social efforts are made to bring about such change.

Resocialization efforts sometimes are concentrated in special settings apart from the rest of society (such as a military training camp), where the individual is almost totally surrounded by an environment designed for that purpose. The uncontrolled processes of mass communication seem antithetical to resocialization in such total institutions, threatening their impermeability and reminding socializees of the values of the world outside that they have left behind. Under these circumstances, steps may be taken to minimize people's access to mass communication, especially during initial periods of indoctrination when "recruits" are being restricted in personal contacts and communications that might make their former social selves and self-images salient again.[28]

---

[27] Howard Tolley, Jr., *Children and War: Political Socialization to International Conflict* (New York: Teachers College Press, 1973), quotations, pp. 111–112, 121.

[28] For an account of some characteristics of total institutions, see Erving Goffman, *Asylums* (Garden City, NY: Doubleday, 1961); also Gecas, "Contexts of Socialization."

Some adult socialization and resocialization occurs during adult participation in the more or less everyday activities of the society, such as adult immigrants learning new customs from people at work, on the streets, in stores, and elsewhere. Although resocialization through confinement in total institutions is more dramatic, leading to what Gecas has labeled "radical resocialization," much adult socialization and resocialization usually takes place in the more commonplace and open context of everyday life. Here, mass communication contributes to the process in various ways. We will explore some studies that focus on the role of mass communication and personal communication in the socialization of immigrants to the United States, an interesting topic in its own right, but also one that I consider a promising area for future communications research.

International Migration

International migration is a good example of a major status change in adult life that usually requires some new socialization and perhaps resocialization.[29] Even temporary visitors to a foreign land, who may be given privileged statuses (tourists, foreign students, or invited guests) which exempt them from some of the country's customs, are nevertheless expected to obey the laws of the land and to respect (if not adopt as their own) many of the folkways and customs of the people they are visiting. Preparation for these temporary statuses may be as casual as getting a few tips from seasoned travelers or hints from an article in a travel magazine. It also may be more formal and elaborate, as in special orientation meetings held for students going abroad or for citizens who are about to visit politically sensitive or dangerous places.[30]

Those who wish to work in a foreign country or to live there for an indefinitely long time as resident aliens are likely to be subject to more pressures for socialization. They are expected to comply with the host country's customs, at least in public, and to make an effort to speak the local language if their stay is a prolonged one. And persons who seek fuller membership in the new society may require substantial socialization experience, even resocialization, before making certain of its values, allegiances, views, and social behavior part of their own personal code.

In the earlier parts of this century, mainly prior to World War II, studies of

[29] See Dennis H. Wrong, *Population and Society*, 4th ed. (New York: Random House, 1977), esp. chap. 6; and Douglas S. Massey, "Dimensions of the New Immigration to the United States and the Prospects for Assimilation," *Annual Review of Sociology*, vol. 7 (Palo Alto, CA: Annual Reviews, Inc., 1981), pp. 57–85. Massey uses the term *assimilation* in the sociological sense of integration of the new immigrants into the society.

[30] For an example, see Richard T. Morris, *The Two-Way Mirror* (Minneapolis: University of Minnesota, 1960). Morris's study of foreign students in America argues that a foreign visitor's adjustment is related to his or her beliefs about how much prestige or status the host society gives to his or her homeland. The foreign student experiences severe changes in status upon arriving in the new country, which affect his or her self-image. The foreign visitor's own nationality becomes an especially salient and important personal characteristic once abroad. It would be of interest to know, although not investigated in the study, the parts played by mass communication and personal communication in helping to shape the foreign visitor's ideas about whether Americans regard his or her country relatively favorably or unfavorably, and why.

immigrants to the United States often focused on their *assimilation* (sometimes called Americanization), a process through which immigrants' old norms were more or less replaced by American ones and the newcomers became assimilated into their new country. More recent sociological work has stressed the pluralistic character of American society, arguing that immigrants and their descendants do not and need not replace all of their ethnic heritage (and never did) in order to participate fully in American society. "The surprise for many analysts," remarks Melvin Seeman in a recent review of the social psychology of intergroup relations, "has been the tenacity of minority solidarities in American life, especially in view of the power and pervasiveness of mainstream cultural definitions."[31] But even though subcultures (ethnic and otherwise) coexist in a pluralistic society, members nonetheless share much of the mainstream culture, and acquiring this culture requires socialization or resocialization for those coming from another society.

Sociological research on immigrants and their assimiliation in the United States shows an early awareness of the possible role of mass communication in this process. A good example of this sensitivity to the potential power of the mass media can be found in a study by Robert E. Park, a sociologist at the University of Chicago in the early 1920s.[32] At that time there was considerable social and scholarly interest in the social institutions that might help or obstruct the assimilation of immigrants into American citizenship. Among these was the major mass medium of the day, the press. Park undertook a specific examination of the foreign-language press and its apparent role in encouraging or discouraging assimilation.[33]

Park noted that many immigrants at that time, from a variety of ethnic backgrounds, saw themselves as temporary residents here. They were hoping to return to their homelands once they had made enough money to buy property back home or once there was a more favorable political regime there. They were oriented toward the old country. Hence many were not necessarily strongly motivated to become Americans or to adopt any more American ways (in place of their own) than were necessary for survival while here. A variety of ethnic social institutions set up here, such as voluntary associations and local churches, appeared to help preserve the mother tongue and Old World customs and loyalties, and among these was the foreign-language press.

To some observers, it seemed that the foreign-language press kept alive the immigrants' ties to the old countries and slowed, perhaps even prevented, the process of Americanization. But, Park stated, "It is a question whether the foreign-language press is a brake or an accelerator in this process of assimilation." Did it help to segregate and isolate foreign-language ethnic communities and thereby prevent assimilation? Or did it, Park asks, assist the immigrants, "partic-

[31] Melvin Seeman, "Intergroup Relations," in Rosenberg and Turner, *Social Psychology*, chap. 13, pp. 378–410; quotation, p. 405.

[32] Robert E. Park, *The Immigrant Press and Its Control* (New York: Harper and Bros., 1922).

[33] Park's book was one among ten reports on methods of Americanization sponsored by the Carnegie Corporation. Others described the immigrants' schools, homes, and family life, legal protection and correction, health care, naturalization and political life, industrial and economic institutions, neighborhoods and organizations, rural developments, and treatment of their cultural heritages.

ularly the first generation, to orient themselves in the American environment and share in the intellectual, political, and social life of the community?"[34] Park argued that, on balance, the foreign-language press was helpful to the assimilation of ethnic immigrants, many of whom read little or no English.

More than a half-century has passed since these observations by Park on people's concerns about the role of mass communication in the socialization of immigrants. Yet the topic remains timely as a source of social concern and research interest today, in our modern age of television, cable TV, radio, motion pictures, and other new technology.

One consequence of worldwide modern mass communication is that many of today's immigrants arrive with preconceptions about the country to which they are migrating based in part on impressions gleaned from the mass media. Thus a certain amount of anticipatory socialization can begin prior to migration. This experience may be more common for people who have migrated voluntarily than for those who have been driven from their homelands, but even the latter probably have some preconceptions about where they are settling. Some of these preconceptions may come from exposure to that host country's mass media products abroad and from personal communication with persons who have visited that country or migrated there.

Once immigrants have arrived in the new country, they may be assimilated in varying degress. Communication researchers are interested in the extent to which the immigrants' communication behavior is related to their assimilation into the new society.[35] Social science terminology is not standard on this topic. For some scholars, the term *assimilation* has a sociological meaning. It refers to the degree to which a society has absorbed immigrants so that they are functioning as members of that society—able to conduct business, hold jobs, and participate in the social, political, and economic life of the society. Assimilation also has a psychological meaning. It refers to the process by which immigrants have become similar to most members of the host society—resembling them in values, beliefs, customs, behavior, and in other ways. The term *acculturation* also refers to the immigrants' acquiring traits from the new society in place of those from their own culture. Clearly all these uses address important aspects of the immigrants' settlement into a new society. Each might be affected by communication factors. But each term addresses different kinds of research problems, and therefore it is important to determine how a term is being used in a particular study.

Communication research on recent immigrants to the United States tends to use a psychological approach to assimilation. Researchers infer that socialization is taking place from the study of statistical associations between the immigrant's communication behavior and certain personal characteristics (such as knowl-

---

[34] Ibid., p. 86.

[35] An account of a current study of the role of mass communication and interpersonal communication in shaping immigrants' ethnic community identity, as well as their acclimatization to America, is presented in Hannah Kliger, "Mass Communication and Ethnic Identity in Immigrant Communities," paper presented to the Fifth International Conference on Culture and Communication, 1983. Kliger's study focuses on Jewish-American *landsmanshaftn*, voluntary associations formed among immigrants from the same home town or area.

edge about the new society or stated beliefs). These associations are analyzed through such procedures as multiple regression and path analysis—methods used to estimate how much of the variation in some quality (knowledge about America) appears to be attributable to differences in some other matter (reading American newspapers or reading the foreign-language press), in a direct or a contributory way. We will present a few examples that illustrate this work.

In 1977 Young Kim studied the communication behavior of a sample of Korean immigrants in Chicago to see how it related to their acculturation.[36] "Acculturation," as used by Kim, refers to an immigrant's taking over traits from the host culture. More specifically, Kim tried to relate the immigrants' interpersonal communication behavior and their mass media consumption to their perceptions of America. She examined the extent to which these perceptions became less stereotyped and more complex, displaying some knowledge about the variety within American society.

The study reports that Korean immigrants' views of Americans were more likely to be complex—to show an awareness of subgroup differences and similarities in interpersonal relations—when the immigrants had relatively frequent (and intense) personal communications with Americans. Also, heavier users of information media and information content (newspaper reading, watching TV news) seemed more likely to show this "cognitive complexity." The study, however, did not present data on the immigrants' internalization of American norms or their attempts to follow these social norms in everyday behavior.

Another researcher, Jin Kim, points out that the study focused mainly on the immigrants' use of American mass media and personal communications with Americans, but did not consider their use of ethnically oriented communications (reading Korean newspapers and having conversations with other Koreans here in the United States). These ethnically oriented communications might limit acculturation or slow it down, or both.

To investigate this possibility, Jin Kim studied the acculturation of several hundred Koreans living in California. Acculturation was defined, for research purposes, as the "immigrant's degree of similarity to Americans in responding to a series of value statements."[37] Kim tested a formal theoretical model relating variations in acculturation (so measured) and variations in the immigrants' intercultural (American) and ethnic (Korean) communications while here in the United States. The model also postulates that differential exposure to American or Korean mass communications and people are more or less determined by occupational status, family composition, and intra-ethnic contacts at work and elsewhere. For example, immigrants with high occupational status are more likely than others to share American values; some of this can be "explained" as due to the fact that such immigrants use more American mass communication and have more personal communications with Americans than do other immigrants.

[36] Young Yun Kim, "Communication Patterns of Foreign Immigrants in the Process of Acculturation," *Human Communication Research*, 4, 1 (1977), pp. 66–77.

[37] Jin K. Kim, "Explaining Acculturation in a Communication Framework: An Empirical Test," *Communication Monographs*, 47 (1980), pp. 155–179; quotation, p. 166.

Jin Kim interprets the data as confirming the general importance of both ethnic and American communications among immigrants for the process of acculturation. Also, the length of time that a person has been here makes a difference. Kim suggests that during an early stage of assimilation, the immigrant's active pursuit of information about America and his or her communications with Americans seem far more important to acculturation than whether or not he or she also uses Korean communications. But later, Kim suggests, "The avoidance of significant symbols of the original culture becomes almost as important as the active seeking of interaction with the host culture in facilitating one's acculturation in the later stage."[38] At least this seemed to hold for the first-generation Korean immigrants in the study.

The fact that certain immigrants communicate more across ethnic boundaries than others seems to help explain the statistical associations found between some of their personal characteristics and assimilation, according to a study of Korean immigrants in Hawaii by June Ock Yum.[39] The researcher measured immigrants' knowledge of social agencies in Honolulu that provide services for immigrants. She then examined whether the statistical relation between such knowledge and certain personal characteristics of the immigrants (such as education) could be statistically "explained" by differences in their communications behavior, especially communication across ethnic boundaries. Such communication diversity appeared to account for the association between knowledge about agencies and the person's education, occupational status, length of residence in Hawaii, and a "sense of control." (But it did not account for the association with fluency in English and "cognitive complexity.")

These recent studies, among others, thus attack in a new way questions about the contributions of mass communication to the socialization of immigrants that concerned Park and other social scientists earlier in the century. The new studies draw inferences about the mass media's effects from statistical correlations between communications behavior and measurements of immigrant assimilation, within theoretical communications models tested through statistical analytical procedures. Future research may provide more direct information on the social process of immigrant resocialization and the ways in which mass communication fits into this process.

Studies of socialization, from childhood through adulthood, suggest that both mass communication and interpersonal communication play important parts in this social process. We found that both were important in our earlier discussion of research on the social consequences of mass communication surveillance, correlation, and entertainment. This observation, much refined in the materials discussed, thus reinforces our argument that mass communication, from a sociological perspective, should be regarded as a social phenomenon, as part of the total communication institution of a society, which together with interpersonal communication and personal experiences helps shape people's views of the world and influences their social behavior.

[38] Ibid., p. 179.

[39] June Ock Yum, "Communication Diversity and Information Acquisition among Korean Immigrants in Hawaii," *Human Communication Research*, 8, 2 (1982), pp. 154–169.

CHAPTER 10

The Social Impact of the New Communication Technology

As we approach the twenty-first century, major developments in mass media technology are rapidly changing the mechanics of mass communication production, distribution, and reception.[1] Research interest in the new media has grown among social scientists, especially communications researchers, during the 1980s.[2] This promises to become a major direction of future scholarly attention. The research challenge posed, from our perspective, is whether such technological developments significantly affect mass communication as a social institution, and if so, how.

These new technologies certainly sound exciting, if somewhat mysterious. Consider some of the technical devices available now or promised for the near future: broadcast satellites, direct broadcast satellite service, cable television, teletext, videotext, video discs, videocassette recorders and players, fiber optics, lower-power TV, electronic newspapers and magazines, multipoint distribution service, VHF drop-ins, high-resolution TV, flat-screen TV, pocket-size portable TV sets—to mention but a few. Who among us, whether raised on the technological fantasies of Buck Rogers and Tom Swift or Star Wars and video games, can fail to fire the imagination with glimpses of twenty-first century communications?

Among the most popularly recognized of these new devices are communication satellites, which allow broadcast signals to be transmitted back to earth from space satellites, and cable television, with its potential for allowing communication back from the audience member to the communicator (so-called two-way or downstream and upstream transmission). Joined to our ever-improving computer technology, the prospects for social impact seem awesome—but no more awesome, perhaps, than those anticipated during the introduction of other major new communication changes in the past, such as radio broadcasting and television.[3] A sense of recent history helps.

[1] For some examples, see: Frederick Williams, *The New Communications* (Belmont, CA: Wadsworth, 1983), chap. 8, "The New Technologies"; Lynne Schafer Gross, *The New Television Technologies* (Dubuque, IA: Wm. C. Brown, 1984); Ronald E. Rice et al., *The New Media: Communication, Research, and Technology* (Beverly Hills, CA.: Sage, 1984); Robert W. Haigh, George Gerbner, and Richard B. Byrne, eds., *Communications in the Twenty-first Century* (New York: Wiley, 1981); and Mitchell L. Moss, ed., *Telecommunications and Productivity.* (Reading, MA: Addison-Wesley, 1981).

[2] See Rice et al., *The New Media.*

[3] Not all discussions of new technology predict only favorable social consequences. For example, a content analysis of stories about computers in popular magazines from the 1940s to the 1980s

Current forecasts about social effects are, understandably, mixed: Enthusiasts look optimistically toward the future social benefits of the new media; critics fix upon expected social damage. Cable television is seen by some as breaking the bonds restricting telecasts to a small number of broadcast channels, opening the door to a greater variety of shows, programming to meet minority tastes, local program origination, and other social benefits. Pessimists see cable television as evolving (together with subscription television services) into a more expensive array of programs similar to those now available through direct free telecasts.

They foresee it, at its worst, as developing into a tightly controlled propaganda instrument controlled by the government. Two-way cable television could be used for government surveillance of citizens (perhaps under the guise of the public welfare—to reduce crime, to make certain that elderly or ill people are safe in their apartments or rooms) and other oppressive intrusions into the private lives of individuals, not unlike those fictionalized in George Orwell's novel *1984*. Broadcast satellites are seen by some as enabling people-to-people communication across national boundaries; others see them as potential vehicles for international propaganda and cultural invasion.

The social consequences of the new technology, like the old, probably will be mixed: some good, some bad, some trivial. While awaiting the results of future studies of this impact, the functional framework outlined in our opening chapter should serve to alert us to some of the possibilities and should strengthen our ability to be skeptical of predictions of totally beneficial or totally harmful social effects.

The general sociological framework developed throughout this book also suggests some of the key areas that need to be considered in speculation and research on the social aspects of the new media technology—for example, questions about institutional arrangements surrounding these new communication techniques and their use, such as how the new techniques will become institutionalized and incorporated into the society. What will be the organizational framework within which they will work? What will be the restraints on future communicators? Who will have access to these new techniques of communication? What is the social structure of the society within which they operate, and the international scene? Our attention is directed also to the organizational structure and occupational roles in communication production and distribution; to audience behavior and the public or private context of the communication experience, the composition of the audience, the significance of interpersonal communications, and the content of the materials transmitted—to mention but a few of the topics of concern.

Consider, for example, some questions about social norms and institutional controls over new communication technology that bear on our traditional safeguards for freedom in the production and distribution of information, news, and

shows that from 1965 to 1969, "references to predicted social outcomes of a clearly negative nature, like increased unemployment, devaluation of human brainpower, and loss of privacy, either outnumbered or equaled references to positive social outcomes, such as improvements in medicine, increased jobs, greater efficiency in manufacturing, or the solution of social problems." Josephine R. Holz, "Trends in Mass Media Depictions of the Computer," paper presented at the Eastern Communication Association convention, March 1984.

entertainment. Ithiel de Sola Pool, a political scientist and communications researcher, raises critical questions about the impact of the new technology on American social norms and legal protections for freedom of the press, freedom of speech, and freedom of information. There is, he says, a growing convergence of modes of communication—that is, many modes are now capable of performing multiple communication services. The technological distinction between various modes is being blurred. Previous divisions of communication tasks that led one or another medium to have a monopoly or specialization on some kind of communication activity (such as news or point-to-point message delivery) are weakened.

This convergence of technical modes of communication has coincided, more or less, with a historical process of cross-ownership of various mass media—newspapers, radio stations, television stations and networks, computer systems. One social consequence of all this, according to Pool, is that the rights of people to speak freely and to have access to news and other communications free from government control may be endangered, because the laws that apply to electronic modes of communication are less protective than those that apply now, or applied in the past, to the press.

We have a heritage of freedom of the press for the print media, but we have a history of governmental regulation of the electronic media, because in the past they used scarce public resources. For example, the broadcast spectrum limits the number of stations that can be on the air without mutual interference, and therefore we have come to accept government regulation in this sphere. As electronic technology is employed by the print media, however, there is the danger that these media will be treated more like electronic and broadcast media, as proper subjects for government regulation, rather than as newspapers. This may occur even though new technology is making many of our former concerns about the scarcity of electronic resources obsolete through the expansion of such broadcasting alternatives as cable television and direct satellite transmission. A pro-regulatory policy may be applied to newspapers whenever they use electronic technology. And the future will see more forms of "electronic publishing," such as computer news printouts, in the home.

"Civil liberty functions today in a changing technological context," Pool argues; "The new communication technologies have not inherited all the legal immunities that were won for the old. When wires, radio waves, satellites, and computers became major vehicles of discourse, regulation seemed to be a technical necessity. And so, as speech increasingly flows over those electronic media, the five-century growth of an unabridged right of citizens to speak without controls may be endangered."[4] It is something to think about. Of course, in societies in which the press as well as other modes of mass communication have long been under government regulation and control, the new media may be treated with even fewer safeguards for freedom as we understand that term.

The rapid diffusion of new and conventional methods for mass communication holds both promise and threat to the governments and citizens of individual

[4] Ithiel de Sola Pool, *Technologies of Freedom* (Cambridge, MA: Belknap Press of Harvard University Press, 1983), p. 1.

nations and to worldwide international relations. Direct broadcast satellites, which would permit direct reception of television signals in the home (by means of a "dish" antenna), offer the audience an opportunity to view worldwide events, but at the risk of receiving intentional foreign propaganda and perhaps unintentionally conveyed foreign cultural values in entertainment and other programs. These may be mainly hypothetical consequences at the moment, because of the relative scarcity of dish antennas in private homes. When used for reception at the community level, as in some Third World nations, these devices are likely to be institutionalized as part of the total mass communication system, subject to whatever freedoms and controls one finds there.

In 1984, for example, the government of India marked the twenty-fifth anniversary of the start of Indian television by a massive effort to bring television to 70 percent of its 750 million rural and urban population by 1985 (thus making it reportedly the largest potential television audience in the world). The government is relying on an American-built broadcast communication satellite, launched from our space shuttle in 1983, 180 low-power ground transmitters, and 2,000 satellite receiving stations in remote villages.[5] India's late prime minister, Indira Gandhi, was reported as justifying this effort in terms of national security and to have said that television "will be the ultimate tool" in unifying what one reporter describes as "this incredibly diverse nation, where there are 14 official languages, dozens of divergent customs and three major religions."[6]

But others, critical of the content of many programs (particularly those from abroad), fear the "cultural pollution" they might bring. According to one account, information and educational programs dealing with matters of development and rural improvement account for about 14 percent of the program time. The rest, the vast majority of programs, consists of entertainment provided through Indian-produced movies and imported entertainment such as "Star Trek" and "The Lucy Show." The minister of information and broadcasting is quoted as saying: "We want to keep Indian television Indian. We don't want to pollute our culture. We have our own concept of television, but at the same time we are part of the world. The world influences us, and we influence the world. . . . Our programming should be a judicious mixture of information, education and entertainment. Entertainment is an important part of the human character, and we understand the need for it."[7]

Indeed, entertainment provided one impetus for trying to expand television nationally during 1984 in time for the 1984 Olympic Games, which were carried live over India's one-channel network, Doordarshan (meaning distant audience, or distant vision). Many of the government-supplied television receivers are community sets, placed in spots where the public can view them, thus making viewing a group experience, as noted in our discussion in Chapter 2. But sets also are diffusing into private hands, one account stating that "television an-

[5] William Claiborne, "India: The TV Pollution Debate," *The Washington Post National Weekly Edition*, July 30, 1984, p. 18; and Mark Fineman, "The Rural Towns of India Enter the Age of TV," *The Philadelphia Inquirer*, July 27, 1984, p. 2A.

[6] Fineman, "The Rural Towns of India."

[7] Claiborne, "India."

tennas poke through the rooftops of nearly one in five of the mud or brick bungalows" in one village.[8]

New technology sometimes seems to be a means for getting around national or community controls over certain communication content or simply for adding some variety to an otherwise dull state-controlled entertainment industry. Videocassette recorders and players have been used in this way, for example. According to one Associated Press news report, there are approximately 1 million videocassette recorders in Turkey, and reportedly 2,000 video clubs exist in the country. "Video sets can be seen even in some village coffee houses in remote parts of the country where domestic movies and belly-dancer shows are in high demand." These shows presumably provide entertainment preferred over the shows on the one-channel state-run television, on which "Three times a week there is a movie, usually a black-and-white relic from the 1950s. . . . Locally produced shows are few and severely censored. . . ."[9]

New technology also needs to be incorporated into the organizational structure of communication production and distribution and may have important consequences for the organizational roles involved. New occupations are created and older ones modified: some even disappear. An interesting sociological study was made, for example, of what happened to traditional typesetters following the introduction of automation (electronic typesetting) at *The New York Times.*

Traditionally, typesetters comprised a rather special occupational group who tended to see one another often both on and off the job. They shared similar educational backgrounds, were highly knowledgeable and skilled in their work, worked at night or other odd hours that put them out of step with many other workers and hence more likely to turn to one another for company after work, had considerable control over working conditions on the job, had a hand in selecting their own temporary substitute worker if they had to take time off, and had spent considerable time in the union and hiring halls waiting for work. These circumstances, among others, made the typesetters resemble an *occupational community*, a group that shared many interests and activities beyond the job.[10]

Much of this picture changed with automation. The occupational community more or less vanished. Some of the older workers took the opportunity to retire; some of the younger ones retrained to do the work by computer. The highly specialized technical knowledge that these men had was no longer so necessary to the job. The men began to regard typesetting more as a job than as a special occupation or profession. Changes in rules gave them less control over working conditions on the floor and removed the option of selecting one's own substitute. In general, there seemed to be a loss of a sense of deep identification

---

[8] Ibid.

[9] *The Philadelphia Inquirer*, July 2, 1984, p. R10.

[10] See Theresa F. Rogers and Nathalie S. Friedman, *Printers Face Automation* (Lexington, MA: D. C. Heath, 1980). The authors compare their findings with those from an earlier sociological study of the same occupational group, reported in Seymour M. Lipset, Martin Trow, and James S. Coleman, *Union Democracy* (Glencoe, IL: Free Press, 1956), in which the concept of occupational community is employed.

with the occupational role, less use of other typesetters as a reference group off the job, and a loss of the occupational community. It would be interesting to know what happens to occupational identity and role, sense of occupational community, and role-related behavior following the introduction of new technology, especially for those more directly involved in the creative, editorial, or other production aspects of mass communication.

The significance of new technology for audience composition and behavior also seems very important to study. Not all members of the public are able to make use of the new technology, especially initially. For example, television dish antennas are relatively expensive and not readily installed in many neighborhoods or houses. Thus few people can receive direct satellite broadcasts in their homes. Videotext and teletext, while available in some homes, are not mass-marketed at this time; costs and other considerations keep them mainly experimental as home devices. Cable television is relatively widespread in the United States, but not available in many places and not subscribed to by everyone where it is. Home computers, with links to information data banks through modem devices and telephone lines, are not owned by most people.

It takes time for such innovations to diffuse throughout a society. Some segments of the population never use them much, if at all. Communications researchers David Dozier and Ronald Rice cite research suggesting that it took more than 100 years before newspapers were read regularly by more than half of the population of the United States; 70 years before half of us had telephones; 17 years for color television to diffuse to half the population; 10 years for AM radio; and 10 years for black and white television. Thirty years after its introduction, cable television has achieved 20 percent "penetration," and "the prevailing estimate is that 7% of the U.S. households will be using videotex by 1990." They report that market research suggests that the typical initial user of videotext "will be male, white, college educated, between the ages of 25 and 45, of managerial or professional status, and earning in excess of $30,000 per year."[11]

Unequal access to new modes of communication or differential use of them by various segments of the population raises the possibility of serious social consequences over time. There is, for example, the possibility that society may become differentiated into strata of information-rich and information-poor, along the lines suggested by the knowledge-gap hypothesis discussed earlier.

Even when new modes of communication are readily available, not everyone is equally likely to use them. This was evident, for example, in a study of a two-way (interactive) cable television system in Reading, Pennsylvania. This was a closed-circuit cable system especially designed for putting senior citizens in touch with one another and with public officials.[12] Television "studios" were set up in neighborhood apartment complexes and in a downtown community center, where senior citizens could "broadcast" by cable to others who received the programs either over television sets in the other studios, or in their own homes. The idea was to give participants an opportunity to share common problems, ex-

[11] Rice et al., *The New Media*, pp. 115–116. Cable television continues to grow. For later figures see the discussion in Chapter 2.

[12] See Mitchell L. Moss, ed., *Two-Way Cable Television: An Evaluation of Community Uses in Reading, Pennsylvania* (The NYU–Reading Consortium, 1978).

periences, and solutions, to participate in recreational activities, and generally to service some of the needs of the elderly.

But not everyone who was offered (for free) the device that would hook their television receiver into the cable circuit accepted it. Further, residents' attendance at the downtown studio was rare, further limiting participation. Attendance was good at the studios in a high-rise apartment building for the elderly and in a neighborhood garden apartment complex. There the cable system, operated by volunteers from among the senior citizen residents, was judged a success. However, not all residents in the apartments participated equally in producing the programs or in appearing before the camera during televised meetings in order to state their views or speak out about problems. As often happens in voluntary community activities, a selective process makes some people more active participants than others, either through self-selection or selection by others, or both.

Some technical, social, and communication skills are necessary in order to use certain of these new technologies for communication purposes. There is talk, for example, of a need for "computer literacy" before one can effectively use computers as part of a communication system, although exactly what that term means is a matter of interpretation. Researchers Carolyn Marvin and Mark Winther, for example, in a study of people using one large computer network, found that their images of the public could be classified into five types according to the public's apparent level of computer skills. These are (1) nonusers; (2) data-entry users ("tourists"), nonprogrammers who depend on other people's computer programs; (3) programmers, who write computer programs that can meet other people's needs; (4) hackers, who invent new capacities for problem-solving by computers; and (5) wizards, "the most talented and respected members of several high-level expert specialties, including designers of hardware and software systems, analysts, and computer scientists."[13]

Most people who use computers are likely to be at the data-entry level of computer skill, capable of using packaged software for purposes of information processing, retrieval, and "interactivity" with data systems and even with other users in the system.[14] Some would regard this as computer literacy; others would restrict that term to the minimum skills necessary for writing programs. But if computers are to be regarded as links for audience interaction with communicators during mass communication, the ability to use computers at all seems

[13] Carolyn Marvin and Mark Winther, "Computer-Ease: A Twentieth-Century Literacy Emergent," *Journal of Communication*, 33, 1 (Winter 1983), pp. 92–108.

[14] New users of media technology also need to learn the social norms concerning their use. A study of users of two major computer networks, through which subscribers can communicate with one another, suggests that there is a definite set of conventions and norms newcomers must learn in order to be accepted into a particular "community" of participants. There are stages of socialization into these communities. At the core of each community is a small group of "expert communicators," oldtimers or founders of that particular interest group, who admit or reject newcomers and socialize them. Terri Toles, "Socialization into Electronic Communities: Communication on Computer Networks," paper presented at the annual meeting of the Eastern Communication Association, 1984. For a humanistic psychological and sociological study of computer users, from little children through adult "hackers," see Sherry Terkle, *The Second Self: Computers and the Human Spirit* (New York: Simon and Schuster, 1984).

more relevant than the ability to create software—although clearly the user's communication choices are limited by the computer techniques supplied by others.

Both the technical equipment and the skill to handle it are necessary before people can make use of teletext and videotext. *Teletext* is a one-way system using over-the-air transmission of information to the television screen, but allowing the viewer to select from available texts through use of a keypad and decoder box. *Videotext* is a two-way system, involving transmission of text to the home television screen by wire; the viewer makes requests by means of a home-computer modem device and telephone connection. Either system can provide news and information, among other matter, but videotext, because it can feed into a home computer, provides the opportunity for paper printouts of the text—a "home-delivered" printed newspaper of a sort—in addition to the electronic newspaper or news magazine on the television screen. While the level of skill necessary for simple operation of either system may not be very high, they have to be learned and, as noted earlier, these devices have yet to be marketed to the mass public.[15]

Beyond technical skills, these new communication media may require that the user change his or her traditional habits and expectations. Carolyn Marvin suggests, for example, that when cable and information systems are built in as equipment in new apartments and houses as a matter of course, and therefore readily available, people will learn to use them. Changes in the workplace may help too, as people who use computerized information systems at work transfer these skills and familiarity with information systems to their private lives. Still, not everyone who has the necessary skills will abandon traditional newspapers for newer electronic information systems: "An electronic advantage in electronic news formatting is of little importance if the habits of generations of newspaper readers cannot be budged," she states. "Not all newspaper aficionados will want to give up browsing the generalist newspaper for the specialist and narrow efficiency of a dial-up newsscreen, and the modest price and portability of the newspaper will be hard to beat in any electronic form." Of course, she notes, consumers may not have to choose between newsscreens and newspapers so long as both remain available in the market.[16]

Dozier and Rice also argue that the electronic newspaper will not serve as a functional substitute for printed newspapers if it is regarded only as an information retrieval and distribution device. Most heavy, regular newspaper readers "use the newspaper in an elaborate, ritualized" way, for many personal and social purposes. They derive many more gratifications from newspaper reading than merely getting information. Readers are not likely to switch to electronic news services at the cost of losing these other gratifications.[17] Then again, as

---

[15] For one discussion, see John Carey, "Selling Teletext to Archie Bunker," in Moss, *Telecommunications and Productivity*, pp. 245–254.

[16] Carolyn Marvin, "Delivering the News of the Future," *Journal of Communication*, 30, 1 (Winter 1980), pp. 10–20; quotation, p. 14.

[17] Donald M. Dozier and Ronald E. Rice, "Rival Theories of Electronic Newsreading," in Rice et al., *The New Media*, pp. 103–127.

Marvin points out, they may not have to, if they can use both the old and the new media.

The social impact of the new communications technologies also depends in part on what kinds of information and entertainment they will carry to the mass audience. Will there be sufficient diversity of content to meet the needs and tastes of minority as well as majority members of the public? What cultural values will be conveyed? Will one society's values dominate, weaken, or even replace those of societies that receive its communications? These are but a few of the questions that come to mind. Consider as one example what appears to be happening with cable television in the United States. Communications researcher Frederick Williams believes that:

> Despite the emergence of art and cultural programming channels and sports alternatives now offered via cable television, there is still no firm basis for believing that we will have an improved type of TV leisure in our future. . . .
> New technologies are exceedingly expensive. In order that investors may get a return on their money, mass-marketing techniques and advertising are spilling over into cable and satellite television services and into videotape and disk. In fact, the "new" television is becoming disturbingly similar to the old.[18]

We might add the observation that the same thing probably would happen even if there were no commercial investors (in a state-owned communications system, for example) so long as the system aims at using the new technology for mass communication—that is, to reach large segments of the public—as we have defined it here.

This is an appropriate note on which to end our discussion. Much of the new technology offers new methods for communication production and delivery. These changes seem bound to have significant consequences for society and its members. Our functional orientation suggests that some of these may be regarded as potentially beneficial and others not. The relevant questions, from our sociological perspective, concern how the new technology affects mass communication as a social phenomenon. We have raised a few such questions here. These examples reflect, as our discussion throughout the book has done, the need to consider mass communication and other forms of communication within the context of social organization and cultural norms. This is the underlying theme and focus of our sociological approach to the study of mass communication.

[18] Williams, *The New Communications*, pp. 328–329.

Additional Selected Readings

Erik Barnouw et al., eds. *International Encyclopedia of Communications.* Philadelphia: Annenberg School of Communications and Oxford University Press, Inc., forthcoming.

Leonard Broom, Philip Selznick, and Dorothy Broom. *Essentials of Sociology,* 3rd ed. Itasca, IL: F. E. Peacock, 1984.

Robert O. Carlson, ed. *Communications and Public Opinion: A Public Opinion Quarterly Reader.* New York: Praeger, 1975.

George Gerbner et al., eds. *Ferment in the Field: Communication Scholars Address Critical Issues and Research Tasks of the Discipline.* A symposium issue of *Journal of Communication,* 33, 3, Summer 1983.

Morris Janowitz and Paul Hirsch, eds. *Reader in Public Opinion and Mass Communication,* 3rd ed. New York: Free Press, 1981.

Robert K. Merton. *Social Theory and Social Structure,* rev. ed. Glencoe, IL: Free Press, 1957.

Ithiel de Sola Pool et al., eds. *Handbook of Communication.* Chicago: Rand McNally, 1973.

Morris Rosenberg and Ralph H. Turner, eds. *Social Psychology: Sociological Perspectives.* New York: Basic Books, 1981.

NAME INDEX

Abelson, Robert, 117n
Adair, John, 84n
Adams, John, 110n
Alley, Robert S., 70n
Altheid, David, 77n
Anderson, Daniel R., 187n
Andison, F. Scott, 175n
Aronson, Elliot, 95n
Arvidsson, Peter, 147n
Asner, Ed, 165
Atkin, Charles K., 188, 189n, 190.
Auster, Donald, 136n, 141, 142, 173n
Austin, Bruce, 112n, 173
Australian Broadcasting Tribunal, 123n

Bachen, Christine M., 154n, 156n, 158n, 187n
Bagdikian, Ben, 55, 74, 75
Ball-Rokeach, Sandra, 20n, 24n, 26n, 164, 167
Bannerman, Julia, 112n
Barber, Elinor, 80n, 84n
Barnouw, Eric, 50n
Barrington, Thomas, 115
Barton, Allen H., 96
Bate, Barbara, 130
Bauer, Raymond, 94n
Becker, Howard S., 72
Beinstein, Judith, 102, 103, 105
Benet, James, 129n
Berelson, Bernard, 14n, 88n, 89n, 90n, 93n, 95n, 100n, 105n, 125n, 137n
Berger, Arthur Asa, 173n
Berry, Gordon L., 187n
Birdwhistell, Ray L., 4n, 185n
Black, Joan S., 99n
Blumer, Herbert, 85
Blumler, Jay, 13n, 26n, 120
Bogart, Leo, 23n, 112n, 114n, 176, 177n
Bonjean, Charles M., 109n
Bouthilet, Lorraine, 175n, 189n

Bower, Robert T., 113n
Bowman, William, 62, 63n, 64n, 65n
Boylan, James, 29n, 117n, 118n
Breed, Warren, 20n, 73, 74
Brim, Orville G., Jr., 194n
Brinton, James, 110n
Browne, Ray B., 173n
Bryant, Jennings, 187n
Bryson, Lyman, 5n, 18n, 153n, 172n
Buerkel-Rothfuss, Nancy L., 188n, 189n
Bureau of Applied Social Research, Columbia University, 96
Bush, Diane M., 185n
Byrne, Richard B., 202n

Campbell, Angus, 130n
Canadian Radio-television and Telecommunications Commission, Information Services, 123n
Cantor, Muriel G., 50n, 53n, 67, 68, 69, 70, 71, 79, 98, 99, 120, 137n, 173n, 194n
Cantril, Hadley, 18n, 49n, 146n
Carey, James W., 25, 27n
Carey, John, 209n
Carter, Jimmy, 108
Cathcart, Robert, 192n
Center for the Study of Popular Culture, 173
Chaffee, Steven, 108, 195
Chandler, Robert, 49n
Charters, W. W., 173n
Chaudhary, A. G., 30n
Chen, Min, 39, 40n, 41
Choe, Sun Yuel, 108
Chu, Godwin C., 39n
Chu, James, 39, 40n, 41
Ciociola, Gail, 146n
Claiborne, William, 205n
Clarke, Peter, 73n, 159n
Coleman, James S., 206n

213

SUBJECT INDEX

ABOUT THE AUTHOR

Charles R. Wright is Professor of Communications and Sociology at the University of Pennsylvania, where he is a member of the Annenberg School of Communications and of the University's Department of Sociology. Formerly, he was a member of the sociology departments of the University of California, Los Angeles, and Columbia University. He also has served as Program Director in Sociology and Social Psychology at the National Science Foundation.

Professor Wright's publications reflect a broad range of interests in sociology, social psychology, and mass communications. Among his latest books are a coauthored pair *Education's Lasting Influence on Values* and *The Enduring Effects of Education*. His contributions to professional journals and scholarly anthologies include work on such varied topics as social structure and mass communication behavior, functional analysis and mass communication, adult socialization, graduate education, voluntary association membership, methods of evaluation research, and social change.

Earlier editions of *Mass Communication* have been translated into Italian, Spanish, Portuguese, and Japanese.